ALSO BY JOHN F. KASSON

Civilizing the Machine:
Technology and Republican Values in America, 1776–1900

Rudeness and Civility:
Manners in Nineteenth-Century Urban America

Amusing the Million:
Coney Island at the Turn of the Century

HOUDINI, TARZAN,

❧ AND ❧

THE PERFECT MAN

HOUDINI, TARZAN,

◈ AND ◈

THE PERFECT MAN

THE WHITE MALE BODY AND

THE CHALLENGE OF MODERNITY IN AMERICA

JOHN F. KASSON

〰 HILL AND WANG

A DIVISION OF FARRAR, STRAUS AND GIROUX

NEW YORK

Hill and Wang
A division of Farrar, Straus and Giroux
19 Union Square West, New York 10003

Library of Congress Cataloging-in-Publication Data
Kasson, John F., 1944–
    Houdini, Tarzan, and the perfect man : the White male body and the challenge of
modernity in America / John F. Kasson.
        p. cm.
    Includes bibliographical references and index.
    ISBN 0-8090-8862-2 (hc : alk. paper)
        1. Men in popular culture—United States—History.   2. Masculinity in popular
culture—United States—History.   3. Body, Human—Social aspects—United States.
4. Sandow, Eugen, 1867–1925.   5. Houdini, Harry, 1874–1926.   6. Tarzan (Fictitious
character).   I. Title.

HQ1090.3 .K39 2001
305.31—dc21

00-053669

Designed by Jonathan D. Lippincott

For
Joy, Peter, and Laura,
who give me strength,
and for Peter Filene,
who led the way

ACKNOWLEDGMENTS

I am grateful to many individuals and institutions for help in writing this book. The University of North Carolina at Chapel Hill provided crucial support, including fellowships and grants from the Institute for the Arts and Humanities, the Pogue Research Fund, the University Research Council, the Office of the Dean of Arts and Sciences, and the Department of History. A fellowship from the John Simon Guggenheim Memorial Foundation sped the work's completion.

I would also like to thank the following librarians for their assistance and for permission to quote from and to reproduce unpublished materials in special collections: Annette Fern and Jason Radalin at the Harvard Theatre Collection; Wallace Finley Dailey at the Theodore Roosevelt Collection, Harvard College Library; Joan F. Higbee at the Rare Book Collection, Library of Congress; Melissa Miller and Esther L. Mes at the Theatre Arts Collection, Harry Ransom Humanities Research Center, The University of Texas at Austin; Matthew Carpenter at the Houdini Historical Center, Appleton, Wisconsin; Rita Belda at the Wisconsin Center for Film and Theater Research; Josephine Matthews at the Image Library, The National Archives, Public Record Office, U.K.; Therese Babineau at the Phoebe A. Hearst Museum of Anthropology, University of California at Berkeley; Scott S. Taylor at Georgetown University Library; and George McWhorter and Linda Buie at the Edgar Rice Burroughs Memorial

Collection, University of Louisville. I am also especially grateful to Danton Burroughs for his kind permission to quote from manuscripts and to reproduce photographs owned by Edgar Rice Burroughs, Inc.

In conducting research for this book, I benefited from the help of David Avitabile, Matthew Brown, Eric Combest, Jason Dash, Joshua Guthman, Daniel Jolley, Emily Kelley, Michael Kramer, Ethan Kytle, Thomas Newsome, Michael Sistrom, Jill Snider, Shirley Taylor, and Adam Tuchinsky. A host of friends and colleagues also provided encouragement, criticism, and hospitality. Let me thank especially Gavin Campbell, Charles Capper, Michael Claxton, James W. Cook, Jr., the late Robert Crunden, Ann Fabian, Leon Fink, Alison Isenberg, Michael Kammen, Susan Levine, David Lubin, Jennifer Ritterhouse, Daniel Rodgers, Joan Shelley Rubin, Bill Stott, Alan Trachtenberg, and Keith Wailoo. Kent Plemmons gave valuable technical advice on computer hardware and software.

Although I have recorded specific scholarly debts in the endnotes, I wish to acknowledge my three principal subjects' major biographers: David L. Chapman, the late Irwin Porges, and Kenneth Silverman.

Hill and Wang, with which I have worked for a quarter century, remains my ideal publisher. Arthur W. Wang cheered my first stumbling efforts, and Elisabeth Sifton's brilliance and enthusiasm kept me going. Nina Ball-Pesut provided assistance with unfailing grace. Ingrid Sterner's copyediting was impeccable.

Peter Filene, a pioneer in the history of masculinity, has been an incomparable friend, giving encouragement, advice, and insight every step of the way.

And my family has been superb. My brother and sister-in-law, Jim and Betty Kasson, generously supplied computer equipment at critical moments. My children, Peter and Laura, sustained me with their love and sharpened my prose with their suggestions. My wife, Joy, has been indispensable to the project—as she has been to my life.

CONTENTS

INTRODUCTION 3

ONE: WHO IS THE PERFECT MAN?
Eugen Sandow and a New Standard for America 21

TWO: THE MANLY ART OF ESCAPE
The Metamorphoses of Ehrich Weiss 77

THREE: "STILL A WILD BEAST AT HEART"
Edgar Rice Burroughs and the Dream of *Tarzan* 157

CONCLUSION 219

Notes 225
Index 245

HOUDINI, TARZAN,

~ AND ~

THE PERFECT MAN

INTRODUCTION

In 1904 a balding, compactly built banker in Muncie, Indiana, posed for the camera on his forty-fifth birthday. It was not a conventional birthday portrait, however. For the occasion he stripped to the waist, flexed his biceps, and had himself photographed from behind. His business life was sedentary, but during the next forty years he kept up various physical regimens, ranging from lifting light weights to deep-breathing exercises. His name was Albert G. Matthews, and he was my great-grandfather; he died nine days before I was born.

I first saw this portrait in a family album as a child, and it prompted questions that fascinate me still. My initial response was surprise: What was he doing? Other male relatives in photographs showed their bodies, if at all, only in swim trunks as they squinted at the camera, usually holding a fish. Later I wondered, What was his sense of his body, and how was it shaped by the technologies and culture of his time? What models of strength did he admire? What dreams and anxieties did this image contain? Family photographs were one of the earliest ways by which I learned the importance of visual evidence in history, and in retrospect, I can see that this photograph was the first historical fragment that led to this book.

Many years later, I sifted through some thirteen thousand photo-

Albert G. Matthews on his forty-fifth birthday, 1904

graphs at Harvard University devoted to the most famous of all Albert Matthews's contemporaries (ten months his senior), the man who was president when his birthday portrait was made in 1904, Theodore Roosevelt. Here the sense of theatricality that I had first glimpsed with my ancestor burst forth on a colossal scale. Crucial to Roosevelt's success was his ability to turn prized characteristics of manliness into spectacle, literally to embody them. The camera and the pen were essential aids in that effort. Born in 1858 to one of the richest and most socially prominent families in New York, Roosevelt created his own stirring drama of childhood adversity overcome in an account of how he transformed his "sickly, delicate," asthmatic body into the two-hundred-pound muscular, barrel-chested figure of a supremely strong and energetic leader. His *Autobiography*, first published in 1913, included illustrations of Roosevelt in positions of executive authority (assistant secretary of the navy, governor of New York, president of the United States) carefully balanced with portraits of him active and outdoors (on horseback, returning from a bear hunt in Colorado, with hand on hip as Rough Rider colonel in the Spanish-American War, and holding a rifle "in winter riding costume").[1]

The photographic archive showed that Roosevelt had practiced such poses assiduously, and no American of his generation or president before or since—not Lincoln, not Kennedy, not Reagan—developed a broader repertoire. Once past his childhood, when he was pictured in the unisex white dress, long hair, and bonnet worn by upper-class children of the time, he seems to have determined never to appear before the camera in a pampered guise again. In a routine physical examination as a Harvard undergraduate, he learned from Dr. Dudley A. Sargent, the college physician and the nation's leading authority on physical education, that he had "heart trouble" and should lead a sedentary life, taking care not even to run up stairs. Roosevelt replied that he could not bear to live that way and intended to do precisely the opposite.[2] A photograph from about this time shows him outside the Harvard boathouse wearing rowing togs, bare-chested and barefoot, his jaws filled out with a beard, his biceps bulged by his fists.

Theodore Roosevelt as a Harvard undergraduate in rowing attire. Theodore Roosevelt Collection, Harvard College Library

From his college days to the end of his life, Roosevelt appears to have considered no hunting trip complete without recording it either in the field or in a photographer's studio. For his first book, *Hunting Trips of a Ranchman* (1885), based on his adventures in the Dakota Territory, he struck various attitudes, holding a rifle and wearing a fringed buckskin outfit in the style of Buffalo Bill and sporting the holsters, pistols, chaps, and broad-brimmed hat of the ranchman. In 1898, upon his return from Cuba, where he had led his regiment of Rough Riders in victorious charges up Kettle Hill and San Juan Hill, he instantly memorialized his achievements in portraits that displayed a commanding martial bearing. In 1904, the year my great-grandfather posed for his birthday portrait, Roosevelt repeatedly jumped a fence on horseback until a *Harper's Weekly* photographer caught just the right dynamic image for the upcoming presidential campaign.[3] After his presidency, a stage of life in which most of his successors have done nothing more strenuous than golf, he threw himself into new activities—with photographers always at the ready. He recorded his exploits as big-game hunter and explorer (including obligatory poses with animal trophies) in Africa in 1909. Four years later, after his fiercely energetic but unsuccessful "Bull Moose" campaign against William Howard Taft and Woodrow Wilson, he headed for uncharted wilderness and big game once again, this time in Brazil, where he nearly lost his life. He spent his last years, also before the camera, stumping on behalf of the U.S. military effort during the Great War and itching to be in the thick of battle himself.

Many historians exploring manliness in this period have stopped with Roosevelt. But my pursuit has taken me further. And it has led to three immensely popular artists who entertained Americans in the two decades between 1893 and 1914: the strongman Eugen Sandow (1867–1925), the escape artist Harry Houdini (1874–1926), and the author of *Tarzan of the Apes*, Edgar Rice Burroughs (1875–1950). Sandow, Houdini, and Burroughs's Tarzan all acquired immense national and international fame. They literally became part of our language, which suggests that the cultural need for the metaphors they supplied was great, as was the power with which they entered into the lives of their audiences. Viewed in conjunction, these figures assume still greater significance: they expressed with special force and clarity important changes in the popular display of the white male body and in the challenges men faced in modern life.

Although Sandow's name is no longer a household word, he is still revered as the father of modern bodybuilding and a pioneer of physical culture. In his heyday as a vaudeville performer, his position was even more exalted. Physical-fitness experts and journalists alike hailed him as the "perfect man," and his unclad body became the most famous in the world. He established a new paradigm of muscular development and attracted countless followers, ranging from the reformed "ninety-seven-pound weakling" Charles Atlas to the poet William Butler Yeats. His significance for cultural history is still greater. His display of his physique provides a fresh point by which we can assess the changing standards of male strength and beauty that may have inspired men like Albert Matthews to inspect their own bodies in private.

Sandow's celebrity has faded, but Houdini's hold on the popular imagination remains strong even today, though the nature of his feats and the context of his career have been obscured. For the general public, his name dominates the history of magic—to the intense annoyance of many conjurers and magic historians, who rank others superior. Wildly erroneous myths about him persist, such as that he died performing his "Chinese Water Torture Cell" escape (as does Tony Curtis's character in the 1953 Paramount film *Houdini*). Meanwhile, there has been little effort to place him in full historical and cultural context as not only the most brilliant escape artist in the history of illusion but also a magus of manliness, known for some of the most audacious displays of the male body in his time.

Burroughs's fictional character Tarzan is best known of all, but, again, in ways that obscure the significance of his creation. As the subject of twenty-four books written by Burroughs over thirty-five years, and of roughly fifty films, four major television series, a radio serial, and comic books, Tarzan and his adventures have been adapted in ways that hardly resemble the original. The persistence of his popularity testifies to enduring cultural fantasies about manly freedom and wildness. And an examination of the cultural milieu at his first appearance in Frank Munsey's *All-Story* magazine in 1912 illuminates important, if forgotten, aspects of American life a century ago. It reveals why a story about an immensely strong, incomparably free, indomitably wild noble savage could so entrance men who felt locked in the "iron cage" of modern urban, corporate life.[4]

The spectacles of the male body mounted by these three figures built on values embodied in men such as Theodore Roosevelt. In fact, at various points in their careers, all three sought to associate themselves directly with Roosevelt. As a confused young man in 1898, Burroughs wrote to Roosevelt to volunteer for the Rough Riders; he received a gracious but firm refusal. In 1905, at the height of his international prestige, Sandow met with Roosevelt, then president, to discuss their mutual support of the physical-fitness cause. As for Houdini, after entertaining the ex-president on a transatlantic voyage in 1914, he eagerly distributed hundreds of copies of a photograph of himself and his new "pal," in which five other men had been carefully airbrushed away.[5]

Nonetheless, the popular spectacles created by Sandow, Houdini, and Burroughs take us far beyond Roosevelt's performances of manliness, expressing even deeper fantasies and anxieties. All three laid great stress on the unclad male body in ways that Roosevelt would have found unimaginable. This element was crucial to their novelty and impact. They contributed to a new popular interest in the male nude as a symbol of ideals in peril and a promise of their supremacy, as a monument to strength and a symbol of vulnerability, as an emblem of discipline and an invitation to erotic fantasy. In the guise of entertaining, they reasserted the primacy of the white male body against a host of challenges that might weaken, confine, or tame it. Popular spectacles of the female body in this period usually revolved around issues of subordination and transgression, but the overriding theme for these three men concerned metamorphosis. They repeatedly dramatized the transformation from weakness to supreme strength, from vulnerability to triumph, from anonymity to heroism, from the confinement of modern life to the recovery of freedom.

These images of manliness were obviously images of whiteness as well. Neither Sandow, nor Houdini, nor Burroughs was a racial extremist by the lights of his era, any more than Roosevelt himself, who famously invited Booker T. Washington to dine with him at the White House (and infamously issued dishonorable discharges to 170 African American soldiers in the "Brownsville affair"). Yet like Roosevelt, all

Harry Houdini and
Theodore Roosevelt
on board the liner
Imperator, June 1914 . . .

. . . with their fellow passengers.

Library of Congress

three shared—and to various degrees contributed to—the highly racialized views that mark and mar this period. In science, popular literature, art, and daily life, the bodies of African American and Native American men had been frequently displayed, even fetishized, while their dignity and worth were denied. Significantly, the popular exaltation of the white male body took place at the very time when Plains Indians, supposedly a "vanishing race" following the massacre at Wounded Knee in 1890, were forced onto reservations little better than prisons and African Americans were brutally subjected to segregation, disfranchisement, and lynchings. It is as if white American men sought to seize the "primitive" strength, freedom, wildness, and eroticism that they ascribed to these darker bodies to arm themselves for modern life.

Manliness is a cultural site that is always under construction, of course, but in this period it seems to have been undermined on a number of fronts and demanded constant work in new arenas to remain strong. Many men born too late for the Civil War wondered how they would fare in a similar test of courage, and some, like Roosevelt, plunged into the Spanish-American and Philippine-American Wars as opportunities to prove themselves and to build American manhood.[6] Alarmed by the "new immigration" from southern and eastern Europe, composed principally of Catholics and Jews, some Americans worried that the "enterprising, thrifty, alert, adventurous, and courageous" immigrants of past generations were being replaced by "beaten men from beaten races; representing the worst failures in the struggle for existence."[7] At the same time, reports warned that Americans of Anglo-Saxon stock were declining markedly in physical vigor and, by failing to reproduce themselves in sufficient numbers, might ultimately commit "race suicide."[8] Keenly aware of the passing of the frontier, many Americans believed that a nation of farmers was rapidly becoming a nation of city dwellers. Roosevelt's fervent commitment to conservation represented one attempt among many to stay close to the wild lest it be extinguished. Even those such as he who occupied the most privileged positions often worried that society's comforts might weaken their bodies and their wills. Anglo-Saxon Protestants from refined and intellectually cultivated classes were thought to be especially susceptible to neurasthenia, that distinctively modern, characteristically American disease of nervous weakness and fatigue. The founder of this medical specialty, George M. Beard, placed high among its manifold causes excessive brain work, intense competition, constant hurry, rapid communications, the ubiquitous rhythm and din of technology. At the turn of the century, neurasthenia appeared to be reaching epidemic proportions.[9]

Above all, perceptions of manliness were drastically altered by the new dynamics created by vast corporate power and immense concentrations of wealth. Fundamental to traditional conceptions of American manhood had been autonomy and independence, which had to be recast in a tightly integrated economy of national and international markets. Titanic corporations arose with incredible swiftness in all areas of industry: Standard Oil, United States Steel, Pennsylvania Railroad, General Electric, Consolidated Coal, American Telephone and Telegraph, International Harvester, Weyerhaeuser Timber, U.S. Rubber, Pittsburgh Plate Glass, International Paper, Du Pont de Nemours, American Sugar Refining, Armour, United Fruit, American Can, Central Leather, and Eastman Kodak. By 1904, about three hundred industrial corporations had gained control of more than 40 percent of all manufacturing in the United States.[10]

And at the head of these new companies stood a greatly expanded, highly bureaucratized managerial class. Clerical workers, no more than 1 percent of the workforce in 1870, had swelled to more than 3 percent by 1900 and nearly 4 percent by 1910. These nascent "organization men" (and some women) increasingly worked in large buildings where the offices were as hierarchical and rule-bound as armies. A writer in *The Independent* worried, "The middle class is becoming a salaried class, and rapidly losing the economic and moral independence of former days."[11]

Factory workers, for their part, were the foot soldiers in this expanding industrial force. The period 1890–1914 was pivotal in the struggle between them and management over control of production within factories. Skilled workers had treasured a certain autonomy in setting the pace, organization, and distribution of wages for their work, an autonomy they had earned because of their superior knowledge of their craft. As Big Bill Haywood of the Industrial Workers of the World liked to boast: "The manager's brains are under the workman's cap."[12] The new corporate industrial order massively assaulted this power and the ethic of manly pride and brotherhood among workers that sustained it. Through intense mechanization, division of labor, and "scientific management," industrialists endeavored to dominate all aspects of production and to reduce the workers' bodies to components in a gigantic machine.

Americans were in the forefront of this corporate revolution. Whereas in 1870 Britain provided 32 percent of the world's industrial output (followed by the United States at 23 percent and Germany at 13 percent), in 1913 the United States provided an immense 36 percent (Germany and Britain distantly trailed at 16 percent and 14 percent, respectively).[13] Yet to contemporaries, this industrial growth felt not like an orderly process but like a wild, careening ride. Wall Street panics in 1873 and 1893 began two of the greatest depressions in American history, and smaller depressions in 1885 and 1907 jolted the economy. By the mid-1880s supporters of labor and capital alike had come to fear that the strains of the new industrial society might erupt in large-scale riots, even a class-based civil war.

Industrialization accelerated major demographic shifts that were also altering the arenas in which manliness might be exercised. The nation's population continued to be the fastest growing in the world, leaping from fewer than forty million in 1870 to roughly sixty-three million in 1890 and nearly ninety-two million in 1910. This increase was partly due to unprecedented numbers of immigrants, amounting to 16 percent of the population in 1881–1900 and a staggering 24 percent in 1901–1920.[14] The new arrivals clustered mostly in America's cities, particularly along the manufacturing belt from the Northeast to the upper Midwest. In 1910 in New York, Chicago, Boston, Cleveland, Detroit, and Providence, more than one in three residents was foreign-born.[15]

Yet even as the population grew, more and more men deferred marriage; in fact, one historian has called this period "the age of the bachelor." In 1890 an estimated two-thirds of all men aged fifteen to thirty-four were unmarried, a proportion that changed little through the first two decades of the twentieth century. In cities the proportion was higher still, forming the basis for a flourishing urban bachelor culture that included a growing gay subculture. In many respects, this bachelor culture represented a pocket of resistance to—or at least a refuge from—the responsibilities of family and community, the demands of women, the discipline of work, and the pressures of a more regulated society. In boisterous play and aggressive competition, bachelors could enjoy a continuity between boyhood and manhood. They played or watched sports and reveled in contests of physical skill and decisive triumph. At the beginning of this period, their great hero was no exponent of manly rectitude such as Roosevelt became, but boxing's brawling heavyweight champion John L. Sullivan. In newspapers and pulp fiction, they avidly read adventure stories about other heroic men, from Eugen Sandow to Tarzan. Many also indulged in pursuits that more respectable elements condemned: heavy drinking, swearing, gambling, engaging in casual sex with women—or other men.[16]

These urban bachelors had several female counterparts, including the working-class "tough girl," the radical needleworker, the shop clerk, the typist, and the "New Woman." The last was a capacious term for middle- and upper-class women who in various ways conducted themselves with a new independence and assertiveness, whether by shopping in department stores, smoking in public, playing tennis, expressing interest in sexuality, earning advanced degrees, entering traditionally male professions, calling for social and political reforms, or agitating for the ballot. Self-development, not self-sacrifice, was the New Woman's watchword. As one woman writer succinctly put it, "The question now is, not 'What does man like?' but 'What does woman prefer?'" Although neither the term "feminism" nor its full expression emerged until the end of this period, it was already clear that many women were refusing to be bound by traditional notions of women's domestic sphere.[17]

As the structure of both work and urban life changed dramatically, so too did the forms of leisure and communications by which people found release from and perspective on their worlds. Many commercial enterprises offered attractions calculated to appeal to broad popular tastes across different classes, ethnicities, and genders, and they grew into big businesses with some of the same characteristics of systematization, centralization, and managerial control that defined corporate industries. As they intersected, they created the conditions for a new society of spectacle that seemed to ease some of the deep divisions in America's new urban, industrial life. It is here that Sandow, Houdini, and Burroughs flourished.

Vaudeville theater, one of the most popular new entertainments and the springboard for both Sandow's and Houdini's careers, emerged in the 1880s. It represented an extraordinarily successful effort to unite a fragmented theatergoing public: it combined the format of the variety show with standards of morality and settings of refinement that placed it decisively apart from the concert saloons and burlesque houses where variety shows had flourished. With as many as ten or twelve acts, sometimes in continuous performance throughout the day, vaudeville triumphed by offering "something for everyone." "If one objects to the perilous feats of the acrobats or jugglers," observed a critic in 1899, "he can read his programme or shut his eyes for a few moments and he will be compensated by some sweet bell-ringing or sentimental or comic song, graceful or grotesque dancing, a one-act farce, trained animals, legerdemain, impersonations, clay modeling, the biograph [moving] pictures, or the stories of the comic monologuist."[18] Whether in small-time houses or big-time theaters, vaudeville performers prided themselves on being able to engage diverse audiences of men, women, and children from both working-class and middle-class backgrounds in cities and towns across America. Even so, theirs was an industrialized art in which the vaudevillians worked along regional circuits that were dominated after 1900 by the United Booking Office, which spanned the continent.

Sport experienced a similar transformation into commercial entertainment. As once local, informal, and unregulated games became big business, they were systematized and put under managerial control. Yet they did not succumb to bureaucratic rationalization; the most popular sports, boxing and baseball, offered stirring dramas of individual prowess and communal aspiration that some fans treasured for their lifetimes. These professional sports, as well as college football, were heavily freighted with ambitions to revitalize American manhood. Even while seeking to reform their abuses, elite spokesmen extolled the value of these sports in instilling strength, skill, toughness, endurance, and courage. Writing in the dignified pages of *The North American Review* in 1888, Duffield Osborne simultaneously advocated replacing bare-knuckle fighting with regulated glove boxing and defended pugilism, with its "high manly qualities," as a bulwark against the emasculating tendencies of modern life. Without such antidotes to "mawkish sentimentality," he warned, civilization would degenerate into "mere womanishness."[19] Four years later,

"Gentleman Jim" Corbett defeated John L. Sullivan in the first heavyweight championship bout fought with padded gloves and timed rounds under the Marquis of Queensberry Rules. When the African American Jack Johnson won the title in 1908, however, it became abundantly clear that many fans thought revitalization should be for whites only. They raised an insistent call for a "Great White Hope" who could defeat Johnson, which was finally answered by the hulking Jess Willard in 1915.[20]

The transformations in popular theater and sport were sustained by profound changes in journalism. In the country as a whole from 1892 to 1914, the number of daily newspapers rose by more than a third, from 1,650 to 2,250, an all-time high; and their size expanded and circulation doubled. In the vanguard of change marched the great metropolitan newspapers. In 1892 ten papers in four cities had circulation bases higher than 100,000; in 1914 more than thirty papers in a dozen cities could make such a claim. Publishers, led by Joseph Pulitzer and William Randolph Hearst, increasingly encouraged the practice of what was called the New Journalism, by which they hoped to attract as diverse a readership as possible. They offered at low prices a bulging combination of sensational stories (such as those about Houdini's flamboyant escapes), serious news coverage, reportorial stunts, personal interviews (often with vaudeville and sports celebrities), civic crusades, and lavish illustrations. When newspapers were organized into spaces and departments devoted to sports, fashion, Sunday magazine supplements, and special columns, they acquired a variety format that resembled a vaudeville bill. And like vaudeville, these newspapers self-consciously aspired to be the "voice of the city," speaking for as well as to its myriad residents. They expressed this ambition both in their publications and, frequently, in their very offices, exemplified by the Pulitzer Building, which, upon its completion in 1890, surpassed Trinity Church as the tallest structure in New York City.[21]

The birth of the modern metropolitan daily and Sunday newspaper was accompanied by that of the modern, low-priced, mass-circulation magazine. Previously, inexpensive magazines had enjoyed only fleeting success. But in 1893 S. S. McClure founded an illustrated monthly magazine bearing his name that offered both fiction and articles and sold for only fifteen cents rather than the thirty-five charged by his self-consciously genteel rivals. Other magazines, such as *Cosmopolitan* and *Munsey's*, cut their prices still further, and a host of new ten-cent magazines followed in their wake. In 1896, on the strength of his success, Frank Munsey revamped his story weekly, *The Argosy*, printed it on cheap, porous wood-pulp paper, and launched the modern pulp-fiction magazine. In the next few years he created a stable of such magazines, including *The All-Story*, in which *Tarzan* first appeared. By 1903 Munsey could fairly estimate that the ten-cent magazines had gained 85 percent of the entire magazine circulation in the country. Offering a wide variety of stories and articles, abundant illustrations, and a lively tone, such magazines represented a significant cultural challenge to established competitors. The editor of *The Independent* snobbishly defended his magazine's concentration on the "comparatively cultivated class" in magazines and newspapers, saying it was "the only audience worth addressing, for it contains the thinking people." But publishers such as McClure, Munsey, Pulitzer, and Hearst, like vaudeville impresarios such as B. F. Keith and F. F. Proctor, staked their fortunes on their ability to hold a mass following by giving the people plenty of varied materials at low prices.[22]

A number of factors held down the costs of mass-circulation magazines and newspapers, including technological breakthroughs in papermaking, typesetting, printing, and binding. But in their development, revenues from advertising were indispensable. Between 1892 and 1914 advertising in newspapers and periodicals increased by roughly 350 percent, and most of it was from local sources, especially the new department stores. Yet magazines, long the messengers for correspondence courses and patent nostrums, now were key sites for national advertising of standard brands from Victrolas to Grape-Nuts. Older "polite" magazines had once prided themselves on avoiding advertising, but for mass-circulation magazines in the early twentieth century the situation was fundamentally different. "There is still an illusion to the effect that a magazine is a periodical in which advertising is incidental," explained an advertising executive in 1907. "But we don't look at it that way. A magazine is simply a device to induce people to read advertising."[23]

Associated with these transformations in the popular theater, sports, and the press, as well as with the expansive commercial culture as a whole, was the continuing proliferation of photographic im-

Recovering classical manhood through Grape-Nuts, an advertisement in *The All-Story*, December 1911. The University of North Carolina at Chapel Hill

ages. The passion for studio portraits, awakened with the rise of photography, not only seized people of all classes but helped to make possible a new celebrity culture. Innovations in photographic reproduction and display changed individuals' very apprehension of themselves and the world. In 1888 George Eastman introduced his Kodak camera, initially a toy for the wealthy but a device that quickly demonstrated its potential to make virtually everyone an amateur photographer. At about the same time, between 1885 and 1910, the halftone, a new, cheaper technique of photoengraving that permitted the direct reproduction of photographs in newspapers, magazines, and books, effected a visual revolution.[24] Finally, the new mass medium of the movies grew with dazzling speed from Thomas Edison's peephole kinetoscope of 1893 (in which Sandow made an appearance), to large-scale motion-picture projection in 1896 (which was frequently the concluding diversion on vaudeville programs), to D. W. Griffith's controversial two-and-a-half-hour epic of white supremacy, *The Birth of a Nation*, in 1915. What had begun as a novelty became a consuming national pastime.

These popular spectacles were crucial in both maintaining and subverting gender categories. Indeed, one of the most striking elements was that men's and women's bodies were displayed and dramatized as never before in popular theater, sports, photography, fiction, film, and advertisements. Recent studies have highlighted aspects of this process, especially as it affected women. In the popular theater, for example, spectacle could be used to address quite different audiences for vastly different purposes. Burlesque, expelled from "legitimate" theaters and vaudeville houses, offered leg shows for working-class and lower-middle-class men. By contrast, vaudeville theaters, looking to attract middle-class families as well as members of the bachelor subculture, offered women a broader range of roles. Many of these were constraining, but others allowed for freedom, independence, and self-expression that laid the groundwork for an emergent feminism. By the second decade of the twentieth century, protesting women, including socialists, trade unionists, and suffragists, had taken this sense of theatricality from the stage to the streets to gather support for their causes.[25]

Historians have paid less attention to the importance of the *male* body in popular spectacles—and, especially, challenges to the exposed white male body—as expressing the meaning of manliness in this emergent urban, industrial order. That subject lies at the heart of this book. My approach is highly selective. I have chosen to focus on Sandow, Houdini, and Burroughs in order to see how they reveal popular aesthetic and cultural patterns. In a context dominated by the rise of corporate capitalism, the changing character of work, the advent of a skyscraper civilization, and the emergence of the New Woman, they helped to create the Revitalized Man. As a model of wholeness and strength, this figure ostensibly stood above the political conflict and class strife of the period, inviting a broad and diverse public of men and women, blue-collar and white-collar workers, to celebrate common gender ideals. The appeal of Sandow, Houdini, and Tarzan could unite followers of John L. Sullivan and Theodore Roosevelt; readers of newspapers as diverse as Richard Kyle Fox's *National Police Gazette*, Hearst's and Pulitzer's metropolitan dailies, and the socialist *Masses*; admirers of Burt L. Standish's *Frank Merriwell at Yale* and Jack London's *The Call of the Wild*; and fans of the illustrator J. C. Leyendecker's Arrow Collar Man and the painter George Bellows's savage boxers.

Sandow, Houdini, and Burroughs's Tarzan can thus illuminate much about the place of popular culture at the advent of modern society. They help us to understand more about how the shift to an advancing technological civilization was communicated to and apprehended by publics in North America and abroad. They tell us about how modernity was understood in terms of the body and how the white male body became a powerful symbol by which to dramatize modernity's impact and how to resist it. They reveal the degree to which thinking about masculinity in this period meant thinking about sexual and racial dominance as well. They also tell us that hopes and fears, aspirations and anxieties are often difficult to distinguish. Perhaps every dream is the sunny side of some nightmare; perhaps every cultural wish has a dark lining of fear.

ONE

WHO IS THE PERFECT MAN?

EUGEN SANDOW AND

A NEW STANDARD FOR AMERICA

Images of male muscular development and bodily perfection have both a distinguished lineage and a troubled history in Western culture. Though securely established in classical Greece and Rome, their position afterward became highly precarious, particularly in the context of a Christian pursuit of spiritual perfection that denied the body. In response, artists from the Renaissance on have been remarkably resourceful in attaching both male and female nudes to classical, biblical, ideal, or exotic subjects. In addition, beginning in the 1840s, the new medium of photography offered an expanding range of images of the nude in more and less acceptable guises: academic studies for artists; records of medical and scientific subjects; ethnographic evidence of exotic peoples; and pornography. Still, even in the late nineteenth century, to display the unclad male figure, let alone the female one, bereft of divine, allegorical, or alien trappings—not as a god, virtue, ruler, hero, exotic figure, or scientific specimen but simply as a person—was to risk falling from the lofty plane of the nude to the shameful one of the merely naked.[1]

Given this context, the emergence of the unclad male body from the realms of high art, science, and low life into the broader culture toward the turn of the twentieth century demands historical investi-

Sandow dressed in fig leaf and Roman sandals, 1894. Photograph by Benjamin J. Falk. Library of Congress

gation. That body did not simply walk free. It faced suspicious inquiries as to its status. And it carried heavy aesthetic and cultural baggage, into which were stuffed a multitude of claims and aspirations, fantasies and anxieties. This baggage bore various tags, sometimes prominently, about manliness, heroism, power, virility, and eroticism. The figure who could lift them all would be regarded as not an ordinary but a perfect man.

This was perhaps the weightiest baggage that accompanied Eugen Sandow when he disembarked from the liner *Elbe* in New York in June 1893, and it only increased during his appearances across the United States in the next year. Sandow arrived at a key moment: just a month earlier, the stock market had crashed, slowly pulling the economy into a deep depression that profoundly threatened the sense of independence and control once enjoyed by men. Already bankers and businessmen feared ruin; soon millions of workers were unemployed, and tens of thousands of tramps drifted around the country. The depression intensified a widespread sense of gender malaise. To many, manhood seemed no longer a stable condition—absolute and unproblematic—but rather an arduous, even precarious achievement that had to be vigilantly defended. Supposedly a biological category, manhood was also a *performance*.[2] And Sandow quickly emerged as the most brilliant performer of manhood of the 1890s. In his live appearances at vaudeville theaters, in widely circulated photographs, newspaper and magazine illustrations, and in some of the very first moving pictures, Sandow's unclad body became the most famous in the world and his name a synonym for muscular development. He helped to reshape notions of what male bodily perfection—and masculinity itself—might be in modern industrial society. And for all his active participation in this process, this "perfect man" was not simply a figure waiting to be discovered. In significant respects he was created out of the cultural demands of his time.

FROM ADONIS TO HERCULES

An acrobatic strongman on the English music-hall stage, Sandow made his American debut on June 12, 1893, at the Casino Roof Garden at Broadway and Thirty-ninth Street in New York City. He was an unusual attraction for the Casino, whose manager took pride in its being among the most refined variety theaters in the country, offering comic operas and other stylish acts in a theater of fantastic Moorish design. Sandow's six-week run came during the slack season, one made worse by a heat wave that baked the city and by the economy's plunge into depression. After the stock market's collapse in May, credit had tightened like a fist. Businesses failed daily. The Erie Railroad went bankrupt in July, and other railroads rapidly followed. Rich, middle-class, and laboring men alike had reason to feel tense about the future and uncertain about themselves. Depending on their class and political position, they would cast the blame on labor agitators or greedy capitalists, Democrats or Republicans. All were receptive to a man who embodied strength and confidence—as were many women of all classes. The wealthy saw Sandow first, but instantly newspapers and illustrated magazines made him a household name.[3]

Sandow went onstage immediately after a performance of William Gill's musical spoof *Adonis*, one of the most popular American plays of the time. In retrospect, we can see the two acts not simply as diverting offerings on a single variety bill but as contending performances of masculinity, the first of a series of such contrasts that Sandow's American tour entailed. To appreciate the effect of Sandow's performance, we need to watch the previous act closely.

The title role of Adonis, the perfection of male beauty, was taken by a handsome, trim matinee idol named Henry Dixey. *Adonis*, first produced in 1884, when he was twenty-five, had made his career. Dixey was a "master of pantomime," in the words of one critic, and had made "his body . . . a thoroughly trained instrument of expression, of which he has perfect and complete control." He was so successful at embodying this popular theatrical ideal of physical perfection that he was virtually trapped in the role, performing it more than seven hundred times in New York alone, in addition to tours around the country and an acclaimed run in London.[4]

Adonis was a late-Victorian burlesque lampooning the conventions of melodrama, society plays, and gender roles as it presented women in aggressive competition for and pursuit of an irresistibly beautiful man. Gill's play turned inside out the Greek myth of Pygmalion and Galatea, in which a sculptor falls in love with his female creation, whom Aphrodite brings to life. (The Pygmalion story was being freshly popularized at the time both in comic treatments, including a play by W. S. Gilbert performed in New York in 1881, and in paintings by the British artists G. F. Watts and Edward Burne-Jones and the Frenchman Jean-Léon Gérôme.) In Gill's play a sculptress has created in her statue of Adonis a "perfect figure." Indeed, he is so beautiful and alluring that she cannot bear to sell him as promised to a wealthy duchess. Seeing Adonis, the duchess, together with her four daughters, is instantly and passionately smitten as well. The daughters try to conceal their ardor as each offers a refined observation about the figure's artistic merits: "Isn't it lovely." "What grace in that nostril." "What symmetry in that eyebrow." "What indications of strength in those biceps." Until the fourth sighs, "And what lovely calves."

To resolve the question of ownership, an obliging goddess brings the statue to life. Theatrical photographs suggest how Dixey comically achieved this metamorphosis. The determinedly absurd plot combined the spirit of Gilbert and Sullivan's *Iolanthe* (in which Dixey had earlier played) and a college farce. The pursuit of Adonis rapidly becomes entangled with three figures who are burlesques of stock characters of melodrama: the Marquis de Baccarat, a quintessential "polished villain"; Rosetta, a self-declared simple and poor "village beauty . . . pursued by all the lordly vilyuns for miles around"; and Rosetta's rustic father, Bunion Turke, who, doubting his daughter's virtue, repeatedly declaims the necessity of shutting against her his "poor but honest door" and "poor but honest heart"—even as he attempts to steal Adonis's lunch. To heighten the absurdity (and the gender inversion), Adonis ludicrously assumes the disguise of a village maid and is briefly courted by the Marquis. For her part, Rosetta, who promptly falls in love with Adonis and who boasts that she weighs 120 pounds, was played by the hefty Amelia Summerville. (In an earlier production she had been played by the 300-pound George K. Fortesque in drag.) Ultimately, Adonis is cornered by all his female pursuers, who demand that he choose among them. Instead, he beseeches the goddess who gave him life, "Oh take me away and petrify me—place me on my old familiar pedestal—and hang a placard round my neck:—'HANDS OFF.' " Thus, exhausted by his stint as a flesh-and-blood object of desire, Dixey as Adonis reassumed the pose of a perfect work of art as the curtain fell.

Dixey's metamorphoses in *Adonis*.
Photographs by Napoleon Sarony. Theatre
Arts Collection, Harry Ransom Humanities
Research Center, The University of
Texas at Austin

Dixey's Adonis as a village maid.
Photograph by Napoleon Sarony.
Harvard Theatre Collection

Adonis pointed to a new set of attitudes governing gender relations and bodily display, in which genteel women were assuming some of the prerogatives that earlier in the century had been reserved for men.[5] That a man might be the construction and possession of women, valued solely for his beauty, his body openly admired and aggressively pursued by them (as well as courted by his own sex)—such was the stuff of both male fantasies and male anxieties. In its farcical way, *Adonis* played with the meaning of gender in modern life and with the question of whether anatomy indeed determined destiny or merely offered a pretext for roles and disguises. Still, if at the end of the play anyone in the audience were asked who best portrayed the perfect man, the answer would undoubtedly have been Henry Dixey.

Then it was Sandow's turn. When the curtain rose again, Sandow, clad only in a loincloth and Roman sandals, had assumed the statue's pose in Dixey's stead—and the contrast made the audience gasp. One observer wrote, "New York has come to look upon Dixey as a fairly well-made young man. When New York has seen Sandow after Dixey, however, New York will realize what a wretched, scrawny creature the usual well-built young gentleman is compared with the perfect man." Slowly, this new statue came to life as Sandow struck classical poses and moved his "forest of muscles" at will. For almost a decade, Dixey had successfully played the part of a beautiful classical statue come to life, but Sandow took on the dual roles of sculptor and masterpiece. He instantly eclipsed Dixey. In the words of one journalist at the time of his debut: "It was hard for the spectators . . . to believe that it was indeed flesh and blood that they beheld. Such knots and bunches and layers of muscle they had never before seen off the statue of an Achilles, a Discobolus, or a fighting gladiator." Another reporter marveled: "He postures so as to bring the muscles more prominently before the audience, and he appears to be able to make them rise and fall just as easily as he can open and shut his eyes."[6]

In the second part of his act Sandow demonstrated his strength and dexterity. With a crisp, military manner and to piano accompaniment, he performed a series of feats with two fifty-six-pound dumbbells, repeatedly exceeding what the audience thought possible. Holding a dumbbell in each hand, he turned a back flip; he did the same feat with his ankles tied together and his eyes blindfolded. Then, with a great show of exertion, eight men brought onstage a huge barbell with a basket holding a man at each end. Using only one hand, Sandow lifted the two men over his head, stopping momentarily to hold the barbell straight out from his shoulder as a further proof of his strength. In still another feat displaying his powerful abdominal and dorsal muscles, he had his knees fastened to a Roman column and then bent backward to lift two men over his head.

The finale of Sandow's half-hour performance was the human bridge. Making his body into an arch with his chest upraised and his hands and feet on the floor in the "Tomb of Hercules" position, he supported a wooden platform on his shoulders, chest, and knees. Then three trained horses (actually ponies), with an advertised combined weight of twenty-six hundred pounds, stepped onto the platform and stayed there for about five seconds supported by Sandow, whose "every muscle . . . stood out like whipcord."[7]

From the moment of his New York debut, Sandow was seen not simply as a remarkable figure of strength and showmanship but also as a new ideal of the male body which brought to the fore a host of personal and cultural issues. At the height of his career, from 1893 to

1906, he repeatedly toured the United States (the total duration of his visits amounted to nearly seven years, far more time than he spent in his adopted home of England or anywhere else), but already by the end of his second American tour, in 1894, his presence had dramatically altered the discussion. His appearance shattered the prevailing image of the strongman: the thickset, barrel-chested performer in circuses, dime museums, and beer halls who might be mistaken for a blacksmith but never for a gentleman, let alone an Adonis. Sandow brilliantly succeeded in winning the applause of elite theatergoers even before he gained the attention of the broader middle and working classes. To them all, he represented a new standard of male fitness, beauty, strength, and potency. Starkly exposed and thoroughly publicized as he was, he became an icon of the hypermasculine who with his extraordinary muscular development literally embodied characteristics that many men and women believed were threatened by modern life.

Spectators viewed Sandow's body as both an attraction and a challenge, a model of strength and an object of desire, an inspiration, a rebuke, and a seduction. He simultaneously incited superlatives and stirred disquieting controversies and ambiguities. He was touted as the "strongest man in the world" and the "perfect man," yet he was pursued by challengers, imitators, and impostors who claimed they could duplicate or better his feats. He was celebrated as a monument not only of strength but also of classical beauty, yet his body was criticized as abnormal, even decadent. He cultivated prestige in both medical science and sport, yet he was supremely a creature of the vaudeville stage, the newspaper interview, and the photographer's studio. He presented himself as a modern gladiator with a heroic aura, yet he aroused charges of fabrication and deception. He was ostensibly an apostle of asexual health and strength, yet he implicitly promised to restore lost virility. He never acknowledged himself as an object of erotic interest, yet he enlarged the boundaries of the display of the male nude in live exhibitions and in photographs that elicited intense interest from women and especially from men at a time when the categories of heterosexuality and homosexuality did not squeeze so tightly as to inhibit a man's frank admiration of another man's body.[8] He claimed to embody an ancient heroic ideal of manhood that had been lost in the modern world, yet he turned his body into a commercial spectacle and a commodity whose image was widely reproduced and sold.

THE RECOVERY OF LOST MANHOOD

Superlatives and ambiguities began with Sandow's accounts of his upbringing and training. At the outset of his American tour, he concocted an autobiography that emphasized his eminently respectable origins and heroic achievements, and he reiterated it throughout his career in interviews, articles, and amply padded books (beginning with *Sandow on Physical Training*, a compendium of physical instruction, biography, press clippings, photographs, and line drawings.[9] In the process he changed his name from Friedrich Wilhelm Müller to a version of his mother's maiden name, Sandov (frequently Anglicizing his new given name of Eugen to Eugene as well). He preserved his background in Prussia, where he was born on April 2, 1867, but elevated his father from a fruit and vegetable seller in the markets of Königsberg to a successful jeweler and merchant. At the same time he shrewdly insisted his strength was not a gift of nature but an attainment strenuously earned. Indeed, the more he retold the story, the more his health as a youth declined. In some of his earlier newspaper interviews during his first American tour, as well as in his first book, he was "healthy," though less strong than his fellows; in later accounts he grew "very slight and sickly" as a child, and "my parents, as well as the physician, had serious doubts as to whether I would live."[10]

In this way Sandow struck chords about masculine strength and self-determination that have been played by many exemplars of American manhood from his time down to our own. Making his body became a sign of a man's ability to make his way in the world against all adversaries, strictly on his own merits. A strong, muscular body was an emblem of strong character and command. The message could be used equally well to validate the achievements of men from obscure and privileged backgrounds.

Born in the lap of the upper class, Theodore Roosevelt wrote that the turning point of his boyhood was his resolve to remake his "sickly, delicate," and asthmatic body into the strong, vigorous frame of a fearless leader. Significantly, he determined to do so at the age of fourteen after a trip to Maine on which two boys taunted him unmercifully and he discovered himself helpless to lay a blow on either. His transformation was no seven-day wonder, but years of boxing lessons and exercise paid off. A decade later, in the Dakota Territory, when a profane, two-gunned barroom bully called Roosevelt "four eyes" and goaded him beyond endurance, the eastern dude met the challenge decisively: "As I rose, I struck quick and hard with my right just to one side of the point of his jaw, hitting with my left as I straightened out, and then again with my right. . . . When he went down he struck the corner of the bar with his head . . . he was senseless."[11]

From the other end of the social spectrum, the leading American exemplars of physical culture in the early twentieth century credited Sandow for their own youthful conversions of body and will. The once frail and tubercular Bernarr Macfadden (1868–1955) saw Sandow perform in Chicago in 1893 and almost immediately began posing in classical and muscular attitudes himself. In 1899 Macfadden launched a monthly magazine, *Physical Culture*, which crusaded for health, fit-

Bernarr Macfadden posing as Mercury. Photograph by F. W. Guerin. Library of Congress

ness, exercise, and nutrition—as well as the "inspiration" of the muscular male (and occasionally female) body—with what might be regarded as missionary zeal, huckster's effrontery, or both. "Weakness is a crime," the magazine darkly warned readers. "Don't be a criminal."

A decade later, in 1909, sixteen-year-old Angelo Siciliano, a self-described "ninety-seven-pound weakling" and target of sand-kicking beach bullies, fastened a picture of Sandow on his dresser mirror and determined to emulate his hero. Within a few years he was performing as a strongman, first in sideshows at Coney Island, then on the vaudeville circuit. Having adopted the name Charles Atlas, he was proclaimed, in contests sponsored by Macfadden, the "World's Most Beautiful Man" in 1921 and "America's Most Perfectly Developed Man" the following year. For the next four decades, Atlas ruled as the most prominent physical-culture entrepreneur in the nation.[12]

All these men emphasized how, by dint of determination and method, they had transformed themselves from puny boys to men of strength, confidence, and command. The theme of metamorphosis lies at the heart of bodybuilding; and a longing for male metamorphosis lay deep in the culture of the United States and much of western Europe at the advent of the modern age. Sandow invoked it again and again.

Sandow dated his own conversion (almost certainly inauthentic) to the age of ten while on a studious Italian holiday with his father. By Sandow's account, in Rome he and his father pondered in art galleries the magnificently sculpted figures of ancient warriors and athletes "bespeaking power and energy in every limb." Sandow claimed to have asked his father not about the attainment of male power and virility but about their loss: "How is it that these men were so strong?" Why were men today so inferior in strength and stature? His father explained: "The heroes of old, my little Eugen, . . . never lolled at ease in a carriage or a railway train." Modern civilization marked the ascendancy of the brain over the body, but the price was "world-wide degeneration in health and strength."[13] Enraptured by this classical ideal, or so he later maintained, Sandow resolved to reclaim for himself, for men, and ultimately for humanity the health and strength they had lost.

But how? In Sandow's account he avidly acquired every book on athletics and exercise that "I could persuade my generous parents to purchase" and spent every spare moment at the gymnasium, all without much success. Only when he began to study anatomy seriously and to devise his own system of exercises to develop each and every muscle did he find "the key to the secret I had been endeavoring to solve." Here, it appeared, was a wholly individual achievement of almost Promethean proportions: to bring strength to the weak and health to the ill. From Sandow's account, one would never know of the enormously influential gymnastic movement founded by Friedrich Ludwig Jahn (1778–1852) to revive German manhood after the humiliating defeats of the Napoleonic Wars or of the vast revival of enthusiasm for the classical Greek ideal of the male nude dating back to Johann Winckelmann in the mid-eighteenth century.[14]

In this way Sandow appropriated the prestige both of science and of classical art in his career as a bodybuilder pioneering the display of the nearly nude body. Here again, he was not entirely original. Among men, self-declared "professors" of physical culture grew commonplace in variety shows, music halls, and dime museums; and, especially among women, "living sculptures," "*tableaux vivants*," and "model artist" shows had for half a century borrowed classical subjects as the thinnest of pretexts for the display of the female body.[15] Yet Sandow cultivated an air of bourgeois respectability that lifted him above these low entertainments. Though he admitted he served apprenticeships in circuses and wrestling matches on the European continent, he asserted that they came only after he dropped out of medical studies and the resulting rift with his father forced him to support himself. Throughout his career he cannily sought the appearance and demeanor of a gentleman, if a rather flamboyant one. Sandow early sensed, as would Edgar Rice Burroughs in *Tarzan of the Apes*, the importance of social credentials as well as great physical strength. Both Sandow and Burroughs were aware that a privileged class standing was vital in the new ideal of the male body, that class remained inscribed on the body, even the nude body. Class and, in Sandow's case, the incessant cultivation of classicism provided social and aesthetic cover that saved the body from mere nakedness.[16]

While knocking about the Continent in circuses and as an occasional artists' model (labors converted to picaresque adventures in his reminiscences), Sandow met one of the most successful professional strongmen, "Professor Louis Attila" (Ludwig Durlacher; 1844–1924),

The defeated French strongman
Charles A. Sampson. Harvard Theatre
Collection

Sandow triumphant, 1893.
Photograph by Benjamin J. Falk.
Library of Congress

then living in Brussels. A canny self-promoter, Attila eventually claimed among his students Tsar Alexander III, King George of Greece, and Britain's King Edward VII. Under the professor's tutelage, Sandow vastly developed his physique through progressive weight training, and, even more important, he honed his abilities as a showman.[17] Attila also orchestrated Sandow's first great breakthrough: his successful challenge in London for the title "strongest man on earth."

Challenges were a mainstay of stage strongmen, as they were of other stage performers (as we shall see with Harry Houdini) and of prizefighters such as John L. Sullivan. Formal challenges—including standing offers to best all comers and published challenges (known as cards) aimed at a specific rival—flourished on both sides of the Atlantic. These challenges, borrowing elements of the aristocratic duel, gave working- and middle-class men occasions to participate vicariously in dramas of strength, courage, and honor. And, of course, they contributed considerably to publicity and box-office receipts.[18]

In the fall of 1889 a French strongman who had taken the name Charles A. Sampson packed London's Royal Aquarium music hall as he nightly reiterated a dramatic challenge. Appearing with his protégé Cyclops (the Pole Franz Bienkowski), he offered a cash prize of five hundred pounds—as well as his self-awarded title, the "strongest man on earth"—to anyone who could duplicate his feats. In earlier appearances Sampson had performed such prodigies of strength as lifting a barbell that supposedly weighed an imperial ton (2,240 pounds) and raising a platform that supported an elephant. Yet like most stage strongmen, he accomplished these exploits far less through strength than through showmanship, deception, and special equipment that blurred the line between strongman and magician. A successful challenger to his title would need not only strength but also cunning.

With Attila's aid, on October 29, 1889, the unknown Sandow rose from the audience at the music hall to accept Sampson's challenge. He first surpassed Cyclops in a series of lifts. The following week he triumphed over Sampson himself, duplicating, if not as gracefully, the Frenchman's tricks of bending an iron bar, snapping a wire by expanding his chest, and breaking a chain with his arms.[19] With this triumph Sandow supplanted Sampson as the leading strongman on the

British music-hall circuit, a position he retained until his debut in the United States almost four years later made him an international star.

THE CHALLENGE OF SANDOW'S BODY

Sandow was not simply an athlete but also an actor, a man of the theater even more than of the gymnasium, and it is no accident that his career flourished during the great age of the music hall in England and of vaudeville in the United States, both of which placed a premium on specialty acts that could be reproduced for broad audiences night after night in a kind of industrialization of the theater. Onstage and off, he performed compressed dramas of masculine strength, agility, and physical development. These demanded great skill and training, to be sure, those not merely of sport but of showmanship. (Even his bent-press lifts might be regarded as less a proof of strength than a spectacular balancing act. Modern bodybuilding has continued to exist uneasily between sport and spectacle.) He offered his body not so much as an instrument of his achievements but as an achievement in itself: a heroic sculpture come to life. For muscular strength, development, control, and proportion, that body seemed instantly to set a new standard. To an unprecedented degree, Sandow made his body a subject of immense popular attention and cultural debate from the moment of his New York debut, as his press coverage clearly attests.

His extraordinary body fascinated observers, first, because it could be so successfully cloaked in a mantle of ordinariness. A Barnumesque giant who could lift a five-hundred-pound weight with his middle finger, break iron rods across his arms and legs, perform a regulation army drill with a good-sized man instead of a musket, or defeat three large and expert wrestlers at once would be impressive enough. That these and equally prodigious feats were achieved by a handsome young man of middle height who, when conventionally dressed, easily blended into a crowd seemed almost incredible. Sandow learned to cultivate this surprise and to startle spectators with the speed of his transformation from late-Victorian man-about-town to modern Hercules. When he had emerged from the music-hall audience to challenge Sampson in London, he had come onstage sporting

SANDOW.

13 AND 15 WEST 24TH ST. N.Y.
•MADISON SQUARE•

Sandow as a well-dressed gentleman. Photograph by Benjamin J. Falk. Harvard Theatre Collection

a monocle and evening clothes especially designed to be whisked off, like the unveiling of an artist's masterpiece, to reveal his powerful, sculpted body. So American viewers repeatedly marveled how this genial blond man, who was "nothing like so formidable in appearance as many men one [met] on the street every day," could reveal a body of almost superhuman development.[20] Thus, to his gradual transformation from sickly youth to strongman Sandow added a second, virtually instantaneous metamorphosis: from man of the crowd to marvel of muscle. This simultaneously placed Sandow in a class by himself and appealed to fantasies of self-transformation in boys and men, much as Clark Kent was to inspire later generations to dream of stripping off their street clothes and eyeglasses in a telephone booth and turning into Superman.

With his triumph over Sampson, Sandow claimed the title "strongest man on earth," and upon his arrival in America, he immediately won a new title: the "perfect man." Bodybuilding stresses muscle mass, definition, symmetry, and proportion, and Sandow embodied these to an unprecedented degree. His body's combination of well-proportioned, articulated, and extraordinary measurements fascinated trained observers and novices alike. By Sandow's own report, he stood five feet eight and a half inches and weighed 190 pounds. He boasted a neck of "18½ inches; biceps, 19½ inches; forearm, 17 inches; chest, normal, 52 inches; contracted, 46 inches; expanded, 58 inches; waist, 29 inches; thigh, 26⅔ inches; calf, 18 inches." These numbers prompted one reporter to observe that Sandow's waist was "not much bigger around than" the renowned beauty Lillie Langtry's, while his chest was "a good deal bigger . . . than [President] Grover Cleveland's." A century later, in a world of specialized equipment, systematic training, sophisticated diets, and anabolic steroids, Sandow's measurements would not earn even a second glance from experienced observers, but in 1893 they were staggering. Still more impressive was his overall muscular strength, control, and definition; before the names of the major muscle groups were common parlance, Sandow seemed a walking anatomic chart. "With the fond pride of a mother displaying a large family of children," he showed off his "collection of muscles one at a time and . . . [dwelled] modestly but lovingly upon their merits." A reporter exclaimed over his triceps ("much bigger than the calf in an ordinary strong man's leg"), the external obliques covering his ribs (each "twice as big around as a man's thumb"), and the erectors, lats, and other muscles on his back ("so thick, so deep, that the backbone, which is quite invisible, runs along at the bottom of a deep gorge"). Sandow proudly exhibited his trapezius muscles ("as thick through as the back of a man's hand is broad, and thicker in some places") and his abdominal muscles ("each about as big as a man's wrist"), which gave the impression of a corrugated washboard.[21]

He delighted still more in examinations by physicians and other experts, stripping for their inspection even as he shrewdly wrapped himself in their scientific and social prestige. The day before his public debut at New York's Casino Theatre, Sandow offered a private demonstration before a group of two hundred, including many physicians. Perhaps the most knowledgeable among them, Dr. Ramon Guiteras, a member of the New York Athletic Club and a former amateur boxer, declared him far stronger and faster than Sullivan, as well as "about the most perfectly developed specimen of a man I have ever seen."[22]

Mention of Sullivan reminds us that while Henry Dixey stood (especially among middle-class theatergoers) as one contender for the title "perfect man," because of his physical beauty, John L. Sullivan for a decade claimed that title (especially among working-class men), on account of his violent physical strength and fighting skill. Heavyweight boxing champion from 1882 until his loss to James Corbett ten years later, Sullivan attracted a greater following than any previous sports figure in American history. He early earned the nickname the "Boston Strong Boy," which stemmed from such feats as lifting barrels of flour and kegs of nails above his head; and during his boxing career he acquired numerous other appellations—"the Boston Hercules," "the Boston Miracle of huge muscles, terrific chest, and marvellous strength," "the finest specimen of physical development in the world."[23]

Born in Boston in 1858 to an Irish hod carrier, Sullivan worked as a plumber's apprentice, a tinsmith, then a mason, all before he was out of his teens. He was quarrelsome and restless. By temperament and physique as well as by class and culture, he proudly displayed the tough, manly bearing by which workers sought to affirm their independence in a time of shrinking respect and autonomy. His frequent

disputes and occasional fights lost Sullivan his early jobs, but his aggressiveness and bravado were to distinguish him as a boxer and to
make him a beloved hero to the working class.

In Sullivan's career as a boxer, as in Sandow's as a strongman, sport
and stage melded in intense performances of manliness. Sullivan began his boxing career at the age of nineteen, slugging in exhibitions at
local variety theaters and music halls. Though he catapulted to fame
on the basis of bare-knuckle prizefights, generally fought outside the
law, his fortune and following were sustained by stage bouts in which
he challenged all comers to last four gloved rounds of three minutes
apiece. "My name's John L. Sullivan," he would boom from the
stage, "and I can lick any son-of-a-bitch alive." (However, in an era of
growing racial segregation, Sullivan refused to fight black contenders
such as the Australian heavyweight champion Peter Jackson.) If there
were no takers, he sparred with a fellow member of the troupe. On
other tours he did not box at all but posed or acted. Exploiting the enthusiasm for "living statues," which Sandow would transform, Sullivan struck poses as "the biggest undressed heroes of antiquity": "the
Dying Gladiator," "Hercules at Rest," "Cain Killing Abel," and so on.

Dudley A. Sargent. Library of Congress

In 1890–1891 he played the part of a virtuous Irish blacksmith in the tailor-made melodrama *Honest Hearts and Willing Hands*. With Sullivan's ascendancy, prizefighting moved from the shady pursuit of gamblers and saloon keepers to a more respectable mass entertainment that attracted solidly middle-class and professional patrons as well as the working classes.[24]

In 1892, as the thirty-four-year-old Sullivan trained for his championship bout with the Californian James Corbett, his celebrated body was rigorously examined by the nation's leading figure in physical education, Dudley A. Sargent. Sargent was best qualified to determine who the perfect man was from a purely physical standpoint, and, because he also examined Eugen Sandow the following year, he is best qualified to help us compare the two figures.

Sargent was both a scientist keenly interested in the possibilities of bodily perfection and a onetime circus acrobat who knew firsthand the kind of theaters in which both Sullivan and Sandow got their start. After a brief stint as a performer in his teens, he left such entertainments behind for the life of a college athletic instructor. He took charge of the Bowdoin College gymnasium in his native Maine at the age of twenty, two years before he enrolled as a freshman. He went on to receive a medical doctorate from Yale, transforming that college's gymnastic instruction in the process. Since 1879, as director of Harvard's Hemenway Gymnasium, he had trained numerous teachers of physical education and devised an array of muscle "developers," equipment sold throughout the country.[25] He also took detailed body measurements of all Harvard and Radcliffe students. The distribution of variants among these measurements formed a bell-shaped, or normal, curve, which to Sargent, as to many would-be scientists in the nineteenth and twentieth centuries, seemed an empirical revelation of natural law. If the statistically "typical" man stood at the absolute mean, or center, of the bell curve, then, Sargent believed, the "ideal" man possessed equally symmetrical measurements while improving all, so that not only was each element strong and well developed in itself but together they plotted a straight line in their relation to the typical man. Anthropometry proved, according to Sargent, "[t]here is a perfect form or type of man, and the tendency of the race is to attain this type." Yet one price of civilization, he believed, had been the contravention of this law. The specialization of tasks in modern life, as well as the use of conveniences, discouraged balanced exercise of the whole body and contributed to improper physical development and, with it, disease. Furthermore, because bodily health and moral vigor were interconnected, this imbalance and debility inevitably invited moral decline as well.[26]

Sargent was thus John the Baptist of fitness, preaching the gospel of physical education and longing for the coming of a messiah, a "perfect man" who would show forth the way to all. He had beheld this vision in classical "statues of the Gladiator, the Athlete, Hercules, Apollo, and Mercury," and as he composed his anthropometric charts on thousands of young men, he eagerly awaited the second coming.[27]

It was not Sullivan. Sargent examined the heavyweight champion twice during the summer of 1892, first on June 2, at the beginning of training for the match with Corbett, and again on August 13, a month before the fight. Like other physical educators of the period, Sargent believed that concentration on a single activity or sport created a physical imbalance and, with it, a potential moral distortion. He claimed that he not only could identify a gymnast or a baseball player by his distinctive muscular development but also could tell his particular event or position.[28] So Sargent's perfect man would have no mark of specific endeavor or work. Not surprisingly, he found that Sullivan had the body—and presumably the morals—of a slugger. (Although Sullivan was toasted for his lordly generosity at the bar, he was notorious for drunken rages and flagrant affairs.[29]) In fact, the dissipation of the Boston Strong Boy was starkly evident in the first examination. Standing five feet ten and a half inches, he weighed 236 pounds, 20 of which he managed to shed in the next two months. Nor did his bodily measurements present the model of symmetry that the physical educator so esteemed. (The measurements of Sandow, who was two inches shorter and at least twenty-six pounds lighter, are included in the table for comparison.)

Sullivan	June 2	August 13	(Sandow)
Neck:	17.1	16.5	(18.5)
Chest:	46.1	44.5	(52)
Waist:	42.1	38.2	(29)
Hips:	46.1	42.9	(—)
Thighs:	26.4	25	(26.67)
Knees:	—	17.5	(—)

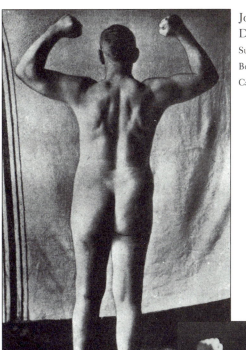

John L. Sullivan as examined by Dudley Sargent. From the copy of Sullivan's *Life and Reminiscences* in The Rare Book Collection, The University of North Carolina at Chapel Hill

Sandow, 1893. Photograph by Napoleon Sarony. Library of Congress

Even the trimmer Sullivan of the second examination had a girth in waist, hips, thighs, and knees that approached and in one instance exceeded any comparable measurements in Sargent's extensive tables. Sargent tried to put the best face on these figures. Euphemistically, he commended Sullivan's "large trunk" as "a reservoir of vital action" and his "powerful . . . thighs as a basis of support." Sullivan, he concluded, exemplified "the brawn and sinew that conquers both opponents and environments and sustains the race."[30] But he was certainly not the perfect man.

Most telling of all were the full-length photographs of the nude Sullivan at the second examination, showing him with arms at his side and with arms raised and muscles flexed, when he was supposedly in fighting trim. Sargent emphasized that they displayed the champion's "strong points," and Sullivan and his book publishers were proud enough of them to include them in his *Life and Reminiscences*. Still, they show the great divide that was just opening between different conceptions of the exemplary male body and how Sullivan was on the verge of losing not just his championship but also his centrality as a manly physical ideal.

No one could mistake Sullivan for a classical nude; he is merely a man undressed. He is massive and powerful but markedly lacks both the proportion and the articulation of musculature that Sandow would do so much to popularize. He has a thick waist, big buttocks, solid but undefined legs. His body is a blunt instrument, shaped to give and receive hard blows and difficult to topple. With some effort, a present-day reader may imagine why in his prime Sullivan could be called a Hercules. But it takes no effort to understand why he was never regarded as an Adonis or Apollo. With Sandow's New York debut ten months later, however, a figure emerged who was hailed as both Hercules *and* Apollo, even as Sargent's prophesied "perfect man." So it is also not hard to understand why, when asked by Joseph Pulitzer's *New York World* to conduct an examination of Sandow, Sargent jumped at the chance.

For Sandow, this examination was in an important sense a title bout, and he went to it eagerly. He arrived at the Broadway hotel in which Sargent had assembled an array of equipment, shed his cutaway coat and steel-gray suit, and presented himself to the physician. Sargent had already made clear his skepticism about mere muscle size in discussing his examination of Sullivan: "We often read of seventeen inch biceps, and seventeen inch calves, but these proportions are more likely to be found on dime museum freaks than on well developed athletes."[31] Nonetheless, Sargent was immediately struck by Sandow's muscular development, especially in the upper arms and back. The first measurements—of height and weight—must have disappointed Sandow. He tipped the scales at only 180 pounds (10 pounds less than his reported weight) and measured five feet eight inches—a half inch shorter than he claimed. (Undaunted, Sandow would later maintain that he stood over five feet nine inches.[32]) But once past these preliminaries, Sandow excelled in the tests, including those measuring both his reaction time and his strength.

Even so, moving an indicator up a scale hardly satisfied Sandow's sense of drama, and he proposed tests of his own. Searching for the heaviest man in the room, he chose the 175-pound Sargent. The strongman knelt down behind the physician and had him step with one foot onto Sandow's open palm. Then with his arm straight, Sandow lifted the surprised Sargent up and placed him on a table. He performed other feats of strength with Sargent, including one that might have been billed "The Human Trampoline." Sandow lay on the floor and asked Sargent to stand on his abdomen. With the doctor in place, Sandow kept his abdominal muscles relaxed for a moment, then suddenly contracted them, popping Sargent into the air. Sandow concluded by making the muscles on his arms and legs dance as Sargent marveled at his control.

Sargent had at last found the figure whom he had so long sought. His enthusiastic judgment was a press agent's dream:

Sandow is the most wonderful specimen of man I have ever seen. He is strong, active and graceful, combining the characteristics of Apollo, Hercules, and the ideal athlete. There is not the slightest evidence of sham about him. On the contrary, he is just what he pretends to be. His behavior under the tests was admirable. I might add that he combines with his other qualities that of a perfect gentleman. He has a considerable knowledge of anatomy, and can call the muscles by their proper names. I shall be glad to have him come and lecture before the students of Harvard.[33]

The "perfect man" was also the "perfect gentleman." With Sargent's examination all Sandow's claims had been authoritatively verified. Having defeated the lightweight Henry Dixey, he had now knocked out the heavyweight champion John L. Sullivan just as assuredly as had Corbett in the ring.[34]

Ultimately, however, the challenge posed by Sandow's body affected much more than perceptions of public figures such as Dixey and Sullivan. His supposed recovery of the classical ideal made men reevaluate their modern bodies in private and look in the mirror with new eyes. A reporter found Sandow "not only inspiring because of his enormous strength, but absolutely beautiful as a work of art as well. . . . One look at him is enough to make the average young man thoroughly disgusted with himself, and to make him give up his nightly habit of standing in front of the [looking] glass in his pajamas [the sense of the passage suggests without pajamas] and swelling his chest with pride." More immediately and intensely than any figure before him, Sandow aroused a desire among men to emulate another man's body, a desire that, depending on the individual, might be more or less mixed with an erotic impulse to possess it. As if to shake off this ambiguous desire, the reporter thrilled to imagine how that manly power might prove itself in a fight: "There is . . . no doubt that he could kill any man with a blow very easily. He could crush in the chest, break the neck, or fracture the skull of any man, and not use one-half his strength."[35] Sandow always emphasized his composure and restraint, even when others picked a fight, but he would not have disagreed with the reporter's assessment. Here was a figure who combined the qualities of Adonis and Hercules.

ASSAULTS ON MANHOOD

This image as Adonis and Hercules was one that Sandow and his managers carefully promoted, and it proved enduring. Yet it was never uncontested. Questions and controversy started to swirl around Sandow within weeks of his debut at the Casino. They began, perhaps surprisingly given the newspapers' stress on Sandow's great strength and potentially murderous capacities, with a violent assault on the vaunted strongman. Still more surprising, the assault came at the hands of a woman.

As Sandow left the Casino after his nightly performance on July 1, 1893, a woman in her thirties stepped from the crowd of admirers and demanded to speak to him. He tried to move past her, whereupon she struck him several times with a horsewhip, cutting his face. This was an act of contempt, an effort to reduce Sandow to the level of a beast. White with anger, Sandow raised his walking stick as if to retaliate. Three bystanders leaped forward and held him. The woman was immediately arrested and charged with assault and blackmail.

Almost as quickly as the bystanders leaped forward, the press seized on the incident. The assault on the "perfect man" fascinated them. It was already a familiar theme. The *National Police Gazette*, the most popular men's weekly of the era and a staple of barbershops, specialized in exuberantly illustrated stories of women attacking men, whether in a good cause or not. Accounts of women horsewhipping husbands, lovers, and slanderers frequently emblazoned its pages, together with stories of (preferably young, ideally scantily clad) women,

"Horsewhipped an Editor," in *National Police Gazette*, April 1, 1893. Library of Congress

ranging from "plucky" to "insane," who punched, bit, stabbed, slashed, bludgeoned, and shot men. Plainly, these accounts aroused male readers, who found such gender-crossing punishments both provocative and disturbing. Already in the 1890s, it was clear that some women were not content to rely on male protectors, either at the ballot box or in the bedroom, but would assert their own claims vigorously, even violently. Thus the female attack on the "strongest man in the world," the "perfect man," had crucial if unspoken sexual implications. If Sandow was a Hercules, who was this queen of the Amazons?

The day after the horsewhipping, an excited press identified Sandow's attacker as "Lurline, the Water Queen." A "vigorous woman" who "looks as if she could wield a cowhide with considerable effect," she had been born in Boston "as plain Miss Sarah E. Swift." Lurline, as the press insisted on calling her, had acquired her sobriquet as an aquatics performer in a revealing costume, and her association with Sandow dated back to his beginnings as a strongman under the tutelage of Attila in Belgium. He was, in her account, a lowly servant in a circus and occasional artists' model when she advanced the money for lessons and clothes to transform him into a strongman and gentleman. Besides bankrolling his success, Lurline maintained, she had given him crucial assistance when he triumphed over Sampson in London: as Sandow passed around the chains and coins that he proposed to break in his competition, she deftly switched them with others made to snap easily. She had now come forth to remind Sandow—and, because he had turned a deaf ear, the public—of his debt. Not only did she cast him as a charlatan in his feats against Sampson, but also Lurline and her lawyers appeared eager to bring forth details from Sandow's past, including his family history, that would undermine his claims to respectability. Their insinuation that Sandow had no money, no clothes, and nothing to eat when he came to Lurline for aid made him hardly better than a beggar, perhaps even a kept man.[36]

Feeding the controversy, Lurline brought Sandow's former mentor, Attila, to New York. Whether Lurline intended to blackmail Sandow, as seems probable, or to humiliate him and so be revenged, it was hardly in his interest to keep the story alive and in the papers. The two settled matters privately, and the blackmail charge was dropped.

If Lurline represented an obvious threat to male power and dominance, others were more insidious. The genital power that men were encouraged to see as the core of their identity could, it was believed, be easily sapped by the temptations and strains of modern life: from overwork to overindulgence, from solitary masturbation to the perils of the brothel, including the venereal diseases that afflicted more than one man in ten. Sandow's splendidly self-made physique must be understood in relation to the anxieties of men who often felt unmade and unworthy. The pages of the *National Police Gazette* that carried stories of vengeful women and strongmen such as Sandow bulged with advertisements addressed to "WEAK MEN" that offered cures for various symptoms of impotence, or "lost manhood," and other afflictions, ranging from the supposed effects of "self-abuse" to syphilis. These home remedies, in the golden age of patent medicine, were purportedly devised by fellow sufferers and extended in a philanthropic spirit:

FREE CURE I was Quickly and Permanently CURED of Nightly Emissions, Complete Impotency, Varicocele and Small, Wasted and Shrunken Organs caused by Self-Abuse. Thousands have been fully restored through me. I will mail the means of this UNFAILING SELF-CURE (sealed) FREE . . .

CERTAIN PARTS Of Body Enlarged. Beware of Bogus Free Cures. Send for the common sense method. Surest and safest developing tonic known! Cures all weak men. Increases Sexual Power. Sealed information Free . . .

WEAK MEN suffering from Lost Manhood. Youthful Errors, Spermatorhoea, Gonorrhea, Gleet, Syphilis, and all Private Diseases, should read my 64 p. Book and learn how to cure themselves quietly at home . . .

ELECTRICITY FOR WEAK MEN Only cure for lost manhood, emissions, debility, weakness of man or woman, varicocele. I will send you Dr. Judd's Electric Belt and Battery combined . . .[37]

Whereas some men were anxious about their ability to perform sexually, others worried about the loss of sexual power that intercourse itself might entail. In a diary entry of 1898 a young Virginian, Stephen D. Boyd, expressed conventional medical wisdom when he steeled himself against the temptation of sex with a young woman: "There would be a great drain of nerve force and much useful time and energy would be more than wasted. . . . It is only a momentary physical pleasure, and where indulged in with high nervous excitement causes certain sclerotic changes in the spinal cord and exhaustion of the brain and injury to the medulla."[38]

Such advertisements and reflections suggest some of the deeper fears about manly power and virility, and the keen sense of shame that attended them, to which Sandow's body so eloquently spoke. The average young man's "nightly habit of standing in front of the glass" might not involve "swelling his chest with pride" so much as an anxious self-appraisal. And Sandow's body both highlighted other men's inadequacies and, together with the photographs, exercises, books, and muscle developers he sold, offered another self-help restorative for lost manhood.

LOOKING AND TOUCHING

After his successful New York run, Sandow performed at Boston's Tremont Theatre in July, where he followed a light opera in a program that *The Boston Daily Globe* called "Mirth and Muscle." In a city concerned about artistic and moral propriety, Sandow achieved a noteworthy triumph. One reporter wrote, "It was very agreeable to observe the delighted enthusiasm with which ladies and gentlemen of the highest culture and refinement witnessed an exhibition of animal strength which had not the remotest suggestion of vulgarity."[39] Yet he was still not the stupendous attraction he was to be a month later in Chicago.

The lavish world's fair, the Columbian Exposition, which had opened on May 1 and was ultimately to attract 21.5 million admissions, was then at its height at Jackson Park, six miles from downtown Chicago. Its exhibits created a special context for anyone purporting to be a "perfect man." At the fair various human "types" were on display in both formal and commercial settings. The colossal sideshow that formed the Midway presented peoples and cultures from around the globe with the intention of suggesting a hierarchy beginning with the most westernized nations and stretching on to the least "civilized," such as the Dahomey Village. Then, in the Anthropology Building at the fair proper, visitors could survey an even greater range of types from prehistoric times to the present, beginning with North American native peoples. Fair goers might then consider "typical" modern American men and women in relation to these, as exemplified by "anthropometric statues" based on Dudley Sargent's measurements and photographs of thousands of Harvard and Radcliffe freshmen. Many visitors paid a small fee to have their bodies measured and compared with the standards Sargent had devised. In this way, fair goers might consider exotic bodies, typical bodies, and their own bodies during a single visit.

But where stood a model of white male perfection? Not in the "White City" of the fair or along the Midway. Yet such a marvel

Sandow supporting the Trocadero Vaudevilles. Florenz Ziegfeld sits directly above him. Wisconsin Center for Film and Theater Research

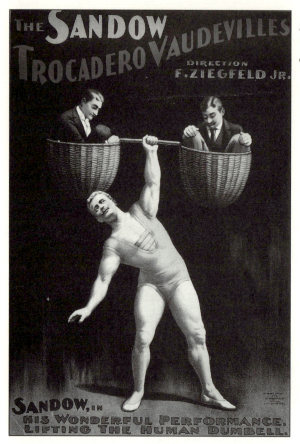

Sandow lifting the "Human Dumbell," c. 1894. Library of Congress

awaited the fair goer willing to travel to downtown Chicago: "The perfection of physical manhood," "the strongest man on earth!" "the sensation of the century," "the modern Hercules." On August 1, Sandow began a three-month run at the Trocadero Theatre, as well as an immensely profitable three-year partnership with the impresario who so trumpeted his abilities. The Trocadero owner's twenty-six-year-old son, Florenz Ziegfeld, Jr., would make the stylish display of bodily perfection a specialty, although he would soon concentrate on female beauty. Sandow was the springboard for his extraordinary career as a theatrical producer, which lasted four decades until his death in 1932.

Billed as "America's only refined European theatre," the Trocadero offered a range of tickets (fifty cents for general admission; seventy-five cents and one dollar for reserved seats) and a diverse

program of exotic attractions: songs, dances, specialty acts (later including "Scott, the calculating collie"), and bands. But it quickly became apparent that to lure tourists from the fairgrounds to Michigan
Avenue, near the Art Institute, the theater needed a headliner. The
young Ziegfeld had taken notice of the strongman's success in New
York and, in a bold gamble, engaged him to play at the Trocadero for
the last three months of the fair.

Sandow's performance as the tenth act on the bill served as the
grand finale of the evening's entertainment. Keeping alive the drama
of challenge that had distinguished the strongman's career from the
outset, Ziegfeld offered ten thousand dollars "to any athlete duplicating his performance."[40] Ziegfeld spent lavishly on advertising. He
cultivated publicity both in high society and in the press, emphasiz-
ing Sandow's dashing figure and erotic appeal, and he added greater
showmanship to Sandow's feats of strength. When his musical accompanist came onstage with his piano, Sandow effortlessly lifted the
man with one hand and then lifted the piano. The snug silk shorts he
wore in the opening portion of his act may have been more modest
than those he had favored in New York or Europe, but his body and
his feats so captivated spectators that they sometimes forgot to ap-
plaud. Ziegfeld also arranged private receptions for specially invited
guests, including, in addition to all the reporters he could muster, scientists and physicians qualified to authenticate Sandow's muscular
development, athletes prepared to admire his feats, artists and sculp-
tors educated to appreciate the classical beauty of his body, and
Chicago's leading socialites to ogle and swoon over it. Among these
last were Harriet S. Pullman, wife of the sleeping-car manufacturer
and civic leader George Pullman, and Bertha Honoré Palmer, wife of
the merchant and real-estate magnate Potter Palmer and herself a
leading force behind the Columbian Exposition.

Sandow eagerly invited their inspection. Even more than in New
York or Boston, spectators remarked on his extraordinary combination
of strength and beauty. The drama critic for the *Chicago Daily News*,
Amy Leslie, meticulously inventoried his "blue eyes and wealth of
golden, close-cut curls," "pink and white" skin, "red lips," "even,
shiny, and white" teeth, and "soft" face "lighted by a smile that is just
short of girlish." "Mr. Sandow," she concluded, "is a dangerously
handsome young man." Others marveled over Sandow's fair com-

plexion, too. One Chicago spectator remembered his skin as "velvety and most extraordinary," "a transparent white without blemish."[41] Sandow heightened the effect by shaving his body hair to display his musculature (as have bodybuilders ever since).

Sandow's skin was an emblem in two respects. Its whiteness testified to his status as a gentleman whose body had not been exposed to the sun. Still more important, it was a sign of racial purity. Sandow represented not simply a male physical ideal but a *white* European male ideal. Appropriately for one whose career was inspired by classical European statues, he was selected in 1901 as the model for a statue of the "perfect type of a European man," and his body arduously cast. One statue thus cast was enshrined in the British Museum, and a duplicate was exhibited in the lobby of B. F. Keith's vaudeville theater in Boston, then presented by Sandow to Dudley Sargent on behalf of Harvard University.[42] In later travels in India and elsewhere, Sandow extolled the virtues of physical culture to people of color. Yet a clear sense of racial hierarchy remained. In accounts of his first American tour, he cheerfully related how he punished an impudent "nigger" bellhop by dangling him over a stairwell sixteen stories high.[43] Sandow's anecdote was in keeping with a period of blatant racism. (The Supreme Court decision enshrining segregation in *Plessy v. Ferguson* was only three years away.) Beginning in Chicago, with the ethnographic displays as a sort of backdrop, he became, in an important sense, the great white hope, a figure whose ideal physique confirmed the place of white European men on the top of the racial hierarchy.

Sandow appealed not just to the eye but also to the touch. He would strip to his tights to display his muscular development and control, make gnarls of muscle bulge and disappear at will over his body, and, at his receptions, urge spectators to feel the size and hardness of his muscles for themselves. The result was a curious mixture of intimacy and distance. Earlier, in New York, a male journalist had described such an experience: "He took my hand while I was in his dressing room and rubbed it across his abdominal muscles, and the feeling was just about the same as it would be rubbing the hand over an old fashioned washboard."[44] With women, the encounter was much more charged. Ostensibly an invitation to verify his muscular development, it carried obvious if unspoken erotic elements. In

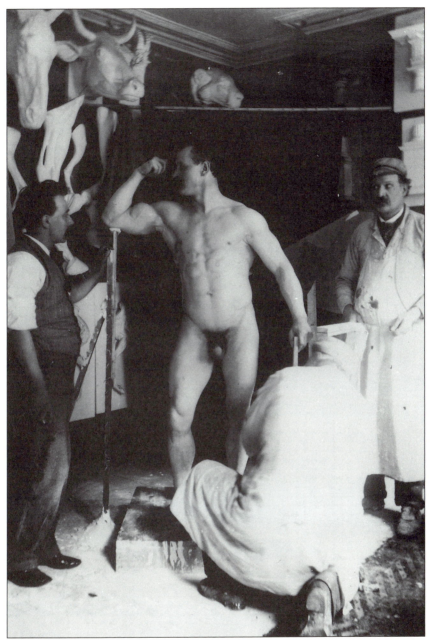

Sandow posing for the cast of a statue of European man, 1901. Image Library, The National Archives, Public Record Office, U.K.

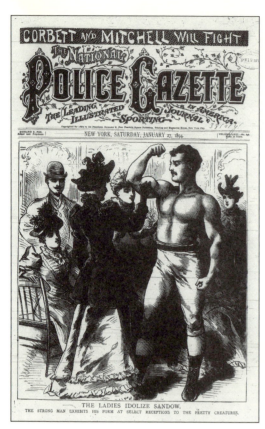

"The Ladies Idolize Sandow," in *National Police Gazette*, January 27, 1894. Library of Congress

Chicago, Amy Leslie reported how Sandow "walked over to me and threw out a stack of corded muscles under the white, smooth skin of his chest in a sort of mechanical way that rather stunned me." When she did not immediately feel his chest, Sandow took her gloved hand and "said amiably, 'hit me hard; you will not hurt me.' " Mrs. Potter Palmer was less shy. Reportedly, she stroked Sandow's massive chest and declared she was "thrilled to the spine."[45]

These receptions became an established part of Sandow's appearances on his early American tours and fortified his image as an irresistible ladies' man.[46] The *National Police Gazette* portrayed one such event with all its erotic titillation, more powerful because never overtly declared, in an article the following year. The writer emphasized Sandow's dominance and his female admirers' timidity as the strongman bade each to touch his body. "I want you to feel how hard these muscles are," he urged them. "As I stop before you, I want each of you to pass the palm of your hand across my chest." The first woman he approached drew back timidly. "Oh, please," she remonstrated. "Never mind." "Ah, but you must," Sandow replied. "These muscles, madam, are hard as iron itself, I want you to convince yourself of the fact." The reporter described Sandow tenderly taking the woman's gloved hand in his own and passing it slowly over his muscle. "It's unbelievable!" she gasped, staggering backward, and an attendant rushed to her aid with smelling salts. It is as if the phallic power of Sandow's body toppled her with a touch.

The drawing that accompanied this article, in all likelihood a product of the illustrator's imagination rather than direct observation, set forth its own fantasy of phallic power and female response. Its fashionable young women are far from timid. They surround the shirtless strongman and vie for the pleasure of feeling his muscles and appraising his body. Conceivably, the seated woman on the left represents the overcome figure described in the article, but she may have taken a chair to gain a better view of the strongman's massive chest. Here is a scene recalling the pursuit of Dixey's character in *Adonis*, the only instance we have seen thus far where the erotic appeal of the male body was openly (if comically) recognized. In this illustration Sandow performs a double legitimation: of the unclad muscular male as an object of desire and of women as active admirers.[47]

A more searching and provocative study of these receptions appeared in a drawing and unsigned article in *Frank Leslie's Illustrated Weekly*. The fact that the artist clearly based his drawing of Sandow on an earlier studio photograph where the pose is identical, then elaborated it as the text and his fancy dictated, undermines its status as reportage but makes it all the more revealing of responses to Sandow's body. Here Sandow stands at the center foreground, dumbbells on the floor behind him. He wears Roman sandals as a token of classicism—and almost nothing else. So lightly drawn are his shorts that they seem to fit like a second skin. In contrast to his virtual nudity, the spectators are all in evening dress. The picture thus shows a confrontation between two kinds of power: social and financial power, signaled by the viewers' clothes; and physical power, signaled by Sandow's naked muscularity, which commands the attention of men and women alike.

People cluster around him, approaching with a frank curiosity and admiration as if he were a classical statue or scientific specimen—two models of viewership to which he appealed. A half century earlier even exhibitions of nude sculpture, such as Hiram Powers's acclaimed *Greek Slave*, often included special showings for women, so that they would not have to view undraped works in mixed company. Male nudity in art was more easily accommodated, but the issue of the exposed male body in daily life remained highly charged. Although men frequently swam naked among themselves, for example, they would wear tank tops for mixed bathing at least into the 1920s; and as late as 1934 men were arrested, fined, and rebuked for appearing topless on a Coney Island beach.[48] Yet here, before a live semi-nude subject, women and men peer eagerly. To the extreme right, a woman holds a lorgnette to her eyes. A second feels Sandow's bare forearm with her gloved hand. Sandow himself returns her gaze as he offers himself for her inspection. Both his fists are clenched, his arm muscles hard. To the left, a bespectacled older man leans forward, intently examining his body. No one speaks.

This is a study of male exhibition—perhaps tinged with exhibitionism. The scene crackles with tension between the genteel disavowal of erotic interest in the male body and the obvious (if unspecified) gratifications of gazing on and touching this essentially nude man. The success of the event depends on the preservation of its ambiguities. The woman feeling Sandow's bulging arm and marveling at its hardness, the spectators appraising his body—all seem to participate in a connoisseurship that, to be sustained, cannot permit the nature of its interest to be clearly defined. An essential attribute of the ideal nude was its impersonality; that is what saved it from mere nakedness. But is it here a work of art (or subject of science) that these spectators consider or a specific individual in a state of undress?[49]

On another level, the scene becomes a study in a different set of ambiguities between the natural and the artificial, between physical development and social decadence. Although Sandow presented himself as reclaiming from the degeneration and torpor of modern life a classical masculine ideal in heroic action, the text accompanying the illustration sounded a dissenting note. Both aesthetically and morally, the author recoiled from the spectacle of Sandow's body and of its admirers. Instead, the writer interpreted Sandow as an instance of "ab-

Sandow, 1893. Photograph by Napoleon Sarony. Library of Congress

"The Latest Society Fad," drawing by B. West Clinedinst, in *Frank Leslie's Illustrated Weekly*, March 29, 1894. The University of North Carolina at Chapel Hill

normal development" and his success as part of a modern hunger "for the *outré.*" Sandow's body struck him as not beautiful but grotesque, reminding him "of some great, massive, gnarled oak, petrified and as relentless as stone." When he thought of ancient Rome, he remembered its decadence: "when the nobles of both sexes visited the gladiators in their quarters and admiringly examined their brawn and sinews" before they placed their bets.[50]

Thus article and illustration left the relationship between Sandow and his admirers ambiguous. Were they "fans" courting him "at his private levee," as the headline implied? If so, it might attest to how male physical development was superior to all social hierarchies. Or were those hierarchies still intact, and was Sandow the spectators' pet, their plaything, ultimately their victim, as were the ancient gladiators? And if he was a gladiator, what contest was at issue? Sandow versus contenders for the title "perfect man"? Virility, embodied by Sandow, versus the debilitating tendencies of modern life, epitomized by his admirers? Sandow as the male representative in the war between the sexes? Sandow as the great white hope? Sandow was extraordinary in his ability to stand center stage simultaneously in these multiple arenas.[51]

By means of these illustrations and texts, the circles of men and women who looked at and, in imagination at least, felt Sandow's body widened to tens of thousands of readers and were extended still further by drawings of his body that accompanied newspaper articles and advertisements describing his exploits. In intimate detail, his body became better known to more people than that of any previous man in history, apart from those depicted in religious art. Important as the illustrator was in this process, the crucial role was played by the commercial photographer.

From its inception in 1839, photography stimulated and satisfied demand for intimate knowledge of the body, and beginning in the late 1850s, souvenir photographs became a major industry throughout North America and Europe. Would-be celebrities of all sorts—stage performers, writers, and politicians—came to depend on the work of studio photographers. For Sandow and for the nascent bodybuilding business, the photographer was essential. The camera captured moments from Sandow's onstage performances, of course, just as it recorded conventional actors in their roles; but it also permitted him

Sandow showing how he won the title "strongest man on earth," 1889. Photograph by London Stereoscopic Company. Harvard Theatre Collection

Sandow in leotard, flexing his
right arm. Photograph by Napoleon
Sarony. Library of Congress

Sandow seated, wearing a fig leaf.
Photograph by Napoleon Sarony. Library
of Congress

to display far more of his body than even his scanty stage costume would permit—and it allowed each viewer to examine it singly and anonymously, to view Sandow not in public but in private.

From the moment of his 1889 triumph over Sampson, Sandow posed often for leading theatrical studio photographers. That same year, equipped with assorted weights, he made one series of photographs for the London Stereoscopic Company and another in classical poses, wearing only a fig leaf, for the London photographer Henry Van der Weyde. During his first American tours, he made still more, including a series for the foremost theatrical photographer in the country, Napoleon Sarony, and for one of his leading competitors, Benjamin J. Falk, both of New York, as well as for the Los Angeles photographer George Steckel.

Sandow carefully distanced himself from circus performers and human oddities, the subjects of popular photographs, and made pic-

Sandow in a leopard-skin leotard.
Photograph by Benjamin J. Falk. Library of Congress

tures that showed he wanted to be ranked with leading actors and even works of art. He offered himself in a number of roles—as classical ideal, polished gentleman, and thoroughly modern athlete—and assumed various guises: he posed in tights (adorned with a medal), in leopard skins (secured by a belt), in evening dress (sporting a boutonniere), and in the nude (shielded only by a fig leaf). He flexed an array of muscles, lifted weights, demonstrated exercises, and dreamily stared into space; he reclined against Roman columns, and he rode a bicycle. In classical poses that still figure prominently in bodybuilding, he struck a range of attitudes from the triumphantly erect (the Farnese Hercules) to the submissively prostrate (the Dying Gaul).[52] He held his emotions within relatively narrow limits: pensive rather

Sandow seated, wearing
a leotard and medals.
Photograph by Napoleon Sarony.
Library of Congress

Sandow as the Farnese Hercules. Photograph by Napoleon Sarony. Harvard Theatre Collection

Sandow exercising with dumbbells. Photograph by Napoleon Sarony. Theatre Arts Collection, Harry Ransom Humanities Research Center, The University of Texas at Austin

Sandow performing a provocative push-up. Photograph by Napoleon Sarony. Theatre Arts Collection, Harry Ransom Humanities Research Center, The University of Texas at Austin

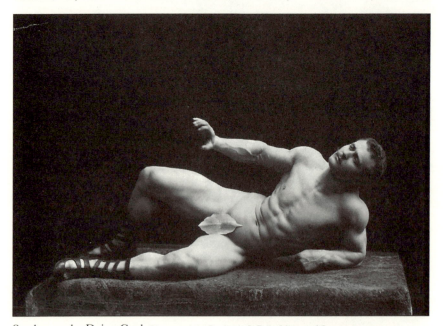

Sandow as the Dying Gaul. Photograph by Benjamin J. Falk. Library of Congress

than weary as the Farnese Hercules, elegiac rather than tortured as the Dying Gaul. Just as photographic reproductions of classical sculpture were helping to disseminate ancient conceptions of the ideal body, photographs of modern muscled men in classical poses offered compelling, apparently objective proof that these ideals could indeed be achieved. In the photographer's studio, makeup and lighting enhanced muscle definition and created a monumental physical presence. Careful retouching and printing in the darkroom did the rest. The smooth, monochromic print completed the process of abstraction and idealization and placed the contemporary body on a plane with classical sculpture. Multiple perspectives on Sandow's body furthered the parallel, giving the viewer the impression of appraising a statue from various angles.[53]

These images were sold at theaters, hotels, and photographers' studios and by mail in various sizes, including the popular cabinet format on stiff cardboard (roughly four by six inches when mounted) for perhaps $.35 and the larger panel size (roughly seven by thirteen inches) for $1.50.[54] And as the basis for newspaper and magazine illustrations, they were widely circulated and took Sandow from the theatrical spotlight into the hands and imaginations of countless thousands of individual owners, who could amass their own collections.

These images of muscular display were (one suspects intentionally) left open to the widest range of constructions and responses, allowing viewers to make of them what they pleased. They attracted women, inviting thousands to participate in intimate encounters with Sandow and to gaze on his body with all its thrilling force and eroticism. A Frenchman visiting the summer resort of Newport, Rhode Island, was startled to discover Sandow's nude portrait displayed in fashionable ladies' sitting rooms. But in all likelihood, these photographs fascinated men even more, with an exhibition of muscularity that sustained many fantasies about physical prowess, virility, strength, and eroticism across a broad spectrum of sexual orientation. All the while Sandow managed to skirt censorship, even though its sentries were especially vigilant. In 1883 Anthony Comstock, the organizer and secretary of the New York Society for the Suppression of Vice, had listed photographs of classical nudes among the many immoral "traps" for the unwary. In a similar spirit, in 1910 a judge upheld the Sandow-inspired health reformer Bernarr Macfadden's conviction for sending obscene materials through the mails, basing his ruling in good part on a magazine cover showing the Venus de Milo, the Discus Thrower, and the Flying Mercury.[55] By avoiding any declared erotic intent and by cultivating an urbane dignity, Sandow became the first great male pinup in modern history.

MODERN GLADIATORS

Among all Sandow's poses, the gladiator deserves special remark. The role of the gladiator, in which Sandow frequently cast himself and was cast by others, underwent a revival in the late nineteenth century. To be sure, the gladiator had been a complex and controversial figure even in ancient Rome, and (as the piece on Sandow in *Frank Leslie's Illustrated Weekly* has already shown) in the late nineteenth century he could easily be associated with the brutality and decadence that led to the ancient empire's decline and fall. Yet the gladiator remained a compelling positive figure as well, which legitimated and popularized the unclad muscular male body in situations of violent and often primitive combat. (Gladiator movies did the same for the bodybuilder Steve Reeves in the 1950s and 1960s, making him the first bodybuilder since Sandow to become an international celebrity.[56])

This positive image was congenial to a growing celebration of America's historic encounter with the primitive. In July 1893, less than three weeks before Sandow's Chicago debut, the young historian Frederick Jackson Turner delivered his famous address in that city, "The Significance of the Frontier in American History." For Turner, the frontier, the "meeting point between savagery and civilization," was the historic site not only of American individualism and democracy but also (though he did not make this claim explicit) of American manhood:

> The wilderness masters the colonist. It finds him a European in dress, industries, tools, modes of travel, and thought. It takes him from the railroad car and puts him in the birch canoe. It strips off the garments to civilization and arrays him in the hunting shirt and the moccasin. . . . Before long he has gone to planting Indian corn and plowing with a sharp stick; he shouts

the war cry and takes the scalp in orthodox Indian fashion. . . .
Little by little he transforms the wilderness, but the outcome is
not the old Europe. . . . The fact is, that here is a new product
that is American.[57]

So when Turner added that the frontier had, as of the 1890 census,
vanished, and with its passing an era in American history had closed,
a fair inference was that an era of American manhood was passing as
well.

The frontier might be gone, but Americans might still savor the
spectacle of gladiatorial combat in other realms of history and contemporary life through art. The French artist Jean-Léon Gérôme explored both its heroic and its brutal dimensions in a number of
paintings and sculptures of warriors and martyrs in the Roman Colosseum. Some of the most famous of these, including *Pollice Verso*, popularly known as "Thumbs Down" (1872), were quickly purchased,
even commissioned, by American collectors; and they became still
more widely known and admired through reproductions.[58] In addition, several of Gérôme's American students at the École des Beaux-
Arts carried this interest back to the United States. Preeminent
among these was the great Philadelphia artist Thomas Eakins, who
found modern analogies to the gladiatorial arena in the surgical clinic
(*The Gross Clinic*, *The Agnew Clinic*) and the boxing ring (*Between
Rounds*, *Taking the Count*, *Salutat*). Such works evinced the hunger for
a modern heroic warrior who, contending in the arena and commanding the eyes of the multitude, could achieve a splendor and purity
akin to the combatants of old.[59]

As promoters of modern boxing and wrestling did their best to
reach larger audiences in the late nineteenth century and to distance
themselves from their rowdy working-class antecedents, figures involved in both sports cultivated the gladiatorial analogy. Contestants
were often referred to as gladiators and given the names of ancient
warriors by the press. Among the many nicknames bestowed on John
L. Sullivan, for example, was "Spartacus Sullivan," and his 1892 autobiography was grandly titled *Life and Reminiscences of a 19th Century
Gladiator.*[60] Similarly, the New York policeman turned Greco-Roman
wrestling champion William Muldoon adopted the studded breechcloth and high-laced sandals of the Roman gladiator for his matches

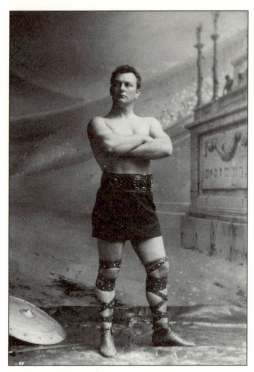

William Muldoon as the Fighting
Gaul. Photograph by Benjamin J. Falk.
Library of Congress

and added still more gladiatorial props for publicity photographs. Like Sandow, he found in Roman models of strength, muscular development, and courage a fit manly context for displaying his body.

Sandow disdained many of these competitors for the gladiatorial ideal, particularly professional boxers. "A man cannot fight a prize fight," he sniffed, "and be a gentleman." At the same time, he told stories to show that although he was slow to anger or respond to provocation, if forced he could teach any bully a lesson he would never forget. Even as Sandow modestly denied he was a perfect man, he added, "If any man thinks he is stronger than I—well, then, I should try to be nearer perfection than he when we meet."[61]

Indeed, much as Sandow endeavored to stand alone as a resurrection of the ancient gladiatorial ideal, he attracted both challengers and counterfeits. The first impostor claiming to be Sandow reportedly preceded the strongman to America, though his feats were decidedly inferior. In Chicago, as Sandow appeared at the Trocadero, another strongman, Sebastian Miller, twisted horseshoes at the nearby Grotto

Theatre but aroused scant interest. The Grotto then booked Sandow's former rival Charles Sampson, who persisted in claiming the title the "strongest man on earth." Sampson specialized in breaking chains and bending coins, but he challenged Sandow to a competition involving any feats of strength, adding accusingly, "providing trickery is not employed."[62] Sandow ignored these taunts, and Sampson quickly sank back into obscurity.

When Sandow arrived with Ziegfeld's Trocadero company in San Francisco in the spring of the following year, 1894, he discovered another impostor appearing under the name Sandowe already performing at the Orpheum Theatre. Imitating Sandow's latest feat, the pretender balanced a grand piano and four musicians on his upraised shoulders, chest, and knees. More galling still, he affected the appearance of the Prussian strongman right down to the cut and curls of his hair. Ziegfeld obtained a court injunction, forbidding Sandowe (alias Irving Montgomery, a Birmingham, England, strongman) to appear in the area under his assumed name. When Montgomery violated the injunction, the matter went to court. As in the earlier contretemps with Lurline, the Water Queen, the case hugely amused the press but did

A Sandow Impostor: Irving Montgomery as a Discobolus.
Harvard Theatre Collection

Sandow little good, even though he was vindicated. Inevitably, it identified him as a man of the theater rather than a self-made titan of strength and beauty, and his feats appeared more as stage tricks than as heroic accomplishments.

More profoundly, Sandow's great appeal lay in his claim to being an original, a man who stood apart from the crowd. Although his achievement may have been based on his imitation of classical models, he seemed to have attained his ideals to an unparalleled degree. All his accolades—the "strongest man," the "perfect man"—rested on that foundation. Of course, Sandow encouraged emulation and purported to share his methods. (He advocated the use of five-pound weights, but this would not have achieved his muscular bulk.) Nonetheless, followers were meant to understand there could be only one Sandow. And the extent to which his body and his feats might be successfully duplicated, even counterfeited, destroyed his mystique. From the lost world of manly strength and heroism, he sank into the modern world, where there were no longer originals, only copies.

Perhaps in part goaded by the controversy with Montgomery, at the end of his San Francisco appearance in May 1894, Sandow promised to pursue the gladiatorial ideal in an audacious spectacle: he would wrestle a lion with his bare hands. The proposition recalled not only the one-sided contests between lions and Christians in the Roman Colosseum but also the first labor of Hercules, in which he slays the Nemean lion (to which Sandow often alluded in his poses). Under Ziegfeld's management, the event was ballyhooed as "the sensation of the century," and Sandow expertly stoked the fires of prefight publicity. "The lion is a coward" before a man, Sandow sneered. He claimed to have earlier killed two wild lions in hand-to-paw combat for the pleasure of the Turkish sultan.[63] But the San Francisco event was to be a wrestling match rather than a duel to the death. In consideration of Sandow, Commodore, representing the king of beasts, was to be muzzled and his claws covered with leather mittens. In consideration of the lion, the "perfect man" was to carry no weapons and had agreed to a bar on strangleholds.

On the night of the contest, the press reported, three thousand spectators, including "prominent citizens" and "ladies of wealth and fashion . . . burning up with eagerness to see Sandow, the modern Sampson, twist the daylights out of the four footed athlete," gathered in a large tent in Golden Gate Park. But from the start, something was clearly wrong, and "the sensation of the century" quickly turned into a ludicrous farce. Only after attendants poked and prodded the lion did the "aged," "worn and weary," "moth-eaten" creature limp out of his box. "As soon as Commodore found himself in the arena he lost heart and fell down." The intrepid Sandow, clad in pink tights, strode boldly forward and eyed his opponent. For his part, "Commodore . . . tried to bury his face in the sawdust." The reporter for the *San Francisco Chronicle* gave a blow-by-blow account of how Sandow tugged Commodore's ear, shook him by the mane, pulled his whiskers, slung him by the tail, raised him by the neck, and generally rolled him to and fro in an effort to arouse some response. But the lion was either too old, too sedated, or too abused, possibly all three, to offer resistance. Shouts of "fake" and hisses erupted from the crowd. To pose as gladiator required a ferocious antagonist, a worthy natural opponent by which to measure the qualities of civilized man. Now the heroic ideal fizzled. Perhaps lions had degenerated even faster than human beings! When officials at last intervened and Sandow was congratulated "for his gallantry in entering this den of wild beasts," the crowd laughed derisively. Sandow departed with his winnings as fast as he could and never "fought" a lion again.[64]

Despite this debacle, Sandow's position as a celebrity was secure. Changing his act little, he continued to tour extensively in the United States until 1906, when he was nearly forty. In 1894 he recorded some of his vaudeville feats on brief filmstrips for Thomas Edison's kinetoscope. Two years later, he made two similar projected film shorts for W. K. L. Dickson, an erstwhile Edison assistant, at the Biograph Company. Both films concluded with his astonishing back flip. Nonetheless, they lacked the immediacy of his live performances and the intimacy of his still photographs.

In ensuing years he endeavored to build on his success as a performer in both England and the United States by encouraging men and women to embrace physical fitness through his sponsored gymnasiums, special equipment (for example, "Sandow's Patent Spring Grip Dumb Bells"), magazines, and mail-order course. A 1903 advertisement for the last, issued in conjunction with the opening of his College of Physical Culture in Boston, broadened his targeted audience to anyone seeking relief from such ailments of modern life as "consti-

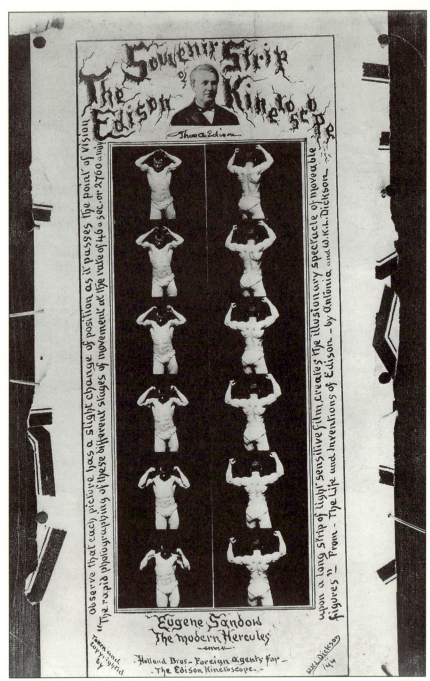

Sandow in an Edison kinetoscope, 1894. Library of Congress

pation, indigestion, or disordered nerves." He also revisited Dudley Sargent, who reiterated his abiding conviction that Sandow was "the most perfectly developed man the world has ever seen."[65]

In 1906 Sandow formally became a British subject and thereafter concentrated on affairs in England. Although he was appointed "Professor of Scientific and Physical Culture" to King George V in 1911, the honor did not altogether shield him from anti-German sentiment during the Great War. In response, the old master of self-invention claimed his mother's Russian heritage rather than his father's Prussian stock. He also pressed physical fitness into the war effort, seconding Prime Minister David Lloyd George's concern about the "lost army of the rejected," the dismaying number of men who failed the army's physical examination. Indeed, in his zeal he contended that by following his methods, society could virtually eradicate disease.[66] When Sandow died in 1925 at the age of fifty-eight, newspapers attributed his death to an injury sustained in a final feat of strength. Sometime earlier, after a road accident, he had, single-handed, lifted a car out of a ditch. The strain reportedly resulted in a burst blood vessel in his brain. Obituaries sealed his legend: the "weakling" who became the "world's most perfect man," the extraordinary individual who had devised a program of training whereby "the average man" could also "become strong and vigorous."[67]

Sandow's success was filled with ironies that illuminate the passage from Victorian to modern culture. He helped many Americans (as well as countless others, especially in the English-speaking world) to negotiate this transition, not by clearly delineating what was at stake but by keeping ambiguities suspended. In the name of ancient ideals, he adroitly tapped antimodernist sentiments and fears of an emasculating civilization. Yet ultimately he raised a new, potentially more punishing "scientific" standard against which to measure one's inadequacy. The concept of a perfect body, ostensibly devised in opposition to modern industrial society, in fact capitulated to the presumption that perfection lay in materially defined, standardized, and repeatable processes and products. He helped to displace the Victorian conception of the body as a moral reservoir and instrument of productive labor with a modern conception of the body as an expression of individual desire and site of pleasure. In place of pride in manly bearing and competence in the workplace, he exemplified a compensatory "working out," a concentration on manly strength and beauty off the job. At a time when the nascent field of "scientific management" was pressing for workers as specialized in their bodies as the work they performed, Sandow offered a vision of the reintegrated male body—yet one that might easily become a product in its own right. Elevating his background and presenting himself as a gentleman, he fortified the ideal of manly dominance based on the body, but in the process he surrendered the assertions of working-class power that had frequently accompanied this ideal. On the music-hall and the vaudeville stage, he adapted older traditions of manly physical challenge to promote a new mass culture of entertainment. And as he made the exposed male body a compelling spectacle in live performance, he also drew on classical art traditions to pioneer its dissemination in still and moving pictures. Lastly, Sandow revealed how the erotics of the male body could be broadly exposed precisely because it was never explicitly mentioned. Studious concentration on antique sculpture and muscular development provided the crucial fig leaf.

Ultimately, Sandow's success as a performer of masculinity suggested the changing status of gender in the modern world. His physique was widely interpreted not simply as an individual achievement but as a reaffirmation of male identity at a time when it seemed to be losing authority and coherence. By stressing the potential for strength, control, heroism, and virility in the male physique, he reassured a broad public of the continuation of these qualities—and their potential for further development—in the modern world. Yet for many who scrutinized Sandow's body and its meaning, nature and artifice were hard to separate. A triumph of man's natural potential to some eyes, his body appeared the epitome of the artificial to others. If his manliness was a performance that impostors could counterfeit, what were the deeper implications for gender imposture? Even as Sandow claimed to return to ancient ideals of male strength as the core of male identity, the possibilities of gender as a repertoire of assumed roles and cultivated performances rushed in.

TWO

THE MANLY ART OF ESCAPE

THE METAMORPHOSES

OF EHRICH WEISS

The period from the 1890s to the mid-1920s was not only the golden age of vaudeville, in which Sandow excelled, but also the end of the golden age of stage magic that flourished in vaudeville's format and settings: live performances of specialized acts before a diverse public. Just as we might ask why the exhibition of masculine strength and physical perfection became so compelling at a time in which the practical need for such strength was lessening, we need to inquire why demonstrations of magic gripped audiences just when modern science and technology were supposedly supplanting the need to believe in magic at all. "Magic is dominant when control of the environment is weak," declared the pioneering anthropologist Bronislaw Malinowski in the 1920s. It was "to be expected and generally to be found whenever man comes to an unbridgeable gap, a hiatus in his knowledge or in his powers of practical control, and yet has to continue in his pursuit." With the rise of more powerful, rational procedures and mechanisms, in science and technology especially, Malinowski confidently asserted, reliance on magic withered away.[1]

Whatever the strengths and shortcomings of Malinowski's functionalist explanation of the place of magic in "primitive" societies, ironically it illuminates some of the lure of stage magic in his own cul-

Houdini stripped and chained. Library of Congress

ture and time. By the 1890s, several generations of stage magicians had forsworn the pretensions of wizardry for demonstrations of "scientific" or "rational" magic, and many had taken special aim at those who used conjuring skills to claim supernatural powers. Still, as entertainers, modern magicians (overwhelmingly male) appealed to people's hunger for the semblance of miracles in a disenchanted world. Much as Western "man" (in the collective sense in which Malinowski used the term) might claim to control events, the individual male frequently faced "an unbridgeable gap" between his powers and his ambitions. By performing amazing feats of mastery over objects and situations, the magician became an exemplary masculine figure to complement the strongman. Both spoke to dreams of dominance and authority in the modern world.

The career of Harry Houdini must be understood in this context. What allowed him to become one of the most celebrated performers of the twentieth century was his skill in making themes of risk and control, helplessness and mastery central to his art and to the male body. A number of talented rivals bested him in straight magic and sleight of hand, including Howard Thurston (1869–1936) and, later, Harry Blackstone (Harry Boughton [1885–1965]), but none approached Houdini in his specialty. He was indisputably the greatest escape artist in the history of illusion. Much has been written describing his extraordinary feats: How he freed himself from the most cunningly designed handcuffs and leg irons. How he escaped from massive packing crates and zinc-lined piano cases, from office safes and bank vaults, from the jail cells of notorious criminals and from entire prisons, from straitjackets, first onstage and then suspended upside down high above city streets. How he extricated himself from a padlocked can filled with water, milk, and even beer, then from an even more spectacular "water torture cell." How, wrapped with chains and ropes or locked inside a weighted box, he plunged into rivers and harbors and swam free. How, lashed against the open barrel of a cannon with a time fuse, he vowed to free himself or "be blown to Kingdom Come." How he consented to be buried alive under six feet of earth and clawed his way back from the grave.[2] Devotees of magic have long discussed how he managed to perform these and other feats.[3] Biographers have probed the personal issues that drove him to do them in the first place.[4] Yet cultural historians have paid little attention to the larger meanings of his tricks and the significance of his career.

When Sandow was making his American debut at the most prestigious variety theaters in the summer of 1893, the nineteen-year-old Houdini was a struggling magician in dime museums. Yet beginning in 1899, his career climbed like a steeplejack, and he soon became not only a leading vaudeville and music-hall entertainer across North America and Europe but an international celebrity. Just as Sandow was the most brilliant popular performer of manliness in the 1890s and his unclad body the most famous in the world, Houdini might be accorded this title for the decade and a half preceding the Great War. The gender meaning of escape art is less obvious, though no less profound, than that of bodybuilding. But Houdini dramatized his naked body as audaciously as any performer of his time. And, naked or clothed, fully exposed or hidden from sight, he relentlessly explored issues of the body and of masculinity. He adapted Romantic and melodramatic themes of the nineteenth century in compelling ways to modern life at the beginning of the twentieth. Although some of his feats have been performed at different times, before his day and since, the way he presented them, as well as his special appeal and fame, was deeply embedded in the cultural needs of his time. In part these needs were epitomized in Houdini himself: he was driven to his performances of manliness by intensely personal issues, which he brilliantly converted into popular art. In addition, as with Sandow, his career is best understood as an intense interaction between the performer and his public in which he learned to select and refine his feats according to his audiences' responses.

ORIGINS OF AN ILLUSIONIST

Like Sandow, Houdini was a self-made man with a self-bestowed name and a keen desire to escape, first and foremost, from his humble, at times humiliating, origins. Over the course of his career, he gave many versions of his family history and his youthful beginnings, almost all embellished and some wholly fictitious. He was born Erik Weisz (later spelled Ehrich Weiss) in Budapest in 1874, the third son of Cecilia and Mayer Samuel Weisz. Two years later, his father immi-

Rabbi Mayer Samuel Weiss, Houdini's father. Boldt Collection, Houdini Historical Center, Appleton, Wisconsin

grated to the United States to take a position as rabbi of a small German Jewish congregation in Appleton, Wisconsin. Mayer Samuel's wife and five sons, including one by an earlier marriage, joined him in 1878. Soon one of the greatest waves of Jewish immigration in history, totaling more than two million people by the time of the Great War, surged after them to the United States.

At first, the family's passage from Budapest to small-town Wisconsin, buoyed by the father's education and prospects, seemed in stark contrast to the more common plunge from eastern European *shtetl* to urban tenement. But in 1882, Weiss (as his name was now spelled) lost his honored position as rabbi to a newly emigrated German evidently more to the congregation's liking. At the age of fifty-three, still speaking little English (the language of his household and congregation was German), now with seven children, he found that the American ladder pointing upward to success also descended toward failure. Rapidly he slipped down the rungs from shabbiness to want to despair. He moved his family to Milwaukee, which had a larger Jewish community than Appleton, and tried to support them by conducting occasional services without a formal congregation, by offering private lessons in Hebrew and perhaps German, and by working as a *shocher*, or kosher butcher, and as a *moyel* performing ritual circumcisions. Soon the family, pursued by creditors, was shuffling among furnished rooms. On at least one occasion, they appealed to the local Hebrew Relief Society for coal and grocery money to survive the winter. As Houdini later summarized this period: "Such hardships and hunger came our lot that the less said on the subject, the better."[5]

In 1886, the Weiss family moved to New York, where the once exalted father again desperately sought any rabbinic occupation at hand, printing business cards that offered "all religious services," including weddings, *brises*, and funerals. Evidently, he achieved no more success than in Milwaukee. Houdini remembered these as "hard and cruel years when I rarely had the bare necessities of life."[6] Ultimately, like many other Jewish immigrants, both literate and illiterate, the elder Weiss was reportedly reduced to working in a necktie factory on a bench alongside Ehrich. He died of cancer in 1892 at the age of sixty-three when Ehrich was eighteen. He left, in addition to Ehrich and two older sons (the first son had died of tuberculosis), three children ages sixteen, thirteen, and ten and a fifty-one-year-old widow. "*Weiss, Weiss*," Houdini recalled his mother, Cecilia, exclaiming at the time of her husband's death, "*du hast mich verlassen mit deiner Keinder!!! Was hast du gethan?*" [Weiss, Weiss, you've left me with your children!!! What have you done?][7]

If in Houdini's recollections his father was a revered but failed rabbi, his mother was a figure of transcendent love and selfless devotion, an "angel." "I am what would be called a Mothers-boy [*sic*]," he later acknowledged, and despite his five siblings, Houdini would claim throughout his life a special relationship to her, as, apparently, she did to him.[8] To cite but two examples: her pet name for him was "Tateleh" (Little Papa), and she would insist that even as a baby, he never cried. If he started to fret, she would hold him to her breast, and the sound of her heartbeat soothed him. Well into his adult life, Houdini and his mother would gratify each other by reenacting this embrace. Houdini spoke of it as one of those "little peculiarities that mean so much to a mother and son when they love each other as much as we did."[9] But in 1913, when she was seventy-two, her heart stopped beating; and upon receiving the news, he immediately fainted. Until his own death thirteen years later, he would extravagantly mourn her absence and try to reconstitute her presence, even making efforts to speak with her through spiritualist mediums—and when they offered only bogus messages, he would rage against them.[10]

His father's decline and his mother's vulnerability appear to have been shaping experiences of Ehrich's childhood. Many stories he later told of his father have a strong compensatory quality: exaggerating his education and degrees, supplying a romantic past (including a victorious duel with a nobleman that supposedly impelled him to emigrate in the first place), and stressing the special bond that united father and son in the protection of Houdini's mother. Houdini claimed that in moments of crisis, including once when Ehrich was twelve and again on the father's deathbed, Mayer Samuel made his trusted son (his siblings are notably absent from these memories) solemnly promise to take care of his mother as long as she lived.[11]

Yet such a pledge—whether made to his father or only to himself—might put Ehrich in a double bind in which he surpassed his father if he succeeded and let down mother and father both if he failed. At the age of twelve, Ehrich ran away from home in what may have

Houdini with his mother and his wife, 1907. Library of Congress

been a confused response to his father's plight and to the pressures he felt. A postcard to his mother, mailed from Missouri, announced his intention to proceed to Galveston, Texas, and to "be home in about a year." It was signed "Your truant son, Ehrich Weiss." In fact, it appears that he was gone only several months and spent most of this time about fifty miles from Milwaukee, in Delavan, Wisconsin. Working as a shoeshine boy and calling himself Ehrich White (his first tentative shedding of his Jewish name and racial identity in favor of a more generalized whiteness), he was taken in by a couple who thought him homeless. Houdini later offered various explanations for this escapade, perhaps reflecting the confusion he felt at the time: that he "ran away from home to earn some money" (and so was a dutiful son after all); that he sought to "seek my fortune" (like the younger son in a folktale); that he intended to "join a small circus" (under the spell of which he had already fallen and styled himself "Ehrich, the Prince of the Air"); and, more vaguely, that he "resolved to see the world."[12] In such an incident one glimpses both the future Houdini's fierce independence and his wish to be seen as not really a truant but an exemplary and devoted son. Much of Houdini's tremendous desire for success sprang from the painful sight of his father's failure and the ambitions kindled by the warmth of his mother's embrace.

THE ROLE OF THE MAGICIAN

Houdini claimed to have seen his first magic show as a boy in Milwaukee, accompanied by his father. It was, in his recollection, a performance by the celebrated English conjurer Dr. H. S. Lynn (1831–1899).[13] The trick called "Palingenesia" (regeneration) especially impressed him; in fact, he recalled it vividly in his diary three decades later and still later incorporated a version of it into his own act.[14] In this trick, Dr. Lynn (or possibly an imitator) administered chloroform to a man onstage, secured him in a cabinet, then sharpened a butcher knife with the blade of a scimitar and exuberantly dissected his victim, lopping off first a leg, then an arm, and, finally, the head. "I really believed that the man's arm, leg, and head were cut off," Houdini remembered. As the audience gasped, the magician calmly gathered the body parts inside the cabinet and drew the curtain; within seconds the man stepped forward intact.[15]

Such a performance might fascinate anyone, but it appears to have struck a special chord with the future Houdini. Like many magic tricks, Dr. Lynn's unorthodox surgery offered a form of playacting about bodily risk and miraculous recovery that might give expression to unconscious fears and forbidden desires. In Dr. Lynn's role as a coolly ironic assailant ("another man cut up tonight," his advertisements promised), he tapped spectators' fears of mutilation and their aggressive urges. Witnessing this magic show with his father—who like the magician was a wielder of knives (as a *moyel* and *shocher*) and was also a figure of esoteric learning (as a rabbi), though one who could no longer command an audience—Ehrich may have found the illusion particularly powerful. He may have felt he was seeing, in displaced but recognizable form, elements of his subconscious come to life. For whatever reason, the drama of bodily risk and recovery, mutilation and integration, death and rebirth consumed him throughout his career.

During Ehrich's adolescence in Manhattan, as he toiled on the bench at the necktie factory, the dream of being a circus acrobat gave way to the dream of being a magician. With a friend and fellow worker, Jacob Hyman, his younger brother Theo, and others, he spent hours practicing magic tricks, including rope tying and escape—with Ehrich usually taking the role of the bound victim. It is of course impossible to say what private meanings such games held for them. In such play, magic can overlap with adolescent male "damage games," in which participants enact fantasized scripts of bodily privation and injury in order to reassure themselves of their phallic mastery and integrity. Like other acts of exhibitionism, this play, with its demonstration of invulnerability, might soothe the uncertain sense of self that is characteristic of adolescence.[16] Such an interpretation is obviously highly speculative. But what can be said with certainty is that Ehrich discovered in magic more than an intriguing diversion: it gave him a powerful identity.

The turning point seems to have come when Ehrich read a secondhand copy of the memoirs of the great French conjurer Jean-Eugène Robert-Houdin (1805–1871).[17] Packed with adventures and triumphs, this book chronicled the extraordinary career of the father of modern magic. (Like many such accounts, including Houdini's later autobiographical statements, it also mixed fact and fiction in a powerful act of self-invention.) The son of a humble clock maker, Robert-Houdin was from boyhood fascinated by ingenious mechanisms and magical feats. Though his father wanted him to enter a respectable profession such as law or medicine, the son followed his bent and ultimately became a mesmerizing performer who astounded multitudes and monarchs throughout Europe. Rejecting the trappings of wizardry, Robert-Houdin produced apparently supernatural marvels such as the "Floating Boy" (in which he suspended his son in midair) and "Second Sight" (an illusion of thought transference and clairvoyance) by what he emphasized were entirely rational means. He capped his memoirs with a thrilling account of how, on behalf of French colonial rulers, he single-handedly bested the sorcery of Marabouts and thus quelled an incipient Muslim revolt in Algiers. In his hands, modern magic was both a source of wonder and a tool of Western imperialism and "enlightenment."

Robert-Houdin's colorful account and commanding persona seized Ehrich's imagination. Houdini later recalled that he "re-read his works until I could recite passage after passage from memory."[18] The memoirs offered Ehrich an irresistible example of one who had created a profession combining science and spectacle, rationality and illusion. In his performances Robert-Houdin fed a public hungry for the uncanny, the inexplicable, and the miraculous. And for Ehrich Weiss, he did more than this: he provided a romantic father figure who, in contrast to Ehrich's own father, offered him an opportunity to claim a charismatic identity that might lead to fame and fortune.[19] "A conjurer is not a juggler," Robert-Houdin famously declared, distinguishing himself from the low carnival performer; "he is an *actor* playing the role of a magician."[20] As Ehrich Weiss grew up, he adapted the theatrical possibilities of this role, along with Robert-Houdin's name, to his own professional and personal needs.

Of course, magic held an attraction for many adolescent boys at this time and since, which publishers explicitly recognized in titles such as *The Boy's Own Conjuring Book*.[21] Even so, everything we know about Ehrich Weiss's childhood and future life and career suggests that for him magic held a special fascination. In its play with appearance and reality, deception and illusion, imposture and grandiosity, magic offered a means by which he could negotiate his anxieties and fantasies about manliness in a household in which he both desired and feared to take his father's place.[22] The magician was a role by which he could sustain a fantasized self of miraculous powers. More specifically, it offered a grandiose *masculine* role by which Ehrich could proclaim his complete independence, even invulnerability. This was, in addition, an *assimilated* role. The downward spiral of his father's career would not be his. Tricking others could fortify his sense of mastery and of mental and bodily integrity. The line between an actor playing the role of a magician and a boy imagining an imposture as a masculine hero might for Ehrich Weiss have been a fine one.

His first and crucial feat as a magician, then, was to reinvent himself. Beginning on a part-time basis in 1891 (the year before his father's death), and soon as a full-time performer, Ehrich Weiss metamorphosed into Harry Houdini—the given name deriving from his nickname Ehrie, the surname from the great French master.

Here was a kind of escape art in itself. Shedding his Jewish name gave him additional means to throw off the burden of his father's fate. More generally, with the name change, he proclaimed a new identity that would not be confined by Old World conceptions of what it meant to be a Jew. Rejecting any suggestion of weakness or effeminacy, he emphasized his masculine toughness, fearlessness, and invincibility for the rest of his life. In his performances, he came to radiate confidence and command. The trace of an accent remained, but in time he shed his guttural voice for the stentorian, bell-shaped tones of a polished orator. Playing the role of magician allowed him to transmute rabbinic failure into assimilated success. He dressed in refined evening clothes to perform stunning illusions on a secular stage while disavowing supernatural means altogether. Although he never denied his Jewishness, he defined himself first and foremost as a free man and only incidentally as a Jew. Yet the ease with which he was mistaken for a Christian occasionally exposed him to the depths of anti-Semitism, particularly in Europe. He once wrote from Munich, "It is awful what I hear from people that are Jew Haters and don't know that I am a Sheeney."[23] And behind his back, even in the United States, detractors occasionally muttered their regret that "this low-minded Jew has any claim on the word American."[24]

Bess and Harry Houdini, 1894. Library of Congress

"Mysterious Harry" and "La Petite Bessie," "The Master Monarchs of Modern Mysteries," promoting their act. Library of Congress

At the beginning, he was half of the Brothers Houdini, though initially not with an actual brother but with his friend Jacob Hyman. Styling themselves "The Modern Monarchs of Mystery," they performed in dime museums and cheap variety theaters around New York and in the Midwest alongside minor blackface minstrels, Wild West imitators, fat ladies, giants, midgets, and legless wonders. Most of the performers, like themselves, had scrambled onstage from immigrant or working-class families, lured by dreams of success. For white performers with talent and drive, and bereft of education and capital, the institutions of mass entertainment offered tempting rewards—at very long odds. Minnie Marx, mother of the Marx Brothers, spoke for their ambitions when she explained why she sent her children into show business: "Where else can people who don't know anything make so much money?"[25] In the summer of 1893, shortly before Sandow's run at the "refined" Trocadero in Chicago, the Brothers Houdini appeared for several weeks along the Midway at the Columbian Exposition. But soon Hyman struck out on his own, and *his* brother Joe briefly joined Harry in the act, until a genuine Weiss brother, Theo, replaced him. Then in the summer of 1894 this partnership, too, dissolved after Harry, in the space of a few weeks, met and married a member of a song-and-dance act, Wilhelmina Beatrice Rahner. Known as Bess, she was a petite eighteen-year-old Brooklynite from a German Catholic family. With their marriage, he took another step away from Jewish orthodoxy, and she immediately replaced Theo as part of a new magic act, the Houdinis.

Though the shift was fortuitous, it decisively transformed key elements of the performance. As part of a brother act, such as with Theo, who was taller and sturdier than he, Harry Houdini could not play the role of the commanding male nearly so effectively as when offset by his diminutive wife. Gradually Houdini forged his body into a muscular instrument of escape, but as yet he appeared slight and boyish. He was also short—though he sometimes seemed determined to will himself taller. On passport applications over the course of his career, he declared himself variously as five feet four inches, five five and a quarter, five six, and five seven.[26] (The first was undoubtedly nearest the mark.) Because Bess was less than five feet tall and weighed ninety pounds, she was an ideal partner.[27]

The importance of the change is most evident in a trunk trick that

Stages in the Houdinis' "Metamorphosis." Library of Congress

had originally been a staple of the Brothers Houdini and that Harry and Bess performed many times throughout their careers. "Metamorphosis," as Harry billed the trick with Bess, created a drama of simultaneous entrance and escape. Volunteers from the audience were invited onstage to examine an ordinary-looking box or trunk, into which a crouching person might fit, and a large cloth sack. Then, as an early promotional bill described the feat:

> Mons[ieur] Houdini's hands are fastened behind his back, [he] is secur[e]ly tied in a bag[,] and the knots are sealed, then placed in a massive box which is locked and strapped[;] the box is then rolled into a small [curtained] cabinet, and Mlle. Houdini draws the curtain and claps her hands three times[.] [A]t the last clap of her hands the curtain is drawn open by Mons. Houdini and Mlle. Houdini has disappeared, and upon the box being opened she is found in his place in the bag, the seals unbroken and her hands tied in precisely the same manner as were Mons. Houdini's when first entering the bag.

The basic trick was familiar among magicians. J. N. Maskelyne had presented a version in England as early as 1865, and the French conjurer Bernard Marius "Le Commandeur" Cazeneuve made a rendition with his wife one of his most brilliant effects. In describing the basic feat, an 1897 book on magic noted, "The whole credit of the trick is due to the cabinet maker who constructed the trunk." Although volunteers might not detect anything remarkable, one of the trunk's ends, "instead of being nailed, is secured by a pivot to the two long sides, so that it can swing. The swinging motion is arrested by a spring plate bolt. When the person in the interior presses upon a point corresponding to this bolt, the pivot turns freely and the end of the trunk swings."[28]

Nonetheless, no successful magic feat depends on apparatus alone. Presentation is everything. As Houdini boasted at the bottom of the bill promoting the trick: "Just think over this, the time consumed in making the change is THREE SECONDS! We challenge the World to produce an act . . . with greater Mystery, Speed, or Dexterity." Houdini gradually added refinements, such as beginning by borrowing a coat from a member of the audience and using a smaller trunk, but even in the 1890s the couple's speed and showmanship drew audiences. The exchange also deeply fascinated Houdini himself, making him feel as if he had left his own body.[29]

The illusion of "Metamorphosis" could be read in at least two ways. First, it might be viewed as a man's magical release from redoubled confinement—and a woman's corresponding capture. In the zero-sum stakes of this game, only one could be free, and the Houdinis clearly knew which result audiences would find most dramatically satisfying. Second, and still more magical, the trick might be viewed as a bodily and sex change between Houdini and his wife. The French titles that the performers assumed—Monsieur and *Mademoiselle* Houdini rather than Monsieur and *Madame*—further suggested that the two were potentially one person in different sexual guises rather than a husband and wife. (Bess's page-boy appearance in tights and flowing blouse—what Houdini called her "boy[']s suit"—only accentuated this aspect.[30]) In such ways "Metamorphosis" played with the boundaries of gender and the mystery of gender differences. It seemed to affirm the rightness of clear sexual divisions (with man unbound and woman dependent) but simultaneously suggested that such boundaries might collapse with startling speed.[31]

THE METAMORPHOSIS OF JULIAN ELTINGE

To appreciate its significance, we must understand the Houdinis' "Metamorphosis," like all Houdini's performances, as highly compressed popular theater. The fascination with gender boundaries and their crossing characterized much of American theater around the turn of the century. Henry Dixey was still spoofing gender roles in *Adonis*. A still more illuminating—and arresting—series of performances of gender differences and gender crossings began when Julian Eltinge (originally William Dalton, 1883–1941) launched his career as the "World's foremost [male] delineator of the fair sex."

In 1904 Eltinge made his New York debut in the musical comedy *Mr. Wix of Wickham*. In a plot reminiscent of *Charley's Aunt* (1892), he played a young college man compelled by circumstances to impersonate a pretty girl. Productions of this sort had customarily based the farce on the transparent absurdity of the disguise, but Eltinge astonished viewers with the charming plausibility of his performance and his mastery of "the many little details of apparel with which women are very familiar."[32] During the next few years he achieved spectacular success on the vaudeville circuit as a female impersonator, depicting various contemporary and historical "types," including the Bathing Girl, the Bride, Salome, and Marie Antoinette. Then he returned to Broadway to win still greater acclaim in a series of plays of gender disguise beginning with the musical comedy *The Fascinating Widow* (1910). His star shone so brightly that a New York theater named in his honor opened on Forty-second Street in September 1912. He continued to tour the country as a headliner for another decade and appeared in several films.

Eltinge fascinated men and women with what one critic called his "ambisextrous" abilities.[33] As an illusionist of femininity, he attracted a remarkably broad audience. In Cincinnati a reporter eavesdropped on theatergoers' excited conversations as they awaited an Eltinge matinee. Young women gushed to one another, without intentional irony, "I think he is the loveliest girl" and "the prettiest woman I ever saw." One woman hoped "to get a few new ideas on the latest gowns." A man in line fully shared their admiration: "I want to see him because I think he's the swellest looking dame that ever wore down the boards, tripping the light fantastic."[34] Theater critics smiled and squirmed at the gender confusions inherent in these remarks. They felt an anxious need to distinguish between Eltinge's illusions and the reality of his sex and to direct all desires in safely heterosexual channels. The completeness of his gender transformations seemed an unsettling feat of magic. A critic for *Variety* wrote, "Eltinge is a good-looking fellow on the street; well-built and perhaps a little beyond the ordinary attractive man to an impressionable young woman. As a girl on the stage any man would rave over the genuine reproduction of Eltinge's impersonation. . . . To those who know him, how he accomplishes these impersonations is marvellous. Eltinge is as great an artist in his line as any artist is or has been in any other."[35]

Like a magician eschewing sorcery, Eltinge insisted that his illusions were based on prolonged and meticulous study rather than unnatural gifts. He prided himself on his knowledge of fashion, his skill with makeup, and his expertise in all the accoutrements of femininity. And just as magicians often described a few elementary tricks, he dis-

Eltinge as a dapper young man. Theatre Arts Collection, Harry Ransom Humanities Research Center, The University of Texas at Austin

Julian Eltinge in costume, 1905. Theatre Arts Collection, Harry Ransom Humanities Research Center, The University of Texas at Austin

pensed advice on dress and beauty secrets to women directly in interviews and in the short-lived *Julian Eltinge Magazine* that was sold at his performances. Such success involved considerable paradox. As a man who could claim to have mastered femininity from the outside, he instructed women in how to be modish in their dress yet thoroughly traditional in their concept of femininity. Reinforcing gender stereotypes, he noted the rise of woman suffrage to defuse it playfully in a song:

> *I've set the heads of men a-whirl,*
> *Since I was but a little girl.*
> *I lead the world of fashion, yet*
> *I'm just a Suffragette.*
> *Look me over carefully*
> *And with them you'll agree.*[36]

Eltinge also gently satirized women's new athleticism in his vaude-ville song "The Modern Sandow Girl." Performing calisthenics in a stylish gym slip, he sang of the gender reversals caused by modern feminism:

> *In the days gone by all the girls were shy*
> *And domestic in their way,*
> *They would never roam, they would stay at home*
> *And they'd sew and they'd cook all day. . . .*
> *But the girl of to-day is a wonder, they say*
> *She goes in for athletics and sport. . . .*
> *Years ago the man saved the drowning maid*
> *Now-a-days the maid will save him. . . .*[37]

Here the ironies flew thick and fast as a feminized man satirized the masculinized woman. Eltinge assumed women's roles ultimately to instruct women in their duties to be charming and alluring to men. Though men might find the degree of his success as a female imper-sonator disconcerting, they also discovered in it consoling proof of male power and control. "It takes a man after all," one critic exulted, "to show women the path to beauty."[38]

Yet as Eltinge himself knew best of all, this power could only be accepted if his stage illusions were anchored in a thoroughly mascu-line demeanor offstage. He seems to have studied the arts of mas-culinity as carefully as those of femininity, only with the former he never acknowledged the degree to which his was a conscious performance. Contrasting his position with that of other female im-personators, whom he kept at a great distance, and elaborately con-cealing his homosexuality, he maintained, "Off the stage I do not have to try to be a man."[39] In fact, he tried hard and succeeded well. He grew adept in striking strong, manly poses for the camera and emphasized his love of boxing, rowing, and outdoor activities, as well as his fondness for gambling. He often spoke in a bluff man-ner, swore freely in a baritone voice, and, to anyone who questioned his masculinity, delivered well-publicized two-fisted rebukes. Indeed, Eltinge and his spokesmen occasionally confided to reporters that he believed his specialty was something a real man should move be-yond—if only he weren't so good at it. As one journalist wrote:

The idea of a man masquerading in women's clothes is repellent to normally constituted people, and, according to this actor's manager, Mr. Eltinge himself is not in sympathy with his work. In private life he is a manly fellow, ready, if necessary, to back up an argument with his fists, and he is ambitious to gain legitimate honors as a player of romantic roles. He assumes feminine garb merely because he is successful in impersonating the fair sex and because of the considerable money there is in it.[40]

The magic of the Houdinis' exchange in "Metamorphosis" emphasized speed. As Eltinge performed his own magical metamorphosis from a robust he-man to a curvaceous feminine beauty before reporters in his dressing room, he emphasized (as Houdini was to do in some of his future escapes) the effort and time required. Over ninety minutes, he shaved and applied greasepaint and powders to his face, artfully prepared his eyes and lashes, rouged his lips, moistened and powdered his arms and shoulders, and applied still more powder, paint, rouge, polish, and pencil to his hands to make them look smaller. To shrink his waist required considerably more exertion. Eltinge's height of five feet eight and a half inches and normal weight of 185 pounds, it is startling to realize, virtually matched Eugen Sandow's. For his stage appearances he strove to reach 178 pounds, although this goal became increasingly difficult. Nevertheless, he managed to squeeze into a corset (one he commercially endorsed but privately called "Old Ironsides"). When tightly laced and breathing only from his upper chest, he achieved an hourglass figure by squeezing a thirty-eight-inch waist to twenty-six inches.[41] Whereas Houdini escaped from tight confinement as an emblem of male freedom, Eltinge painfully entered it in pursuit of femininity. Like Cinderella's stepsisters but more successfully, he then jammed his feet into tiny satin shoes. As a crowning touch, he carefully styled and donned his wig, and his metamorphosis was complete.

Julian Eltinge was but one of many female impersonators to emerge on the American vaudeville circuit. His unrivaled success stemmed from his unique ability to present dramas of gender crossing without a disturbing sense of transgression. He carefully preserved a normalizing framework of traditional gender oppositions to the satis-

ELTINGE'S METAMORPHOSIS

 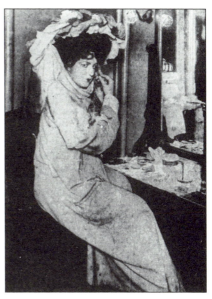

"Penciling the Eyebrows," in the *Chicago Tribune*, September 27, 1908. The University of North Carolina at Chapel Hill

"Beading the Eyelashes." The University of North Carolina at Chapel Hill

"Pressed into Shape." The University of North Carolina at Chapel Hill

faction of men and women alike. By rooting his performances, on-stage and off, in gender stereotypes and by reassuring his public that for the "real" Julian Eltinge, sex and gender, biology and appropriate social roles were one, he could evoke fantasies of possessing both male and female powers while muting their attendant anxieties. He was then in a position to work as an escape artist in reverse. Eltinge, in effect, entered the female body in order to assert male mastery over its secrets. But he did so in such a way as to garb the Freudian figure of the phallic mother—herself a male fantasy of a woman who combines female and male powers, breasts and a penis—in modish fashions that made her safe for the multitude. As sexologists, reform-ers, and the police patrolled with increasing vigilance for signs of sex-ual deviancy, Eltinge eluded their grasp. Denying any pleasure in his feminine masquerade and shielding his sexual orientation behind talk of marriage, he insisted that his metamorphosis started and stopped at the dressing-room door.

FROM DIME-MUSEUM MAGICIAN TO ESCAPE ARTIST

What Eltinge did for female impersonation, Houdini was to do for es-cape art. Just as Eltinge enacted the female body and claimed mas-tery over the secrets of femininity, Houdini made his ability to triumph over any threat to the male body the central theme of his ca-reer. And just as Eltinge neatly skated over the thin ice of sexual de-viancy, Houdini made elements that in other contexts would have been deemed perverse—exhibitionism, bondage, mutilation, entrap-ment, suffocation, criminality, insanity, flirtations with death—the stuff of manly spectacle and riveting popular entertainment.

But these developments did not happen all at once. Only gradu-ally did Houdini learn how to tap his own deep concerns and to pre-sent them in ways that held audiences spellbound. Indeed, his success came within an ace of not happening at all. Through the first four and a half years of his marriage and partnership with Bess, Harry struggled to distinguish his act from the scores of similar acts that jostled for a step on the lowest rungs of the business.[42] Far from specializing in es-cape art at this time, he did various tasks as entertainer. In 1895 he and Bess served a stint in Pennsylvania with the Welsh Brothers Cir-

IN THE CIRCUS. THE HOUDINIS ARE AT THE RIGHT OF THE FRONT ROW. MRS. HOUDINI WEARS A LORD FAUNTLEROY SUIT.

Harry and Bess Houdini (seated on right) with the Welsh Brothers Circus. Library of Congress

cus, which offered a series of acts (but no animals) under a single tent: Houdini worked as a magician, barker, puppeteer, and, briefly, "Wild Man," and Bess as a singing clown. Then for roughly half a year, beginning in September, Houdini served as co-owner and manager of a traveling burlesque troupe, the American Gaiety Girls, in which he not only put on "Metamorphosis" with Bess but also acted in farcical skits. When that venture sank in debts, Harry and Bess leaped on one shaky venture after another, only to see each collapse. They joined a short-lived troupe doing magic tricks in the Canadian provinces; they shunted through obscure variety theaters and dime museums, attempting new acts, revamping the old, trying to stay on their feet. As the Rahners (after Bess's maiden name), they briefly became a comedy act. As "Cardo," Harry offered an evening of card magic; as "Professor Murat," he was a hypnotist. During the winter and spring of 1898, as part of a medicine show slogging through Kansas and the Oklahoma Territory, Houdini offered spiritualist effects, including communicating messages from beyond the grave. After the show itself died, the couple attempted to continue on their own. Their mixed bill of magic and spiritualism won praise in St. Joseph, Missouri:

In sleight-of-hand work Prof. Houdini is very clever. His card tricks, palming and shifts are unsurpassed by any magician on the stage today. The "spirit work," if you wish to account for his feats in that way, was good. Slate writing and reading and answering unseen questions which had been written by the audience were successful. The professor was quickly released from several pairs of handcuffs which had been brought in by people in the audience and locked upon his wrists. This was done in a cabinet, and the agency by which it was accomplished was left for the audience to decide—whether spirit force or his own cleverness. The entertainment concluded with his trick mystery, called "Metamorphosis." In this he was assisted by Mrs. Houdini.[43]

Despite this notice and other spiritualist effects of the sort Houdini would later condemn, the Houdinis could not survive on their own. They rejoined for a new season the Welsh Brothers Circus. This time, in addition to performing "Metamorphosis," Bess played skits and Harry served as an acrobat and clown.

Houdini learned from these years of struggle, first, discipline and craft. "[W]hen I was playing Dime Museums, and being classed a 'freak,' " he later recalled, "i [sic] generally kept very quiet, and tried to make a living, not knowing that I was developing my dexterity by working ten to fifteen times daily."[44] He also learned from other performers, the "freaks" especially—sword swallowers and fire-eaters, "legless wonders," spirit mediums, and sleight-of-hand artists. Whenever he saw someone do a trick that interested him, he studied it intently. One accomplished sideshow performer gave him a lesson in how to swallow objects and bring them up again, beginning with a small potato attached to a long string (a technique highly useful in sleight-of-hand tricks and escapes). Strongmen such as William Le Roy, "the Human Claw-Hammer," who could hold a nail in his teeth and push it through an inch-thick plank or draw one out from a depth of two inches, held a special fascination.[45] From such performers, Houdini learned to develop his body's resources for his own special effects.

Nonetheless, by the end of 1898 the hardships and vexations had grown "so bad," he later recalled, that he "contemplated quitting show business," taking a conventional day job, and running a school of magic in the evenings, in which he would sell the secrets of his act.[46] His dream of escaping the fate of his father by becoming a master magician seemed near an end. Still, he sought new bookings.

Then, in the spring of 1899, his persistence was rewarded. Houdini's career took an astonishing turn, beginning his dizzying ascent from minor vaudeville houses, dime museums, medicine shows, ten-cent circuses, and rented halls to international stardom. These small-time houses, in which performers typically played three to six times daily in short bills and brief engagements, were distinctly inferior to the big-time theaters. Big-time engagements ran an entire week or more, with the players generally appearing twice daily, in a matinee and evening bill of at least eight acts, including a main attraction or headliner. The major vaudeville theaters throughout the country were organized into circuits controlled by theater owners and booking associations. The two largest syndicates worked together to create a network that stretched across the United States and Canada, with an eastern circuit controlled by B. F. Keith and Edward F. Albee, and the Orpheum circuit, extending from Chicago to the West Coast, managed by Martin Beck. While performing at a beer hall in St. Paul, Minnesota, Houdini was "discovered" by Beck himself. Up to this point, Houdini had aimed to be a generalist conjurer. In a diffuse act with various props, he produced pigeons and silk handkerchiefs and performed card tricks, as well as "Metamorphosis." Still, Beck saw the escape artist struggling to get out. Big-time vaudeville emphasized specialties in conjuring as in everything else. He urged Houdini to make "Metamorphosis" and his handcuff escapes the focus of his act and offered him a trial booking on the Orpheum circuit. Soon the Houdinis had a contract with Beck and vaulted to the top vaudeville theaters across the country.[47]

THE HANDCUFF KING

Houdini brilliantly exploited his new prominence. Now a "theme" act instead of an all-purpose magician, he intimately engaged his larger audiences as he performed dramatic challenges to his body. Almost immediately, he introduced the needle-swallowing trick, which

"The Handcuff King."
Library of Congress

became a staple of his act for the rest of his career. The basic trick was simple enough, but Houdini performed it with consummate showmanship. First, he invited members of the audience onstage to inspect a set of sewing needles. He chewed the set noisily, swallowed, and opened his mouth to prove they were consumed. Next, he asked the audience members to inspect a long thread, which one of their number knotted distinctively. Placing one end in his mouth, he gradually swallowed the thread until only the other end was visible in his throat. Then he triumphantly pulled the thread out to display the identical sewing needles neatly strung on it.

Yet Houdini never grabbed headlines by swallowing needles. What distinguished him at this time and soon made him famous were his handcuff escapes—onstage and off. Magicians had been performing handcuff escapes for at least two centuries, and up to this time Houdini had had difficulty injecting new drama into the feat. The release took place out of sight in his curtained cabinet, and initially some theater managers had refused to let him perform the trick.[48] To heighten interest and to prove that the cuffs were not rigged, he challenged members of the audience to place their own regulation handcuffs on him. Almost from the beginning, too, he occasionally sought to fan publicity by inviting local police to restrain him with their toughest handcuffs and allow him only a moment's privacy to escape. He had issued such challenges during the engagement that Beck witnessed in St. Paul. As Houdini later recounted the event, Beck himself had responded to Houdini's challenge by purchasing several pairs of handcuffs, from which Houdini escaped.[49] Meanwhile, the *Minneapolis Times* reported his visit to the local police station, where he defied the authorities to hold him with their best handcuffs and shackles.[50]

On the Orpheum circuit, Houdini became bolder in his handcuff escapes. A month after his fateful meeting with Beck, instead of retiring to the curtained cabinet to remove his handcuffs, Houdini slipped them off within full view of the audience. In a diary he noted with satisfaction, "1st time I took off cuffs with curtain open was the hit of act."[51] Offstage he scored equal successes. MANACLES DO NOT HOLD HIM, marveled a headline in *The Kansas City Times*. The story recounted another police-station challenge. On this occasion the police captain pasted a specially marked postage stamp over each keyhole "so that it would be easy to tell if the stamp had been removed" and the lock picked. Houdini shed the cuffs with the stamps intact.[52]

Houdini persisted in these challenges to the police, making them a frequent and vital accompaniment to his performances onstage. Such challenges appear to have been especially gratifying to him. He was by temperament highly competitive, and he enjoyed nothing more than annihilating a rival or amazing a skeptic. Handcuff escapes gave him the opportunity to create a new kind of metamorphosis: from impotent victim of authorities to manly victor over them. They allowed him to cast himself in the role of the underdog—a modern David pitted against institutional Goliaths—and to come out on top.

The police seem never to have failed to play their part as foils to Houdini. They, too, wanted to publicize their manly prowess. The rise of a uniformed police force superseding the older constable-watch system was a historic innovation of the second half of the nineteenth century. More recently, around the 1890s, municipal police forces shifted from concentration on the "dangerous classes"—those perceived as defective, dependent, or delinquent (including the poor, homeless, transient, and ill)—to professional crime control more generally. The new emphasis reflected a growing corporate ideal of urban safety and efficiency.[53] Mastery over the criminal's body lay at the heart of the police's power and symbolized their efficient command. Time after time, police officers swaggered before the short, slight young man and boasted of their invincibility—only to be stupefied moments later.

In these police-station challenges, Houdini ingeniously varied the terms and raised the stakes. When he arrived in San Francisco in June 1899, he demonstrated his usual wizardry before police officials and two hundred patrolmen. He submitted to a formidable array of restraints: four varieties of handcuffs (including three with double springs) and two sets of leg irons, with the cuffs and irons linked by yet another pair of handcuffs. "This brought him to a crouching posture," a reporter observed sympathetically, "and made him to all appearances helpless to use a key even if he had one."[54] He escaped in seven minutes, gleefully reappearing with the cuffs snapped together to form a long chain.

Houdini's success, like Sandow's, brought forth rivals and detractors. A touring English magician, "Professor" Benzon, ridiculed Houdini's handcuff escapes in William Randolph Hearst's *San Francisco Examiner* and purported to reveal his methods. Relatively few keys were sufficient to unlock all handcuffs made, he asserted. These Houdini "keeps conveniently about him." The way to foil this "professor of trickery," he advised, was to bring to the theater "a pair with a newfangled lock and key." As a parting shot, Benzon offered a general description of the trick behind "Metamorphosis."[55]

This challenge gave Houdini the chance to gain additional publicity and to crush a rival at the same time, and he leaped at it. Not only did he deride Benzon's explanations, but he offered to demonstrate that he needed no cabinet or secret key. Four days after Benzon's article appeared, Houdini once again swept into the San Francisco police station with reporters in tow. This time he demanded that before being handcuffed he be stripped naked and thoroughly searched. (He had undergone a similar strip search by Chicago police the previous December, but this and later searches generated far more publicity.) A police surgeon examined Houdini from head to toe and "certified that it would be an impossibility for him to have any key, wire or other article concealed about him." To ensure that the master needle swallower hid nothing in his mouth or throat, his lips were sealed with adhesive plaster. The police then energetically set to work. They pinioned his arms with handcuffs, attaching them from his wrists up to his elbows. They shackled his ankles, then chained his wrists to the ankles, forcing him into a subservient bow. Weighed down with ten pairs of cuffs, Houdini was shut in a closet. Then, as the presiding police sergeant explained to reporters "the utter impossibility of the feat," the naked and now unbound Houdini blithely strode in with all the handcuffs locked together in a daisy chain. The police surgeon examined the plaster over Houdini's mouth and declared it had not been disturbed in any way.[56]

As if this were not impressive enough, Houdini proposed another trial. He challenged the superintendent of the local insane asylum, who was present, to secure him in a straitjacket. Such jackets had been devised to restrain violent patients from injuring themselves or their guards. Reversing a conventional jacket's design, they were solid in front, fastened in back. The patient's arms were thrust into two closed sleeves, each of which ended in a thick strap. The arms were pulled tightly across the chest and buckled in the rear. Some included a crotch strap.

Houdini had never seen or heard of these devices until three years earlier, when, performing in St. John, New Brunswick, he was invited to tour the local insane asylum. One sight he never forgot:

> Through the small bars of the cell door, I saw a maniac struggling on the canvas padded floor, rolling about and struggling each and every muscle in a vain attempt to get his hands over his head and striving in every conceivable manner to free himself from his canvas restraint, which I later on learned was called a strait-jacket. Entranced, I watched the efforts of this man, whose struggles caused the beads of perspiration to roll off him. . . . But as the straps were drawn tight, the more he struggled, the tighter his restraint encircled him, and eventually he lay exhausted, panting and powerless to move. . . . [The sight] left so vivid an impression on my mind that I hardly slept that night, and in such moments as I slept I saw nothing but strait-jackets, maniacs and padded cells![57]

From this time on, Houdini endeavored to find ways of making this struggle as compelling for audiences as it had been for himself.

Strapped into such a straitjacket in the San Francisco police station, Houdini again retired to a closet (as, up to this time, he retreated behind a curtain onstage). He soon emerged "with the belt in his hand and intact."[58] He left the station bearing a signed affidavit of his escapes.

In an exultant account of his feats in *The San Francisco Examiner*, Houdini, like a heavyweight champion after a prize bout, announced that he was still "king of handcuffs." Though he refused to divulge his secrets—and crowed that all self-styled exposers had been wide of the mark—he stressed that it was a trick others could master. Significantly, Houdini suggested that the strip search and handcuff and straitjacket escapes came at the demands of the police, not on his own initiative. Thus he cast himself in the role of one forced to undergo these trials in order to prove his abilities and to clear his name of slander. Accompanying the article, five photographs recording the stages

Houdini "Handcuffed, Elbow-Ironed, and Thumbscrewed by the Berlin Police, October 1900," in *The Adventurous Life of a Versatile Artist*, p. 11. Library of Congress

Houdini naked and handcuffed by the Vienna police, March 1902. Sidney H. Radner Collection, Houdini Historical Center, Appleton, Wisconsin

by which he achieved his escape showed a virtually naked Houdini (in the first two, his black loincloth is obscured in shadows). Henceforth, such publicity photographs became key images, widely distributed through handbills, programs, and newspapers. Although he could not perform naked onstage, he fixed the image of his naked and shackled body, making it one of the most famous in the world.[59]

Through the rest of 1899 and into the following spring, Houdini repeated his coup in city after city: sweeping into police stations, stripping off his clothes, escaping from handcuffs, manacles, and straitjackets, and carrying away affidavits of his feats. In April 1900 he again raised the stakes, performing nude escapes not just from handcuffs but also from locked prison cells.

Soon afterward, in his first trip overseas as a performer, he showed how brilliantly he could adapt his escapes to European authorities and audiences. In London, he earned a place on the leading music-hall stage after releasing himself from the cuffs of Scotland Yard. A few months later, he appeared in Dresden, where he was photographed handcuffed and manacled by the municipal police, and in Berlin, where authorities obligingly "handcuffed, elbow-ironed, and thumbscrewed" the naked escape artist.[60] In both cities he scored his greatest hits to date. He made such tactics a central element in his European campaign. In every town he played, Houdini declared, "The first thing was to break out of jail."[61]

Indeed, Houdini's success in Europe made his career's trajectory the exact inverse of Sandow's a decade earlier. Whereas the Prussian-born strongman first won fame in Britain, then scored his greatest successes in the United States, Houdini enjoyed such acclaim in Europe that he returned home only for brief respites during the next five years. As he wrote proudly to a Boston friend in 1903, "It may be a long time ere we will work America, as I am actually asking for $1000 weekly salary, and to tell you the truth, I am not even anxious to accept that work at that salary. Over here I stay one, two and even 6 months in one City, and have a G R E A T reputation, and in America it means every week jump to another city!"[62]

THE PRISON DEFIER

When at last he did return to the United States for extensive appearances beginning in October 1905, the "Handcuff King" had become the international "Prison Defier" as well. Abroad he had been escaping from the cells of notorious criminals, then from entire jails. He devised comparable exploits for American audiences. Rapidly he added to his previous escapes in Chicago and Kansas City a string of more than a dozen jailbreaks in eastern cities.[63] Three instances from early 1906 are typical.

In Washington, D.C., during a run at B. F. Keith's Chase Theatre, Houdini defied not one but two prisons. On January 1, he appeared at the Tenth Precinct police station, where he was "stripped and treated as thoroughly as an arch murderer." Then, handcuffed with an "invincible bracelet" used by the Secret Service, he was conducted to a modern steel cell, which had been searched for "any spook assistants or hidden keys." With Houdini securely inside, the police shut the "heavy, barred door with a bar lock that is first set to lock three times. A lever throws another lock, and a Yale padlock completes the quintet of locks. A wire network around the padlock prevents a hand being thrust from inside the cell." One reporter wrote, "Every policeman believed Houdini would give up after an effort. As the minutes crept on, this confidence increased, and there was talk of bets." This complacency burst, however, when, eighteen minutes after the test began, a fully clothed Houdini appeared among them. "This baffles me," confessed the Washington police chief. By Houdini's own count, it was his sixty-second jail-cell escape.[64]

Houdini's success on this occasion triggered numerous challenges from police forces determined to foil him. One came from the warden of Washington's federal prison, a "cathedral-like" structure beside the Potomac. When Houdini arrived, the warden's office was crammed with visitors, police officials, and three jail physicians. They conducted Houdini to the most secure wing of the prison, the massive brick cells of "murderers' row," each of which had a heavily barred door and an intricate lock. He was "stripped stark naked, thoroughly searched," then locked into the cell that a quarter century earlier had held President James Garfield's insane assassin, Charles Guiteau. Not only did Houdini almost immediately escape, but, while still naked, he playfully switched each of the other nine inmates into a different cell. When he presented himself before the authorities, "their amazement passed all bounds." He left proudly bearing the warden's written testimony of his achievement.[65]

Houdini topped even this exploit two months later in Boston. The city police regarded their Somerset Street prison, popularly known as the Tombs, as absolutely "escape proof." Houdini was determined to test it. In a ground-floor cell in front of many witnesses, he shed "every stitch of his clothing," which was then locked inside the cell. On the second floor, the police superintendent and a number of witnesses searched Houdini from the hair on his head to the soles of his feet. The superintendent clamped the department's best handcuffs on Houdini, fastening his left wrist high on the cell door and his right one down at knee level. The superintendent shackled Houdini's ankles "so tightly that the iron sank into the flesh," then locked the cell

Houdini locked in a prison cell in the Boston Tombs, March 1906. Library of Congress

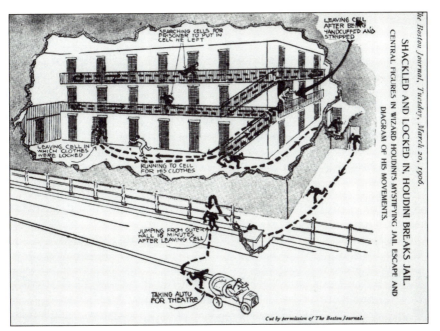

Houdini's escape route as published in *The Boston Journal*, March 20, 1906. Library of Congress

door and led the witnesses to his office, confident of the security of his restraints. Yet only sixteen minutes later, a few reporters waiting outside saw Houdini, now fully clothed, scale the outer wall of the prison yard, vault the iron railing, and jump down to a waiting car. According to one account, from his dressing room at Keith's Theatre, Houdini telephoned the startled superintendent, who thought he was still snugly locked in jail.[66] Police and reporters discovered that Houdini had unlocked not only the cell in which he was incarcerated and the one that held his clothes but also five other cells. He said later that he had planned to scramble the prisoners in different cells, as he had at the federal prison in Washington, until he realized he was the sole inmate. Adding a shiver of excitement, he boasted to reporters, "Were I to turn burglar tomorrow, I feel that I could plan and carry out to a successful end any number of big robberies right here in Boston, for I don't think there is a lock or a safe, guarding valuables in this city, which I couldn't break into and mysteriously dispose of the contents."[67]

Such exploits multiplied many times over made Houdini a celeb-

rity, even a legend. Still in his early thirties and only a few years beyond the obscurity of the traveling medicine show and ten-cent circus, he was one of the most famous entertainers in the world.

MARVELS AND MYSTERIES OF THE
IMPRISONED MALE BODY

What did these escapes mean? Why did they so capture the public's
imagination in city after city, country after country? As Houdini himself was keenly aware, there was nothing inevitably captivating about
handcuff or straitjacket escapes. His first performances of each had
stirred little interest. Furthermore, none of his rivals and imitators
ever enjoyed a fraction of his fame.

Houdini's achievement rested on his unique ability to dramatize
the challenges to his body and to his masculinity. His escape art was
exquisitely attuned to the mass media of his time and their affinity for
spectacle—the synergistic combination of inexpensive, widely acces-
sible vaudeville theater, competitive daily newspapers eager for sensational stories, and theatrical and newspaper photography. It was also
exquisitely attuned to the aspirations and anxieties of millions of people aroused by the spectacle of the naked male body on trial.

That body had become an impressive one. By the time of his
Boston Tombs jailbreak, Houdini had forged it into a powerful instrument of escape. Within a few years the slight young man of the early
1890s had transformed himself into a thickly muscled figure. In a gesture reminiscent of Sandow, he frequently invited people to feel his
body. When in 1904 the future novelist Edna Ferber, then a young
newspaperwoman, obliged by touching his forearm, she declared it
"amazing, as massive and hard as a granite pillar. His neck, too," she
noted approvingly, "is large, and corded."[68] He had acquired not only
strength but remarkable adroitness as well. Houdini's immensely
strong fingers could work through the thickest canvas. With constant
training, his toes acquired the dexterity of fingers, and he could open
knots and buckles with his teeth. He developed a broad, deep chest
by training himself to stay for long periods underwater, even in extreme cold.

Yet these physical attainments were the preconditions, not the essence, of his art. If a magician is an enactor of miracles and a holder of secrets, then an escape artist is a special case: an enactor of the miracles and secrets of his own body. Houdini turned the possibilities created by Sandow and others for the unclad male body to spectacular dramatic effects. Not only did he make his body the nexus of challenges, but, crucial to his success, he made it a subject to investigate and a symbol to interpret, a bearer of meaning and a source of mystery.

The newspaper accounts of his naked jail escapes in Washington and Boston only heightened this bodily drama. On one level, the reporters described contests of literal and metaphoric bodies: Houdini offers his naked body to the police, challenging their ability to hold him; he is innocent of any crime but willing to place himself literally in the position of the most feared and reviled criminals. For their part, the police stand as trusty guardians of law and order, the strong right arm of the metaphoric body of society at large whose central task is to confine and restrain the bodies of accused and convicted criminals, those who threaten to injure that metaphoric body. They appear to relish this job and to be very good at it. The record of dreaded criminals past and present—from the assassin Guiteau to cold-blooded murderers awaiting execution—testifies to their success. They welcome Houdini precisely because they are so confident of their unbreachable cells, formidable clamps, intricate locks—instruments and symbols of their power. How could Houdini possibly escape from such resolute officials and such proven restraints?

This drama of the naked citizen and the uniformed officials of the state was richly evocative for Houdini's contemporaries—and it remains so today. In many respects, it distilled the central elements of earlier melodramatic narratives in which, as the literary critic Peter Brooks has observed, "[t]he body sequestered and enchained, unable to assert its innocence and its right to freedom," is a dominant image. Such melodramas cannot reach their denouement "until the virtuous bodies have been freed" from often nightmarish gothic spaces and their innocence recognized.[69] One such melodrama was Dumas's novel *The Count of Monte Cristo* (1844–1845), and when Houdini read it for the first time, in 1920, while making movies, he wrote excitedly in his diary, "This part was made for me."[70]

At times, Houdini suggested other melodramatic possibilities—for example, a master criminal foiling legitimate authorities: "Suppose the innate and inherent integrity of character that Houdini possesses in common with most men brought up within the circle of a mother's sweet influence, were to be swept aside by the desire for riches not his own." Stoking resentment of the rich, he added, "There are many men of many millions to-day whose money is not their own." Or, in further narrative twists: "Suppose he should be captured by a band of desperate men determined to wrest from Houdini this secret worth millions. Suppose a great hypnotist were to obtain dominance over his mystery-enveloped genius and use his baneful powers for evil designs. What then?"[71] Houdini's naked escapes gained power by leaving such narrative possibilities unresolved and enlisting the viewers' imaginations to complete them.

Behind Houdini's police challenges stood the often sadomasochistic contests between torturers and victims that so fascinated the melodramatic imagination. Another Houdini favorite, Edgar Allan Poe, created tales such as "The Pit and the Pendulum," with its pitiless "black-robed judges" who condemn the narrator to death in a torture chamber.[72] Such punishing figures preoccupied Houdini's contemporaries, among them the fellow German-speaking Jew Franz Kafka. Indeed, it is possible to recognize in the Boston police superintendent who so tightly manacled Houdini a distant relative of the officer in Kafka's short story "In the Penal Colony." The latter worships a machine that executes a prisoner by slowly inscribing on his naked body, with elaborate scrolls and flourishes, a commandment such as HONOR THY SUPERIORS! When the executing machine fails to work properly on an uncomprehending prisoner, the officer administers the punishment on his own body instead.[73]

Houdini's jail and straitjacket escapes anticipated to a degree the themes of Michel Foucault and other historians who have identified prisons and asylums as key institutions in the rigorous disciplining of individual bodies that distinguishes the rise of modern society. Houdini felt a kinship with the inmates of these institutions, visiting them and offering benefit performances throughout his life. In his escapes, he brought the tension between individual liberty and official coercion to stark dramatic confrontation. From the time of the ancient Greeks, Western philosophers have conceived of political freedom in terms of (male) bodily freedom and of political independence in terms of personal autonomy. Houdini was no political philosopher, but what he enacted was the plight of the individual citizen stripped of dignity, imprisoned, immobilized, placed in the position of the most abject slave. Houdini's crouching, inspected, manacled naked body symbolized the consequences of giving the political order free rein over its enemies. Seen in such a light, his challenges to and defeats of the authorities' most strenuous efforts to hold him prisoner constitute a one-man revolution.

Little wonder, then, that Houdini's escapes stirred such popular excitement throughout North America and Europe. And official responses to him offer a rough index of political liberalism in different nations. Police and prison officials in the United States virtually stood in line to accept Houdini's challenges. In Great Britain, except in the largest cities, officials were usually cooperative. On the Continent, however, authorities regarded him more sternly, and when he journeyed to Russia in 1903, he found them deeply suspicious, and he thought the entire country had the atmosphere of a prison. "It does seem strange," Houdini observed in a letter from Paris, "that the people over here especially Germany, France, Saxony, and Bohemia fear the Police so much, in fact the Police are all mighty, and I am the first man that has ever dared them, that is my success."[74]

Beyond these possible political implications, Houdini's display of the unclad male body held deeply personal meanings. In one sense, his stripping and offering his body as an object to be searched was an extension of his rolling up his sleeves for his onstage handcuff escapes—a gesture of disclosure. In an all-male environment, he felt no hesitancy in appearing naked—and apparently neither did such audiences in viewing him—even when concealment was not an issue. (When, for example, he arrived for a performance of his milk-can escape at the Harvard Union in 1908 with only a blue bathing suit—the color of rival Yale College—he offered to perform naked instead, and the male audience readily accepted.)[75] But his nakedness was not incidental to the strip searches and jail escapes, or it would not have been so elaborately stressed in newspaper accounts and publicized in photographs and programs (albeit sometimes with trunks drawn on). He exposed his naked body in situations that highlighted its vulnerability and sought to arouse the curiosity of the police and the public.

That curiosity included specific questions, most immediately whether he concealed a pick, wire, or other device, and if so, where. The effect was to encourage a detailed search, not limited to hair and skin but including orifices and cavities. Newspaper accounts displayed a certain reticence in these matters. Though they emphasized that he was "stark naked" and searched from head to toe, they never described the search *between* head and toe, focusing instead on the examination of Houdini's mouth. Privately it was possible to be more frank. After attending a special handcuff escape before a group of Boston physicians, one doctor wrote Houdini a letter speculating in detail on the ways in which a device might be concealed and retrieved from the nasal and sinus cavities, the mouth and throat, and "many portions of the genito-urinary and rectal regions." ("The urethra could easily be used to hide one or more small keys. . . . The lower colon, above the rectum, will easily learn to tolerate inoffensive foreign material.") The doctor asked not to be publicly identified.[76]

Such speculations inevitably suggest larger psychological, sexual, and gender issues. These searches encouraged Houdini's public to inspect his body for themselves and to imagine secrets—whether special powers or hiding places—within. In effect, Houdini carried the gender dynamics of the substitution trunk trick "Metamorphosis" to a much more daring level. He placed himself in what might be regarded as an especially provocative feminized position: naked, bound, bent over, inspected, even to a degree penetrated. His victimization was thus not only political (a loss of freedom) but gendered (a loss of masculinity). Then, with an extraordinary bit of magic, he confounded his foes and regained at once his liberty and his masculinity. In a sense, Houdini's escapes worked as spectacular practical jokes in which he appeared to be trapped in a position of humiliating gender defeat—unmanned—only to achieve a grandiose masculine triumph. As he put it in his own breathless prose: "He is the man to whom the shrewdest police, the sharpest detectives, and the most watchful jail wardens look with awe and anxiety. . . . [B]uried in the brain of Houdini lies the secret of an unknown power he alone possesses."[77] Houdini appears to have taken the scripts from unconscious performances of male sexual and gender anxieties—exhibitionism and bondage, most conspicuously—and transformed them into brilliant spectacle. A Freudian might see in his mixture of elation and transgression—as a master criminal defying moral authorities—a further element derived from the enactment of private perversions.[78] The great mystery never directly confronted but always implicit in these performances was gender difference: What did it mean if women's bodies were different from men's? What secrets did they conceal? In a period of narrowing gender definitions and widespread anxiety over threats to masculinity, Houdini's performances had enormous cultural resonance.

CHALLENGES OF MODERNITY

The audacious Tombs escape brought Houdini's career as "Handcuff King" and "Prison Defier" to a climax. Beginning in the spring of 1906, simple handcuff escapes onstage and prison escapes offstage fell away. Instead, Houdini embarked on a new series of onstage challenges and offstage escapes that involved ingenious contrivances of all sorts. During the next two and a half years, until his departure for another extensive European tour in August 1908, these would command headlines in cities across the country and pack vaudeville houses wherever he appeared. One of the first was his escape from a wicker hamper at Keith's Theatre in Boston, shortly before his jail-break from the Tombs. Many of its dramatic elements would recur again and again.

A wicker hamper might seem to hold little drama compared with a prison, but Houdini proved otherwise. The Tombs and similar jail escapes had emphasized speed and fixed the image of Houdini's naked body in the public imagination. With the hamper escape he stressed a long, unseen struggle as he took the formula from "Metamorphosis" and, paradoxically, heightened its effect by turning the feat from one lasting seconds to one lasting more than an hour. Assuring his audience, "There is nothing supernatural about the escapes I make," he stepped into the hamper wearing three pairs of handcuffs. The hamper itself resembled the picnic basket of a paranoid giant. Made of tightly woven rattan, it was held by three thick steel bands and secured by huge padlocks, thick ropes, and an iron chain. The keyhole of each padlock bore a seal signed by members of the audience. Then his assistants concealed the hamper behind a curtain. And the audience waited.

The actual escape, like most of Houdini's, took place outside the spectators' view. While the band played, he made his audience imagine his struggle and squirm with anxiety about his safety and success. Some of his previous escapes abroad had lasted even longer. In 1902 in Blackburn, England, a strongman locked him in specially devised handcuffs from which he took two hours and forty minutes and "the fight of my life" to escape. A straitjacket release in Hanover, Germany, took "90 minutes . . . and nearly drove me crazy with pain."[79] Still, these were exceptions, and viewers knew that the hardest stage trick he had hitherto performed in Boston lasted only nineteen minutes. As the clock ticked on, fear of his defeat grew. Finally, sixty-two minutes after he had begun, a freed Houdini pulled back the curtains, revealing the hamper still bound and locked. Every aspect of his appearance testified to the supreme effort of the feat:

> His eye was dim and tired, and all his life and vigor seemed to have departed. His frock coat was dusty, wrinkled and crushed; his linen was soiled, the collar and cuffs were carried in his hands; and his whole appearance was that of a man who has

HOUDINI NIGHT, KEITH'S THEATRE
FRIDAY, MARCH 2nd, 1906

The audience at Keith's Theatre for a Houdini performance, Boston, March 2, 1906.
Harvard Theatre Collection

been through a terrific ordeal. Traces of blood were upon his neck and wrists, and several scratches were clearly to be seen.

"Three cheers for Houdini!!" shouted a man in the balcony, and the audience "simply went wild."[80]

By the time Houdini returned to Boston the following year, he was offering a dizzying array of such challenges. Indeed, he promised a new stunt at every one of his twelve weekly appearances (matinees at four o'clock and evening performances at quarter to ten, Monday through Saturday). Individually compelling, these challenges collectively made him a legend. For the Monday matinee on February 11, 1907, he warmed up with a handcuff escape while bound and nailed to a door. That evening he accepted a challenge from employees of a local boiler works who dared him to escape from a standard galvanized-iron hot-water tank, which had been placed on display in front of Keith's Theatre. Handcuffed and shackled, Houdini crawled feetfirst into the tank as it lay on its side. Six workers then capped, bolted, and, wielding flaming blowtorches, riveted it shut before the curtains of Houdini's cabinet enclosed the whole. When Houdini emerged fifty-five minutes later, "pale, weak and trembling," his "suit . . . torn and dirty, his face . . . bloody and his hands bruised," the audience "rose and wildly applauded him for his success."[81]

Tuesday's matinee brought another challenge, this time to escape from a giant football onstage without disturbing the lacings. On Thursday afternoon he freed himself from a "crazy crib" furnished by an insane asylum. That evening workers from the Derby Desk Company enacted a clerk's nightmare as they locked the handcuffed Houdini inside a massive rolltop desk. He emerged triumphant in fifty minutes. On Friday he escaped from a formidably locked glass box. Then he offered his signature straitjacket escape on Saturday, now performed within full view of spectators, who were moved to feverish excitement and tumultuous applause, even parading him around the theater on their shoulders.

In city after city across the country, Houdini provoked equally demanding and frequently bizarre challenges. Just as he had once invited individual challengers with their handcuffs, police and prison officials, and asylum superintendents, he now appeared ready to take on all comers. Manufacturers and department stores seeking public-

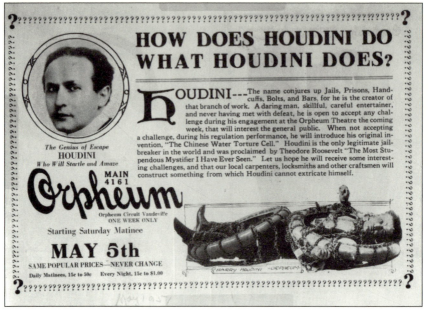

Recalling the Weed Chain challenge. Library of Congress

ity, as well as male clubs and teams, responded with alacrity. Challenges frequently came from male workers eager to display their prowess and skills despite the impersonal corporate economy that surrounded them. Usually they issued printed challenges, which Houdini accepted in writing, circulating the documents as handbills. The contests took on aspects of a formal duel, albeit fought with unorthodox weapons.

For example, on April 10, 1908, in New York City, Houdini submitted to a challenge from the Weed Chain Tire Grip Company, a manufacturer of automobile tire chains to prevent skidding in snow and ice. The company proposed to bind him with its product so that he could not slip away. When workers had completed their installation on the stage of Keith & Proctor's 125th Street Theatre, Houdini's plight was both grotesque and pitiable. They had handcuffed his wrists, shackled his ankles, wrapped his body with six padlocked tire chains, and chained an automobile wheel and tire at both his neck and legs. The entire apparatus weighed four hundred pounds. One spectator exclaimed, "All he needs to run a hardware store is a kitchen stove!" He had to be carried into his curtained cabinet. A few minutes later the audience heard "a shrieking cry for help" as Houdini complained a tire was choking him. It was adjusted, and his struggle resumed. "For many minutes," a reporter noted, "it seemed he would fail in his test." When the curtains were opened again twenty-five minutes later, Houdini had but one tire and a few chains left. He completed his escape within full view of the spectators. "When he appeared again before the audience in answer to cheers," wrote a reporter, "he could not speak and reeled off the stage with an attendant holding him up."[82]

The following month the Weed company demanded a rematch, citing "letters from motorists and others questioning the legitimacy of the test." This time the company proposed to use eight rather than six chains together with two automobile tires, a pair of leg irons, and as many handcuffs and padlocks as it desired, all in "a new and more difficult position." Houdini accepted and triumphed again.[83]

Such challenges permitted numerous variations. In dramas that merged the gothic with the surreal, Houdini struggled against an extraordinary array of objects and situations. The objects might appear formidable (for example, a zinc-lined piano box), macabre (a coffin nailed shut by members of the audience), utilitarian (a long ladder to which he was shackled and chained), startling (a standard Postal Service mailbag), whimsical (the world's largest envelope), intricate (a web of cord and fishing line that took an hour and forty-five minutes to tie), or absurd (a gigantic sausage skin). Whatever their guise, all were converted into the menacing, phantasmagoric materials of a nightmare of modern life. A challenge from the Pittsburg Auto Vise and Tool Company required Houdini to be locked in four vises "designed solely for holding the heaviest type of machinery." Handbills promised that "the contest will be filled with the greatest excitement in the war between MAN AND MACHINE."[84] Some of the challenges that Houdini rejected as impossible carried still further this feel of a modern nightmare: to escape from a gigantic incandescent lightbulb without breaking the glass or from padlocks attached to the bottom of a trip-hammer that struck twice a second. Clearly, part of the dramatic power of many of these escapes was their play with scale, as objects of large or exaggerated size threatened to engulf the individual, who ultimately proved, however, that he could not be defeated.

A Houdini lobby display, from the Salem Theatre, 1906, with (left) pairs of handcuffs, (center) wicker hamper, and (right) packing case. Library of Congress

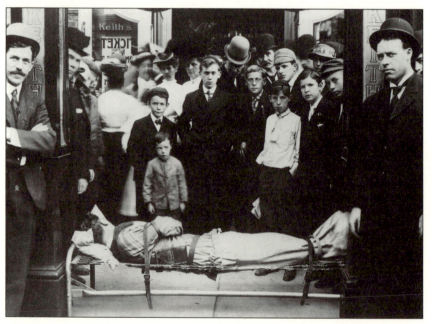

Houdini strapped to a cot. Library of Congress

Houdini regularly encouraged audiences to participate in these challenges. In addition to inviting volunteers onstage to authenticate equipment and procedures, he frequently displayed the device constituting the challenge in the theater lobby for public inspection prior to his performance. With every escape, he kept the question buzzing, How did he do it? His extraordinary success in this regard placed him in a tradition of American entertainers practiced in the arts of pleasurable deception—a tradition extending back to P. T. Barnum, who had invited mid-nineteenth-century viewers to decide which of his attractions were genuine and which hoaxes. Barnum's popular aesthetic was cunningly suited to the antebellum market economy, in which exaggeration and deception thrived. Houdini's operational aesthetic, by contrast, appealed to the amateur's desire to understand technical processes in a secularized corporate age when technology often lay outside the average individual's understanding or control. He invited viewers to look inside the works of his escapes and to match wits with him, all the better to astound them.[85]

This operational aesthetic was largely masculine, and Houdini's cultivation of a supremely masculine persona was essential to its promotion. Significantly, some of the toughest escapes he attempted lacked this critical element and did not become celebrated. These included being swathed to a cot with wet bandages—getting out of bed is not the stuff of legend—and being tied with tarred ropes by Toledo high-school boys. "Hurt like hell," Houdini noted in his diary after the latter.[86] What set him apart from other escape artists of his day was not simply his skill and strength but the remarkable intensity he created in every performance. Though he could be mildly ironical, he permitted no humor at his expense. With each new challenge, he wanted his audience to feel that his entire career—indeed, the entire masculine persona of invincibility he had constructed—was hanging in the balance. At the same time, he communicated absolute fearlessness. He simply would not be defeated.

His enormous celebrity and enduring fame suggest how greatly these qualities appealed to the emotional needs of viewers. At a time when individual male freedom seemed threatened on many fronts, Houdini's dramas were centrally concerned with issues of masculinity and the male body. Intuiting that the primacy of the body may be most dramatically expressed when that body is most at risk,[87] he, more than any other figure of his day, repeatedly and ingeniously put the imperiled male body, agonizingly on the brink of failure, at the center of his art. Eugen Sandow invoked the victorious Hercules, but Houdini's closest analogue in classical mythology was Laocoön, the Trojan priest writhing in the coils of giant sea serpents. Houdini freed himself, of course, and his efforts to do so, the marks of which frequently covered his face and body, elicited a powerful emotional catharsis. Although audience members participated in his confinement, even helping to nail him inside a coffin, they keenly identified with his plight and fixed their hearts on his success. He appealed to both a skeptical rationalism and a deep-seated desire for magical transformation. Dramatic and psychological symbolism conjoined as he moved from vulnerability and impotence, degradation and confinement to a liberation that seemed nothing short of miraculous. In achieving his freedom, he realized fantasies of omnipotent abilities and supernatural powers. Newspaper accounts repeatedly noted the mounting tension that accompanied many of Houdini's challenge escapes and the near hysteria that greeted his triumphs. His celebrated boast spoke to broad public needs and aspirations: "Nothing on earth can hold him a prisoner."[88]

"NEARLY DYING FOR A LIVING"

For roughly the first half of Houdini's career, his feats stressed his powers as an escape artist but not as a daredevil. Then, beginning in the fall of 1906, in tandem with his challenge escapes, and escalating over the next decade, he staged an ingenious variety of challenges to pain, injury, and death itself. Instead of relying on newspaper coverage of prison breaks to generate publicity for his vaudeville appearances, he began his celebrated bridge jumps, in which he leaped, handcuffed and chained, into a river as thousands watched. Onstage he offered new escapes in which spectators feared not simply for his success but for his life. And among his challenge escapes, situations of torture and bodily risk grew prominent. In 1914 and 1915, he capped these feats by introducing his most suspenseful onstage and offstage escapes—the "Chinese Water Torture Cell" and the aerial straitjacket release—in which death itself seemed to have become the jailer in whose clutches he placed himself.

Such feats sprang from Houdini's intense professional ambition and, quite possibly, his equally intense inner demands. The fascination with bodily injury and violent death that captivated him as a boy watching the cut-up man in "Palingenesia" continued to grip him as an adult. He collected articles and photographs of grotesquely mutilated bodies and was grimly attracted to the sites of such casualties. While performing in Cleveland in March 1908, for example, he recorded in his diary a trip to view the remains of schoolchildren whose "arms and legs [had been] burnt off" in a fire.[89] Other males (particularly those with enveloping mothers and emotionally absent fathers) have experienced similar fascination with and dread of mutilation,[90] and if such concerns in fact preoccupied Houdini, then he brilliantly converted them to his professional advantage. As an escape artist, he increasingly made it his business not only to free himself from seemingly inescapable contrivances but to give male anxieties and even terrors powerfully dramatic shape and to triumph over them. He was the self-proclaimed "Handcuff King" and mysterious "Prison Defier," but he aspired to achieve even more. As he declared in a 1910 interview:

> I want to be first. I vehemently want to be first. First in my profession, in my speciality in my profession. For that I give all the thought, all the power that is in me. . . . When I can no longer, goodbye the joy of life for me! So I have struggled and fought. I have done and abstained; I have tortured my body and risked my life only for that—to have one plank on the stage where the imitators cannot come, and one spot where they all fall back and cry, "Master!"[91]

His achievements indeed sealed Houdini's enduring fame as a master magician, fearless defier of death, greatest "self-liberator" of the age. They also brought to a climax an extraordinary career of spectacular performances of masculinity unrivaled among popular entertainers of the day. The innovations he launched reward close examination.

The Harvard Bridge Jump, 1908.
(ABOVE) Houdini just before the
jump. (CENTER) Houdini in the
middle of the jump, legs apart.
Note the spectators on poles,
packed along the bridge and
below it, and on the boats.
(BELOW) Houdini as he nears
the water. Library of Congress

They started with his bridge jumps. To leap from a high city bridge into the water below is generally the act of a suicide. To do so manacled would seem the act of a madman. Yet beginning in the fall of 1906, Houdini made such leaps repeatedly, staying underwater until he released himself. Crowds, mostly men and boys, routinely numbering ten thousand and reaching as many as forty thousand, flocked to these events.

One of his first and most famous jumps took place at Detroit's Belle Isle Bridge on November 27, 1906. Stripping down to his trousers, then being fettered by manacles and two sets of handcuffs, he leaped twenty-five feet to the water as onlookers gasped. After twice surfacing and disappearing again under the water, he gaily held the released bonds aloft. Later accounts by Houdini and others exaggerated the story, turning the chilly water into thick ice, locking Houdini in a trunk, and having him conduct an excruciating search for a hole in the ice to find his way to the surface. (The 1953 film *Houdini* outrageously stretched even these accounts: in it Houdini is directed toward an opening in the ice by his mother's voice—only to learn later that she died in New York at that precise moment, seven years before her actual death.)

Even without such embellishments, Houdini's jumps aroused considerable suspense, and he performed them throughout the country in 1907 and 1908—in Rochester, Pittsburgh, Denver, San Francisco, Los Angeles, New Orleans, Boston, and Atlantic City. Keenly alert to publicity, he offered a prize of ten dollars for the best photograph of each jump. In May 1908 in Philadelphia he plunged forty-four feet into the murky Schuylkill River and remained underwater for an agonizing seventy-nine seconds. As one journalist reported: "The very air seemed surcharged with excitement and apprehension. . . . [S]trong men began to shudder, and women's shrieks of fear filled the air." When at last he surfaced, proudly displaying the unlocked handcuffs and chains, the reporter continued,

how those excited thousands of spectators did cheer and the tug[boats]s added their noises to the din. It was a spontaneous outburst of relief, and it could not have been heartier if this man . . . had been the blood brother of every man of the joy-mad thousands. After all, there is nothing in life, paradoxically, perhaps, which man so loves to see as his fellow-man risk his life in an encounter with danger and death.[92]

Houdini keenly appreciated this paradox. He appealed to a desire for momentousness and risk felt by those caught up in predictable urban routines. Devising new games of challenge and escape, he moved from hide-and-seek to Russian roulette. As he later wrote in an article titled "Nearly Dying for a Living":

[T]he easiest way to attract a crowd is to let it be known that at a given time and a given place some one is going to attempt something that in the event of failure will mean sudden death. That's what attracts us to the man who paints the flagstaff on the tall building, or to the "human fly" who scales the walls of the same building.

If we knew that there was no possibility of either one of them falling or, if they did fall, that they wouldn't injure themselves in any way, we wouldn't pay any more attention to them than we do a nurse-maid wheeling a baby carriage.

Danger was a masculine realm, his language suggests, safety the sphere of women and infants. Houdini walked a fine line as he sought to heighten the drama of his feats and at the same time keep spectators from recoiling in horror. He reassured them that he possessed secrets on how to survive mortal danger but cautioned that if for some reason these secrets failed, all was lost.[93]

Was Houdini actually risking his life? He certainly sought to give that impression. Before the bridge jump in Detroit, he flamboyantly scrawled a one-sentence will on the back of an envelope—"I leave all to Bess"—and handed it to his assistant.[94] Adding to the drama, on this and other occasions, Bess skillfully played the role of anxious wife. Yet privately Houdini wrote to a friend prior to a similar jump, "I have not a single fear of the result, if I had I would not GO!"[95] On still other occasions, he vaguely acknowledged an element of risk, for example, after a jump in Rochester, New York, on May 6, 1907, at which his mother was present: he wanted her there, he said, because "I thought something might happen." That she beheld his triumph also elated him: "Ma saw me jump!" he wrote in his diary.[96] Houdini claimed that the cuffs and manacles he used were never fixed, and he stressed that releasing them underwater was "dangerous business at best." Nonetheless, at the very jump his mother attended, one pair of handcuffs had flown off by the time he hit the water.[97] Perhaps the actual jumps involved as great a risk, because the water was often shallow. Generally, he jumped feetfirst. When in Atlantic City he dived from a pier, he hit his head against the ocean floor.

As in his bridge jumps, in his vaudeville act Houdini devised new ways of satisfying his fellowman's hunger to watch him in encounters with death. In December 1907 he initiated his milk-can escape, his most frightening feat to date. His private description of it expressed pride, not fear: "The new Can trick is the best that I have ever invented. In this I am submerged in a large can, that has been filled with water, and the lid is placed on and locked with 6 padlocks, and in 3 minutes I am free. It is a fine looking trick, and almost defies detection."[98] The trick was accomplished through the ingenious construction of the can rather than through the use of special tools. The can

Houdini in the milk can with police officers.
Library of Congress

contained an inner lining that when turned released a catch. As for the impressive locks on which he focused the audience's attention, they were superfluous because the entire top of the can separated from the base at the shoulder well beneath them.[99]

Houdini performed the feat so as to wring out every last drop of suspense. As a showman, he intuitively grasped the dictum of Leopold von Sacher-Masoch (from whose name the word "masochism" derives): "Everything must be stated, promised, announced, and carefully described before being accomplished."[100] When he left the stage to put on a tank suit, uniformed assistants filled the can to the brim. Upon his return, he invited the audience to make a simple test with him before he attempted his escape. At the moment when he climbed into the can and submerged himself, everyone should hold his breath. Most gasped for air within thirty seconds; a very few lasted slightly longer than a minute. Well after the last had quit the effort, Houdini emerged smiling. Having impressed everyone with the difficulty of remaining underwater for long, he then began the actual feat. Assistants handcuffed his wrists and poured additional pails of water into the tank as he submerged himself inside. They fastened the lid with an ominous clank, attached six padlocks to the hasps, then enclosed the can with Houdini's curtained cabinet. With gallows humor, the band played "Asleep in the Deep."[101] Members of the audience nervously studied their pocket watches. (As he refined the feat, Houdini installed a huge stopwatch onstage for everyone to see.) Then it became a drama of time. A minute passed, then ninety seconds— longer than anyone in the audience had managed to hold his breath. An assistant marched onstage with an ax in hand and stood by the curtained cabinet, listening intently; in an emergency, Houdini had explained, that man would break open the can. Two minutes elapsed, two and a half, then three. Many spectators were now visibly agitated, convinced that something had gone terribly wrong. The assistant himself appeared concerned and lifted his ax to strike—only to see the curtains suddenly swept open to reveal Houdini, panting, dripping wet, but free. The audience burst into a loud ovation.[102]

In tours in Europe and the United States over the next few years, Houdini varied the script to keep interest high. Responding to challenges from dairies, he had the can filled with milk instead of water; to satisfy brewers, he filled it with beer. In 1910, after being locked in a tank of Yorkshire ale, he was so overpowered by the carbon dioxide fumes that he almost passed out in the middle of his escape. He called quietly to an assistant for help and completed his feat without the audience's knowledge of his actual danger.

In 1912 both the bridge jumps and the onstage milk-can escape were superseded by new death-defying feats. Instead of leaping manacled from bridges, he now submitted to the usual handcuffs and elbow irons, then had himself locked in an iron-weighted wooden trunk that was nailed shut and fastened with iron bands. At a signal from Houdini's assistant, the trunk was lowered into a body of water. This was, of course, a variation of the old trick of "Metamorphosis," and in both cases part of the trick was to have virtually completed his escape before spectators were aware it had even begun. (Here, as in so much of Houdini's escape art, the role of his assistants was crucial.) Houdini intended to inaugurate this feat off New York City's East River pier to fan publicity for his opening at Hammerstein's Roof Garden in July 1912, but for once the police refused him permission. Undeterred, he twice performed the feat beyond local jurisdiction in New York harbor—with the press corps eagerly bobbing alongside and thousands of spectators watching from ferryboats. Since, unlike most theaters, Hammerstein's Roof Garden boasted a large pool, he repeated the feat onstage each night.

Two months later, while on tour in Berlin, he unveiled the successor to his milk-can escape, the "Chinese Water Torture Cell." The following summer, he introduced it to American audiences, again at Hammerstein's Roof Garden in New York. It was Houdini's most compelling stage escape, one that he repeated hundreds of times, including in some of the last performances before his death in 1926. What most distinguished the "Chinese Water Torture Cell" from the milk-can escape was that it allowed Houdini to create a spectacle out of his body, which was visible through all the preparations, though the actual escape remained hidden from view. Over the next few years, Houdini refined the trick to enhance this effect.

He began by displaying onstage an imposing metal-lined mahogany cabinet, less than six feet high and less than three feet square, with an inch-thick plate-glass window in front. He solemnly explained its features and how he would attempt an escape under seemingly impossible conditions: locked upside down inside, his ankles

Houdini being lowered into the "Chinese Water Torture Cell," c. 1913. Library of Congress

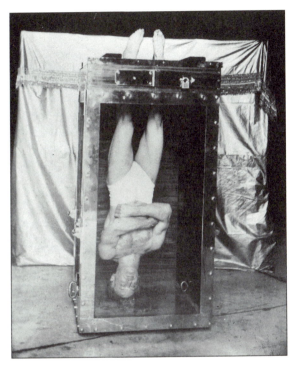

Houdini submerged in a later version of the "Water Torture Cell." Sidney H. Radner Collection, Houdini Historical Center, Appleton, Wisconsin

shackled, and completely immersed in water. He would forfeit a thousand dollars to anyone who could prove he received air inside the tank. "We all know accidents will happen—and when least expected," he continued, heightening the tension, so, "should anything go wrong," one of his assistants would stand ready with an ax to smash the glass front of the cabinet. Houdini would be protected from the broken glass by a full-length steel grill inside the tank, but this cage ostensibly further restricted his movements and made his escape still more difficult. (In a later version, he removed the grill to provide a more unobstructed view of his body underwater.)[103]

Then, while Houdini changed into a bathing suit offstage, volunteers from the audience examined the tank, and his assistants, wearing boots and slickers, filled it to the brim with water. After he returned, his ankles were secured in heavy mahogany stocks, which in turn were fitted into a solid steel frame. Slowly and dramatically, he was hoisted aloft and lowered headfirst into the cell, his entire body visible underwater through the glass. Assistants quickly locked the frame in place, fastened the tank with padlocked steel bands, then curtained off the entire cabinet from view. Thenceforth, the feat followed the script of the milk-can escape. Once again, the orchestra played "Asleep in the Deep." A minute passed, two minutes, as many as three. Spectators invited to hold their breath from the moment Houdini was immersed had long since given up. Once again, a stalwart assistant, wearing fireman's gear, anxiously raised a large ax. Suddenly Houdini thrust the curtain aside and strode forward, dripping wet but smiling triumphantly. The empty cell behind him stood as strongly locked as before. He was inevitably greeted by thunderous applause.

Although Houdini insisted there was "nothing supernatural" about the feat, a prominent British exponent of "psychic science," J. Hewat McKenzie, asserted that to perform such tricks, Houdini dematerialized himself and oozed out. This explanation was embraced by other spiritualist adherents, including Sir Arthur Conan Doyle, the creator of Sherlock Holmes. The exact workings of the water-torture cell remain a mystery, although some biographers have speculated

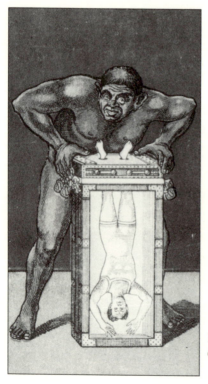

Detail of a poster for the "Water Torture Cell," Cardiff, Wales, 1913. Library of Congress

that the grill allowed Houdini to work his head and shoulders to the top of the tank and to release the catch on the stocks, pull them out like a drawer, and so escape. Later, when he eliminated the grill, the catch may have been automatically released when the water reached a certain level.[104]

The "Chinese Water Torture Cell" also made explicit what had been a growing theme in Houdini's challenges and escapes: torture. (In one poster a gigantic black fiend holding Houdini within the cell made this theme especially lurid.) Many of the modern devices from which Houdini escaped carried strong suggestions of pain and even terror, and he often finished scratched, bleeding, and apparently on the brink of collapse. Other outmoded restraints were occasionally revived to test Houdini's mettle, and these allowed modern spectators to look back with horror at the barbarities of the past. They included a cruel iron body cage used to punish witches in colonial New England; a still more pitiless Scottish body cage, by which criminals "were hung in midair until death released them from their misery";[105] and, in Dover, England, "an old and obsolete Padded Cell Suit, a restraint which has been abolished on account of its extremely cruel nature in holding the criminal insane."[106] Challengers from Liverpool described with sadistic relish ship irons once used to hold mutineers on the high seas. The men proposed to "manacle and truss you up in the old fashioned PUNISHMENT method; you to lay on your back, your hands manacled to your knees, a staff placed behind your knees and between your arms, holding you in an immovable position, also heavy lead leg irons locked on your ankles."[107]

In freeing himself from such antique devices, Houdini seemed to escape from the clutches of history itself and to defeat at last the oppressive authorities that had tortured individuals with impunity. He made these connections explicit in his 1913 escape from the HMS *Success*, the infamous British ship that had supposedly carried many convicts to Australia in the late eighteenth and early nineteenth centuries without ever yielding a prisoner. Moored at a pier in New York City as a floating museum and plentifully equipped with whipping posts, cat-o'-nine-tails, manacles, branding irons, "and other fiendish inventions of men's brutality to his fellow man," it offered Houdini the opportunity to become the first man in history to escape from the cells deep in its hold.[108]

In such escapes, Houdini simultaneously flattered spectators' sense of moral superiority over those who meted out harsh punishments in earlier times and offered them the spectacle of corporeal punishment and even execution that modern Western governments had either outlawed or moved behind closed doors. Whatever personal meanings these cultivated encounters with pain, injury, and death held for Houdini, he demonstrated again and again their fascination for a broad international public. He brilliantly gave the manifold challenges to individual freedom—and, more specifically, to the male body—tangible shape. In moving beyond mere physical privations, such as handcuffs, jail cells, and prisons, to direct confrontations with pain and death, he challenged what the literary critic Elaine Scarry has called the two most intense forms of human negation.[109] In many of his escapes, he turned the process of torture inside out. He gave fear and pain, in both their stark ancient forms and their more diffuse modern guises, compelling dramatic shape and then defied their power either to torment his body or to subdue his spirit. As with his earlier handcuff and jail-cell escapes, such triumphs over torture carried important if unspecified political implications. By dramatizing the isolated male's ability to confront and defeat the most palpable threats to his body, he became a powerful symbol of individual resistance to intimidation and domination. That is why his acts of "self-liberation" assumed an almost messianic character.

Houdini's single most spectacular self-inflicted torture still remained: his aerial straitjacket escape, which quickly superseded all his other outdoor feats and drew the largest crowds of his career. He appears first to have executed this escape in Kansas City on September 8, 1915. By this time he had been wriggling out of straitjackets for almost twenty years but never before while suspended upside down over a city street in full view of thousands. For days *The Kansas City Post*, known for its sensational journalism, had trumpeted the coming event to its readers. The Kansas City police department furnished its "best and strongest straitjacket" for the occasion, and two of its detectives tightened the "straps to the very last ounce of their strength." "If you get out of that you can get out of anything," one told Houdini. Dangling by his ankles, the illusionist was slowly hoisted twenty-five feet above the street by a block and tackle attached to the roof of the *Post* building. As five thousand onlookers craned their necks upward, he began to contort his body wildly. Like a great fish on a line fighting for its life, he put every muscle into the effort. Within seconds, he began to inch his arms under the tight canvas and leather straps. Then with surprising swiftness, he tugged the jacket down toward his shoulders, wrenched it off, and flung it to the pavement.[110]

Houdini performing an upside-down aerial straitjacket escape, suspended from Keith's Theatre across from the U.S. Treasury Building, Washington, D.C., 1922.
Library of Congress

During the next three years he repeated this escape across the country in virtually every city in which he performed that had a tall office building (at times he made do with a crane or tower). He continued to perform the feat at less frequent intervals into the 1920s. Shrewdly, he chose a newspaper building whenever possible, so that reporters were sure to publicize the event. He attracted numerous still and movie photographers as well. His favorite time was half past noon, the middle of the lunch hour. Often he ascended to much greater heights than in his initial effort. "String me up just as high as you can," he told police officials in one city. "If I drop I want to be sure it's going to be the finish. I'd rather have a lilly [sic] in my hand than go through life crippled and a burden to others."[111]

These suspended straitjacket escapes offer striking comparisons with his youthful beginnings. The man who as a boy grandiosely dreamed of becoming "Ehrich, the Prince of the Air," could truthfully boast, as he did after one performance in Boston, "My eye was the axis of the town."[112] The onetime medicine-show and circus performer who had offered free acts to lure small-town customers now turned great cities into his stage. Where once he pitched his feats to indifferent bystanders, now he drew as many as eighty thousand rapt spectators.

Women and especially men and boys streamed to the sites, clogging sidewalks and streets for blocks. Thicker than pigeons, they perched at the windows and roofs of neighboring buildings, drawn by a spirit that mixed Fourth of July festivities, a circus parade, and a hanging.[113] They watched expectantly as police or insane asylum officials vigorously tightened the jacket around Houdini. As his successes mounted, so did the ambition of officials to be the first to defeat him. A San Antonio police chief declared, "We know that he has baffled the officers in other cities, but we have hopes we can turn the trick here."[114] After these men had completed their work, Houdini's assistants carefully raised him aloft. When he reached the desired height, his body became a blur of motion. The sight of a man writhing wildly to free himself from an immobilizing restraint while suspended as much as 150 feet above the pavement, his every movement exaggerated by the swaying rope, offered not just a giddy acrobatic exhibition but an unforgettable example of manly determination and courage. Stiff as his straitjacket was, it served as an elastic metaphor for every-

ABOVE: A crowd watching Houdini. Library of Congress

RIGHT: Soldiers tightening Houdini into a straitjacket, in the *Ladies' Home Journal*, May 1918. The University of North Carolina at Chapel Hill

Stages in Houdini's straitjacket escape, in the *Ladies' Home Journal*, May 1918. The University of North Carolina at Chapel Hill

thing that restrained human movement, liberty, and aspiration. Similarly, his victorious upside-down salute to the crowd—both arms outstretched as he remained suspended high over the city—proclaimed his triumph over privation, officialdom, fear, and death. It renewed hope that in the rising skyscraper civilization, the heroic individual could still claim victory against all odds.

The drama of the aerial straitjacket escapes was unparalleled; and ever since Houdini performed them, people have debated their actual difficulties and risks. Just as Houdini had mastered fear of dark, airless enclosures, he now defied dizzying heights in which a slip would mean certain death. To shed the straitjacket, he tried to gain as much slack as possible, then twist vigorously as he maneuvered inside it. The upside-down position slightly aided in both these efforts. It lengthened his body somewhat and permitted considerable contortions. But the performer paid a heavy price, even assuming he had no fear of heights. His ankles could easily be strained in the process, and rushing blood could cloud his brain. The ropes could snarl, the pulley stick, and he might swing into the side of a building. All these difficulties Houdini encountered on one occasion or another. Only extreme vigilance on his part and that of his assistants prevented more serious or fatal accidents.[115]

MASCULINE VERSUS FEMININE MAGIC

Houdini attempted several more metamorphoses in his career. Though he remained a man of extraordinary physical energy and endurance, the strain of escapes on a now middle-aged body took its toll. As early as April 1911, his wife, Bess, anxiously observed in a letter, "Harry is worked to death, he looks so old." He absorbed numerous punishments over the years. His first lasting injury occurred seven months after that letter, in November 1911, when, freeing himself from a bag tied by longshoremen in Detroit, he ruptured a blood vessel in one of his kidneys.[116] On a number of occasions during this period, publicly and privately, he had wondered how long he could go on performing his strenuous feats.

Also, in July 1913 while on tour in Copenhagen, he suffered the greatest emotional blow of his life, from which he never entirely recovered. There he received news of his mother's fatal stroke. She was seventy-two; Houdini, thirty-nine. Just as Houdini's father's death had defined his entrance to adulthood, his mother's death marked his passage to middle age. She had been unquestionably the greatest love of his life. As he wrote to his brother Theo: "[M]y Heart will ALWAYS ACHE FOR OUR DARLING MOTHER. . . . [M]y very Existence seems to have expired with her." Then he added, "Must try and cheer up and be a man."[117] Against the finality of death, he desperately craved some sort of reunion with her. Ultimately, the struggle between this longing for authentic communion and the bitterness of sham contact, the desire for maternal comfort and the fear of being deceived by a rival's illusions led to his passionate battle against spiritualist frauds in the 1920s. But even before this point, in 1916, expressing his desire to move in new directions, he told a *Washington Times* reporter, "As an escapist extraordinary I feel that I'm about through." "For the last thirty years, or thereabouts," he explained, "I've been getting out of all sorts of things human ingenuity has devised to confine a human being. Hereafter, I intend to work entirely with my brain."[118]

Houdini never abandoned escape art, but the spectacular innovations he had made famous for two decades were at an end. Other developments besides physical and emotional demands contributed to this shift. Even though he was at the height of his career in vaudeville and variety, he felt the looming shadow of the movies, which by then usually closed his vaudeville bills and ultimately, in tandem with radio, eclipsed vaudeville as an institution. In addition, the war had suspended his practice of alternating tours between America and Europe. Seeking new and less taxing outlets, he determined to become both a movie star and an industry mogul. Beginning in 1916, he poured a great deal of time, energy, and money into the Film Development Corporation, a company working to improve processing methods. He went on to make seven films between 1918 and 1923, including *The Master Mystery*, in which he battles a robotic villain, and *Terror Island*, in which (as in a Tarzan film) he foils a tribe of spear-waving black cannibals. But as brilliant as Houdini had been in the compressed dramas of his live-action escapes, he proved a poor writer and a worse actor in these flaccid melodramas. The immediacy, power, mystery, and suspense of his stage and street feats were dissipated on film. As he ruefully concluded: "*No* illusion is good in a Film, as we simply resort to *camera* trix, and the deed is did."[119]

Houdini attempted other metamorphoses as well. Long a passionate collector of materials on magic and magic history, he became a major collector in these and related fields, including theater, mystery, and spiritualism. In the process, he repurchased some of the books his father had long ago been forced to sell and eagerly sought the prestige of a bibliophile and scholar. When the United States entered the war in 1917, the child of German speakers also turned himself into a 100 percent American. Passed over for military service at age forty-three, he threw himself into the war effort: entertaining American troops and performing in a patriotic revue called *Cheer Up*. He also sought to put his knowledge of escape to the national defense. He wrote to the secretary of war offering secrets on how soldiers and sailors might rescue themselves from sinking vessels, and during intermissions of *Cheer Up*, he proposed to teach American servicemen how to escape from German manacles. "Any one can be taught to escape from them," he confided, "if he is willing to endure a little pain in the process."[120]

After almost two decades of specialization as an escape artist, Houdini developed a new and less physically punishing role as a master magician. He had offered a general magic show in 1914, when he was emotionally exhausted after his mother's death. In his performances in *Cheer Up* in 1918, he introduced a new illusion in which he made an elephant disappear, and in the 1920s he offered other magical illusions to supplement his famous escapes.

The most consuming metamorphosis of Houdini's later career, however, was as a crusader against spiritualism. The contest brought many personal and cultural elements into play, including Houdini's skepticism, his longing for emotional comfort, the prestige of science, the lure of the supernatural—and a battle of the sexes. Professional magic was (and remains) overwhelmingly a male preserve—escape art, almost exclusively so. The drama of submission and release, bodily risk and mastery goes deeply to issues of masculine prowess and identity. Spiritualism attracted both sexes, but from its beginnings, women were especially prominent as mediums and as believers. Mediumship offered a means by which women could gain power, attention, and income; it enabled them to accept the tightest bonds of femininity—passivity, spirituality, and suffering—and then slip them off. Such women practiced a form of feminine magic that was in important respects the mirror image of Houdini's masculine escape art.[121]

Modern spiritualism began in 1848 in Hydesville, New York, possibly as a girlish hoax. Two young sisters, Catherine and Margaret Fox, claimed to establish contact with a mysterious spirit in their house that communicated through strange rappings. Soon, joined by their older sister Leah, they were charging admission and became celebrities. Countless other mediums quickly discovered similar gifts, including the brothers Ira and William Davenport of nearby Buffalo, New York. Beginning in the 1850s, spiritualism swept across the country and across the Atlantic to Britain and Europe, leaving its mark on many religious and social issues, from women's rights and

The Davenport brothers with an assistant in their spirit cabinet.
Library of Congress

abolitionism to health reform. At a time when women could not publicly address mixed audiences with propriety, women mediums became, in effect, lay ministers when they took to the stage to perform spirit trances. Spiritualism appeared to offer "scientific" confirmation of immortality without doctrinal complications such as original sin, atonement, final judgment, and hell—all of which it blithely dismissed. It thus provided an optimistic, democratic alternative to sin-sick torment and the dread of damnation. Death had no sting for spirits who merely passed from earthly life to the "Summerland" beyond—from which they might visit the living at will. No soul was truly departed; each continued to grow in body and personality as well as spirit as it advanced through heavenly spheres to ultimate rest.[122]

The dramatic demonstrations of spirit communication inevitably drew investigators and detractors, not only clergymen, scientists, and physicians but also professional magicians. From the eighteenth century through Robert-Houdin's writings, numerous magicians had exposed those who used magic tricks in the name of the supernatural, and the advent of spiritualism intensified this rivalry. As early as 1852, during his first American tour, the celebrated Scottish magician John

Henry Anderson challenged spiritualists directly. He demonstrated their hidden methods so that all could see: "I caused my table to rap as loudly and as intelligently as theirs."[123] Many other prominent British magicians, including Robert Heller and H. S. Lynn, emulated his example. The English conjurer J. N. Maskelyne ridiculed spiritualists' pretensions in his book *Modern Spiritualism* (1876) and exposed their effects onstage. As a volunteer from the audience, he claimed to catch the Davenport brothers red-handed as they slipped their rope bonds inside a spirit cabinet to rattle tambourines, ring bells, and play a tune on the violin and guitar.[124] Similarly, the leading American magician in the generation before Houdini, Harry Kellar, who had worked as an assistant to the Davenport brothers in the early 1870s, launched his own international career by employing and exposing spiritualist methods, especially the Davenports' signature rope-tie release.[125]

Houdini had early learned lessons in escape from such spiritualist-magicians, and, in company with other conjurers, he regarded the Davenport brothers as among the great escape artists of the nineteenth century. He even briefly offered spiritualist effects in the 1890s and saw firsthand their electric result.[126] Yet after his mother's death he came himself to crave the comforts of direct contact with the departed that spiritualism promised. And the extraordinary resurgence of interest in spiritualism following the Great War rekindled Houdini's maternal longing. It also aroused his masculine ire, however. Sir Arthur Conan Doyle sought to convert Houdini to his self-styled virile brand of spiritualism, for which he had become a fervent evangelist after the death of his son in the war. But, flattered as Houdini was by this friendship, their radically different stances toward spiritualism ultimately erupted into a highly public quarrel. After these diverse experiences, beginning in the early 1920s, Houdini devoted considerable energy to unmasking spiritualist charlatans with all the drama and publicity at his command. Wearing disguises, he attended séances and caught mediums in the act. In various publications, including his book *A Magician among the Spirits* (1924), he debunked spiritualist tricks; on the lecture circuit and in stage performances he duplicated their effects for all to see.

Houdini's most formidable antagonist, and the one who most strikingly exposed the gender war at the center of the magic, was a Boston

"Margery" (Mina Crandon), 1924. Library of Congress

medium known as Margery. His encounter with her came in response to a contest conducted by *Scientific American*. The venerable monthly magazine of science and technology had offered prizes, ultimately raised to five thousand dollars, for "an authentic spirit photograph" and for "the first physical manifestation of a psychic nature produced under scientific conditions." The magazine's editor appointed a committee of supposed experts to conduct tests and verify results. A diverse lot, they included Dr. William McDougall, the chairman of Harvard's Department of Psychology and president of the American

Society for Psychic Research; Hereward Carrington, an energetic investigator into psychic phenomena and an amateur magician; Dr. Daniel F. Comstock, an industrial engineer and former professor of physics at the Massachusetts Institute of Technology; Dr. Walter Franklin Prince, the chief research officer for the American Society for Psychic Research, a psychologist, former clergyman, and member of the Society of American Magicians; and Houdini.

During the spring of 1924 a number of mediums, both men and women, came forward to claim the prize, only to be quickly discredited. Margery, however, distinguished herself from her competitors in her social credentials, her amateur status, her aversion to the limelight, and her range of apparent psychic effects. Indeed, the name Margery was a pseudonym intended to shield her during *Scientific American*'s investigations from the publicity her rivals craved—though journalists quickly revealed her true identity. She was Mina Crandon, a blue-eyed, honey-haired woman in her mid-thirties who charmed many psychic investigators and reporters with her beauty and vivacity. In 1917 she had met a prominent, middle-aged Boston surgeon, Le Roi Crandon, whom she soon married. (It was her second marriage and her husband's third.) A former instructor at Harvard Medical School, Dr. Crandon was an ardent rationalist with a dignified, scholarly demeanor. In the early 1920s, he had read and grown excited about spiritualist phenomena, and beginning in the spring of 1923, his wife rapidly discovered her own psychic gifts. The couple began holding frequent, at times nightly, séances within their fashionable social and medical circles at their Beacon Hill home. In December 1923, during a whirlwind trip abroad, Margery astounded leading spiritualist proponents, including the physiologist (and 1913 Nobel laureate) Charles-Robert Richet in France and Sir Arthur Conan Doyle in England. In the summer of 1924, on both sides of the Atlantic, her partisans were already declaring her the most important medium of the twentieth century.

Most mediums specialized in either psychic communications or physical manifestations of spirits; Margery displayed astonishing powers in both domains. Tilting the table at her first séance in late May 1923, she quickly became a medium for coded rappings from spirits. Soon she fluently transcribed messages from the spirit world, including lines in Latin, Italian, French, German, Swedish, Dutch, Greek, and ideographic Chinese. Even as she was claiming to be in contact with the spirit world, her corporeal presence stressed a heightened erotic allure: at her séances, she usually wore just a loose dressing gown, silk stockings, and slippers. To monitor her movements, the sitters not only took her hand but occasionally held her legs in their laps as well. At times during a deep trance, she fell into violent seizures as if possessed. At the end of 1924, after the investigations by Houdini and *Scientific American* had concluded and the controversy over them was at its height, she drew still more attention to her body by producing ectoplasm, which spiritualists regarded as the ultimate proof of ghostly presence. When a spirit's power grew sufficiently strong, they believed, it partially rematerialized through the medium's bodily orifices. In Margery's case, these included her mouth, nose, ears, navel, and vagina. First and last, however, what integrated many of Margery's phenomena and most fascinated spiritualist adherents, investigators, and the public was the personality of the figure called her spirit-control, or principal contact and guide to the world beyond, her dead older brother Walter.

Walter had died in 1911 at the age of twenty-eight, crushed between a railroad car and a tender while working as a fireman on the New York, New Haven, and Hartford Railroad. He was five years older than Margery and still spoke of her, when his hoarse, whispering voice was heard in her séances, as "the Kid." He usually whistled to announce his presence, at times rendering a popular song. He became the star of the show. A lusty, irreverent, and often profane young man, he would banter with the séance circle. When someone greeted his presence familiarly, "Hello, Walter. Where have you been?" he replied jauntily, "Oh, I had to take my girl to a strawberry festival." "Can you read my mind?" another asked. "Yes," he said, "but you wouldn't want me to tell *that*!" "Walter," a third ventured, "when you are relaxed, do you surround yourself with youth and beauty?" Walter would laugh heartily at the lofty sentiment and pat the speaker's head. "No, I'm not relaxed when youth and beauty are around. I'm under fifty!"[127] Wielding props—both supplied and unseen—around the séance room and chuckling like a low vaudeville comedian, he frequently mocked the guests' propriety and hushed expectancy. He recited limericks and parodied hymns:

Onward, psychic soldiers,
Marching as to war,
With the cross of Science
Going on before . . .[128]

He also produced impressive special effects. These extended from commonplace ghostly efforts, such as starting and stopping a record player or a clock and moving furniture around the house, to his own parlor magic: inventorying the contents of sitters' pockets, producing flowers and, on one occasion, a live pigeon. He played many instruments, including the ukulele, harmonica, tambourine, and bass drum, at times whistling an accompaniment in what he once called his own "jazz band." When sitters expressed surprise that he and his spirit crowd should know current popular tunes, "the explanation was offered that they go everywhere to our theaters as to other places." At the conclusion of a séance in 1925, he congratulated himself in terms that made the comparison with vaudeville explicit: "Continuous performance, good as Keith's."[129]

The presence of Walter and his spirit friends seemed still more palpable at Margery's séances because of a variety of touches bestowed on individual sitters, ranging from kisses to kicks, feelings of a powder puff to a hard fist. Occasionally regular participants saw Walter's body parts, such as an eye, hand, or finger, luminously displayed. In response to scientific investigators, Walter could be helpfully interested and occasionally truculent. When so inclined, he patiently participated in experiments, often making suggestions and modifications, like a psychic engineer. But in testier moods, he reminded people that a spirit's life was no bed of roses. In response to a request that he operate an intricate mechanical device brought by one investigator, he snapped, "I have to experiment and work out things in my sphere just as you do in yours. . . . If you think I'm here just to wander around the room making demonstrations, you're damn mistaken."[130]

Walter was, of course, Margery's version of "Metamorphosis," her substitution trunk trick (stuffed full of gender politics) in which she left her body to change positions and sexes in ways that mystified her audience. Inverting the drama in which Houdini assumed a feminized position and released himself, Margery simulated the swaggering masculine presence of Walter while appearing never to escape the clasped hands of her fellow sitters around the table. (Her husband usually sat beside her.) Walter's "vigorous and virile" character (in Conan Doyle's phrase) seemed to many to testify to her authenticity as a medium precisely because they could not imagine that this "most charming and cultivated lady" could step into the disembodied but vividly palpable personality of a rough-and-tumble young man. (In fact, since the mid-nineteenth century, many female mediums, under the influence of their masculine spirit-controls, had assumed the personas of swearing sailors, Indian warriors, and lusty suitors.)[131]

Houdini had no such difficulties. Although he came late to the *Scientific American* investigations of Margery, after thirty sessions had taken place, he approached the case as another challenge. Antagonistic from the outset, he offered to pay one thousand dollars if he could not "detect her in fraud."[132] For their part, the Crandons had already been spoken for by Walter in his singsong taunt "Harry Houdini, he sure is a Sheeny."[133] During their first session together, in late July 1924, Houdini, sitting on Margery's left while her husband sat on her right, tried to control at least her left hand and foot. Walter appeared, ringing an electric bell apparatus designed to measure the psychic force between Houdini's feet and knocking over a screen behind Margery. Most dramatically, he picked up a megaphone and spoke: "Have Houdini tell me where to throw it." When Houdini asked that it be thrown to him, the megaphone immediately landed at his feet.[134]

"All fraud—every bit of it," Houdini announced to his co-investigators after he reached the street.[135] As a magician who performed with his body, he believed that he had detected how Margery performed with her own. In preparation for the evening, he had worn a rubber bandage that made his right leg swollen and sensitive; at the séance he pulled up his trouser leg and pressed his ankle to Margery's. He maintained that he felt her leg slide and her tendons contract just as the bell rang between his feet and he felt her lunge to tip the screen behind her. As for the megaphone, he confessed some grudging admiration: it was "the '*slickest*' ruse I have ever detected." At first he thought it depended on a confederate, but, he concluded, Margery had taken advantage of a moment when someone left the room to place the megaphone over her head like an over-

Houdini in the cabinet he devised for Margery. Library of Congress

size dunce cap. Then it was easy to flip it in whatever direction Houdini asked.[136]

In their second session together, Walter produced some dramatic table tipping, but Houdini groped underneath the table with his hand and discovered Margery's head. She lamely explained she was retrieving some dropped hairpins.[137]

These preliminary sessions were followed in August 1924 by official ones for the *Scientific American* contest. In these the investigation committee, heeding Houdini's suggestions, sought to control Margery's movements by devising a wooden cabinet with armholes and hinged flaps at the top that could be fastened and locked around her neck. In the following séance, Walter taunted Houdini more directly than ever: "You think you're smart, don't you? How much are they paying you for stopping phenomena here?" When Houdini replied, "I don't know what you're talking about; it's costing me $2,500 a week to be here," Walter seemed remarkably knowledgeable about the vaudeville business in the slack summer season. "Where did you turn down a $2,500 contract in August?" he challenged.[138] The session ended without any psychic phenomena.

Before the next session, Margery took a page out of Houdini's playbook by offering to submit to a full anatomic search by a physician or, if he wished, Houdini himself—or so her supporters later claimed. Houdini reported that she asked him (perhaps challengingly, perhaps flirtatiously), "Do you want to search me?" to which he replied, "No, never mind, let it go. I am not a physician."[139] This time Houdini and a fellow committee member, Walter Prince, controlled Margery's hands as she sat in the cabinet, so that, as Houdini declared during the session, if she took out a concealed device by which to ring the bell apparatus on the table in front of her, it would be exposed when the cabinet was searched. When Walter "arrived," he spoke not in his usual hoarse whisper but in a loud, clear voice, strongly insinuating that Houdini or his assistant had planted a carpenter's folding ruler (with which Margery might ring the bell) in the cabinet under his kid sister's feet. "Houdini, you Goddamned son of a bitch," he raged, "get the Hell out of here and never come back. If you don't, I will."[140] The explosion, Houdini wrote, "just expressed Mrs. Crandon's feelings toward me, as she knew I had her trapped."[141] When inspected, the cabinet did indeed contain a folding ruler. For the final session, another member of the investigating committee devised a knee-high compartment to use as a control device in place of Houdini's wooden cabinet. With Houdini and another member tightly holding Margery's hands, nothing remarkable occurred.

By his own account, Houdini both exposed Margery as a magician and triumphed in this battle of the sexes: "I charge Mrs. Crandon with practicing her feats daily like a professional conjuror. Also that because of her training as a secretary, her long experience as a professional musician [she played the cello, piano, and cornet], and her athletic build she is not simple and guileless but a shrewd, cunning woman, resourceful in the extreme, and taking advantage of every opportunity to produce a 'manifestation.' "[142] The manifestations she produced, of course, were not simply spiritualist but masculine. Walter's brash whistle and taunting voice, irreverence, and aggressiveness suggested that a swaggering male sexuality lay within her as well. In exposing Margery's fraud, Houdini also exposed her as a woman who, despite all her guides and talents, could only sham the phallus.

Although the *Scientific American* committee deliberated the Margery case for several more months, ultimately all but Carrington were unconvinced of her powers. In the next few years, other investigators and erstwhile partisans challenged her claims. Nonetheless, she remained the single most sensational medium of her time, retaining loyalists within the American Society for Psychic Research as well as finding new partisans, including the writer Hamlin Garland and the poet William Butler Yeats. As Margery lay dying in 1941, a would-be confidante encouraged her to reveal both how she had achieved her spiritualist effects and, equally pressing, why she had done so. But she adhered to her own magician's code and reportedly replied, "All you psychic investigators can go to hell."[143]

AN UNSOUGHT CHALLENGE

Following the Margery investigations, Houdini continued to make exposures of spiritualist frauds a major part of his activities both on and offstage. For their part, spiritualists railed against him, and Walter warned darkly that Houdini had a year or less to live. Characteristically, Houdini shrugged off this threat: "In the last 10 years my death has been predicted dozens of times, and if the spiritualists (?) guess often enough some time they will guess correctly."[144]

On October 22, 1926, three days after giving a lecture on spiritualist frauds at McGill University, Houdini was visited by three McGill students in his dressing room at the Princess Theatre in Montreal. One of these, a strapping young man named Whitehead, itched to test Houdini's fortitude. "Is it true," he asked, "that you can resist the hardest blow struck to the abdomen?" It was a question more appropriately put to a Sandow than to an escape artist who had never made such a public boast. According to the best eyewitness account, Houdini tried to dodge the issue, inviting Whitehead to feel his forearm and back muscles instead. But the young man persisted, finally asking, "Would you mind if I delivered a few blows to your abdomen, Mr. Houdini?" Houdini reluctantly agreed, and before he could rise from his couch, Whitehead pummeled him with "four or five terribly forcible, deliberate, well-directed blows."[145]

In pain, Houdini completed his final Montreal appearance the following day. He proceeded to Detroit—only to collapse at the end of his evening performance. Three days after the assault, he entered Detroit's Grace Hospital. He wanted to walk from his bed to the operating room where surgeons would remove his ruptured appendix, and when physicians insisted on a stretcher, he bristled. For almost his entire career he had bested police officials, insane asylum attendants, and other authorities. In his aerial straitjacket escapes, he routinely urged a brace of husky men to strap him in as tightly as they could. Now his serene humor was gone, but his tough defiance remained. "Say," he challenged the orderlies, "I can still lick the two of you."[146] He died of peritonitis six days later on Halloween.

Although magic is an ancient art, Houdini demonstrated its appeal for the modern world. At a time when new technologies seemed imbued with magic, he affirmed the presence of magic within the body and spirit of the individual man. In an age of often bewildering obstacles and intimidating authorities, he dramatized the ability of a lone figure to triumph over the most formidable restraints and the most implacable foes and against the most impossible odds.

In such ways, he extended the sense of the male body's special powers that Eugen Sandow had pioneered. Stripping off his clothes in an instant, Sandow delighted in displaying the strength and dexterity of his extraordinary muscles. Houdini, too, was proud of his strength (a pride that may have contributed to his fatal injury), but the masculine power he embodied was a claim of invincibility, which is why news of his death carried a special shock. Whereas Sandow spoke to fears of enervating weakness and hopes of commanding strength and virility, Houdini appealed to nightmares of entrapment and dreams of triumphant release. Making their often unclad bodies the subject of suspenseful challenges and contests, both affirmed the possibilities of individual male heroism in the modern world. Their metamorphoses ultimately emphasized not the fluidity but the stability of gender divisions. Sandow appealed to a male ideal purportedly rooted in both ancient sculpture and modern science. Houdini cultivated illusion in order to reaffirm traditional verities of masculinity. The distance between strongman and escape artist was often surprisingly short.

A third overwhelmingly popular embodiment of masculinity brought these figures into even closer conjunction. Though he, too, ultimately appeared in newspapers, magazines, and films, he first emerged not in dime museums or on the vaudeville and music-hall stage, as did Sandow and Houdini, but from the pen of a frustrated businessman, Edgar Rice Burroughs.

THREE

"STILL A WILD BEAST AT HEART"

EDGAR RICE BURROUGHS

AND THE DREAM OF *TARZAN*

In March 1912, at the beginning of his career as a popular author, Edgar Rice Burroughs wrote to a magazine editor with his latest idea for a yarn:

> The story I am on now is of the scion of a noble English house—of the present time—who was born in tropical Africa where his parents died when he was about a year old. The infant was found and adopted by a huge she-ape, and was brought up among a band of fierce anthropoids.
>
> The mental development of this ape-man in spite of every handicap of how he learned to read English without knowledge of the spoken language, of the way in which his inherent reasoning faculties lifted him high above his savage jungle friends and enemies, of his meeting with a white girl, how he came at last to civilization and to his own[,] makes most fascinating writing and I think will prove interesting reading, as I am especially adapted to the building of the "damphool" species of narrative.[1]

It was, the editor replied, a "crackerjack" idea. "You certainly have the most remarkable imagination."[2]

Edgar Rice Burroughs, 1912. © 1975 EDGAR RICE BURROUGHS, INC.

When Burroughs wrote *Tarzan of the Apes* he was thirty-six years old, married with two young children, and living in Chicago, the city of his birth. He was a sturdy though not especially imposing man, roughly five feet nine inches tall, with strong arms and hands.[3] Far from living a life of rugged individualism, he worked in a minor position, giving professional advice to clients for *System*, "The Magazine of Business." "I knew little or nothing about business," Burroughs later recalled, "had failed in every enterprise I had ever attempted and could not have given valuable advice to a peanut vendor." To mesmerize clients, he took refuge in vague, portentous pronouncements and impressive if irrelevant charts and graphs. "Ethically," he admitted, "it was about two steps below the patent medicine business," in which he had also worked until the passage of the Pure Food and Drug Law in 1906 shut the enterprise down. To make matters worse, his boss was, in Burroughs's words, "an overbearing, egotistical ass with the business morality of a peep show proprietor."[4]

Burroughs thus wrote *Tarzan* as an act of self-liberation. He hoped to cast off the humiliations of a frustrated, insignificant white-collar worker for the independence of a commercial author with a mass readership. But more than merely a means of making money, the story, he hoped, would serve as an imaginative escape for himself and his readers. After he had become one of the most widely read (if never the highest paid) writers of his day, he made this point explicit. Speaking of the appeal of the Tarzan stories, he declared:

> We wish to escape not alone the narrow confines of city streets for the freedom of the wilderness, but the restrictions of man made laws, and the inhibitions that society has placed upon us. We like to picture ourselves as roaming free, the lords of ourselves and of our world; in other words, we would each like to be Tarzan. At least I would; I admit it.[5]

In his own way, then, Burroughs was as much an escape artist as Houdini. The Tarzan escape emphasized not only freedom but also wildness, not only challenge but also combat, and it proved one of the twentieth century's most popular and durable, performed by Burroughs himself in twenty-three additional Tarzan books, which were translated into a host of languages, as well as in magazine articles and newspaper serials, and by others in films, radio and television programs, cartoons, games, and toys.

As Tarzan carried escape art into the realm of fictional adventure, his body recalled Sandow's. Tarzan represented Burroughs's conception of the perfect man, a spectacular nude figure of strength, beauty, virility, violence, and command who extended many of the themes popularized by Sandow. Like Sandow's feats and Houdini's escapes, Burroughs's creation must be understood in historical context. Ubiquitous as the name Tarzan has become, the circumstances of his creation have been largely forgotten. If, however, we see both Burroughs's situation and his protagonist's in historical context, then we also see more clearly the pressures on manhood in the modern world and the urge to recover a primitive freedom and wildness.

BURROUGHS'S BELATEDNESS

Edgar Rice Burroughs never invited the confusion between creator and character that, as vaudeville headliners, Sandow and Houdini did. Instead, he was always acutely conscious of the gulf between his life as an author and the adventures of his alter ego, Tarzan. He was still more aware that until he was nearly thirty-six (an age at which the major portion of Sandow's and Houdini's careers was over) he was not a writer at all and might easily have never written a word of the Tarzan books or the other sixty-eight books, numerous short stories, and articles that he composed before his death in 1950. Had he died in the summer of 1911, just as he attempted his first professional fiction and five months before he started *Tarzan of the Apes*, he would have been virtually unknown. Even within his extended family, he may well have been regarded as a disappointment. Certainly he was a failure in his own eyes.

"Nothing interesting ever happened to me in my life," Burroughs wrote in 1929, in the midst of his success. "I never went to a fire but that it was out before I arrived. None of my adventures ever happened. They should have because I went places and did things that invited disaster; yet the results were always blah."[6] This sense of belatedness, which his rueful humor could not disguise, dogged Burroughs from his childhood. Like many men who came of age in the 1880s and 1890s, he seemed born too late. The great adventures of his father's generation, even of his elder brothers', were over before he came on the scene. If young Ehrich Weiss had to struggle against the undertow of his father's decline, young Ed Burroughs felt the pressure to match his father's success. The very first sentence of the

Burroughs when a boy of about ten.
© 1975 EDGAR RICE BURROUGHS, INC.

unfinished autobiography in which he bemoaned his unexciting life declared, "My father, Major George T. Burroughs, was a cavalry officer during the Civil War."[7] George Burroughs's early adult life certainly did not lack excitement. As part of the Union troops at Bull Run, he had felt a bullet pierce his blouse but, fortunately, not his skin. Four years later, with his new wife, Mary, he watched the bombardment of Richmond in April 1865, and left the service as a brevet major. Three years later he moved his family to Chicago, unquestionably the greatest American city for adventure in the late nineteenth century. In 1871, from the roof of their West Side town house near fashionable Union Park, he saw the most calamitous fire in American history tear through the heart of the city. Seizing on Chicago's position as the capital of the nation's grain market, George Burroughs entered the distillery business and quickly grew wealthy. After a fire in 1885 devastated his distillery, he shifted his enterprise to the American Battery Company, which made storage batteries, and ultimately assumed the position of president.

Ed Burroughs was born on September 1, 1875 (one year after Houdini, eight years after Sandow), into a decidedly masculine household.

Three elder brothers—ages nine, eight, and three—loomed over him. Two other brothers who died in infancy cast shadows as well: Arthur, born in 1874, who survived only twelve days; and Charles, almost six years younger than Ed, who lived five months. "The earliest event in my life that I can recall clearly," Burroughs later said, "is the sudden death of an infant brother in my mother's arms."[8] As the youngest surviving child, Ed aroused considerable anxiety with his boyhood illnesses, which tightened his close bonds to his mother. He made up his first stories and told them to her during the times when he was confined to bed. Burroughs's father valued a strict Victorian order in his household: meals were punctually served to the sound of a gong; all lights were extinguished when he went to bed. So too did he favor a conservative order in society at large. A staunch Republican, as his son would become in his turn, he attended the trial of the Haymarket bombers in 1887 and received a special permit to witness their execution as the city trembled in fear of violent insurrection—another great if grim adventure.[9]

Ed grew up a straggler, always far to the rear of his father's expectations and his brothers' example. In stature and in substance, he never seemed to measure up. His father stood six feet high, and his brothers were tall as well. The two eldest, George and Harry, graduated from Yale in 1889 and dutifully joined their father at American Battery. Almost immediately, however, Harry developed a serious cough from battery fumes, and a physician recommended a change of climate. The tonic of ranch life in the West was the great restorative for many men at this time, including Theodore Roosevelt, the novelist Owen Wister, and the painter Frederic Remington. The two brothers teamed up with a Yale classmate, Lew Sweetser, whose father and uncle ranked among the leading cattle barons in Idaho; backed by their respective fathers, the young men bought land for a cattle ranch in the southeastern portion of the newly admitted state. In the spring of 1892, sixteen-year-old Ed joined his brothers in what was certainly the most exhilarating six months of his youth. Sent west to escape an influenza epidemic, he seemed to step into the pages of a dime novel. Although the romantic days of the great cattle drives had waned, he could at least bask in their afterglow. He joined in roundups, learned to ride all day and all night, and returned brimming with stories of ornery horses (including one that "Sandow himself

Burroughs in Western garb, Idaho. © 1975 EDGAR RICE BURROUGHS, INC.

Burroughs in a football uniform, sporting a mustache, at Michigan Military Academy, 1895. © 1975 EDGAR RICE BURROUGHS, INC.

could not have held . . . when he took it into his head to bolt") and "likable murderers."[10]

He at least glimpsed possibilities of self-transformation as well. A photograph from the time shows him looking at the photographer with the cockiness of a young cowboy, bulked up by his western garb, hand on hip, broad-brimmed hat shading his eyes as if the photographer's studio were a dusty street in Dodge City.

Ed's father wanted less rambunctious models for his youngest son, however. He shipped Ed off to Phillips Academy in Andover, Massachusetts, where another older brother, Coleman, was already enrolled. Ed flunked out after a single semester. His father then sent him to Michigan Military Academy, where Ed chafed under the tight discipline. As a plebe, he excelled chiefly in devising pranks and accumulating punishments. He rode in cavalry drill and played football, exaggerating his height by an inch and a half in a team description. He studied not only military tactics and mathematics but languages and literature as well. A drawing he made of Joan of Arc on the flyleaf of his French text gives us a glimpse of his inner imaginings. No

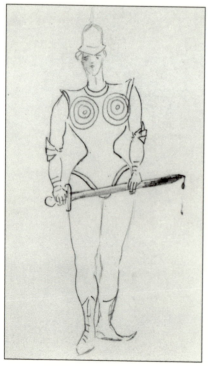

Burroughs's drawing of Joan of Arc, 1895.

slight maid, she is a formidable woman warrior with massive iron breastplates, an hourglass waist, ample thighs, and a conspicuously phallic sword dripping with blood.

Once Burroughs was graduated from Michigan Military Academy in 1895, it was time to gallop on a career, and though he had become an excellent rider, in this effort he found himself bucked and thrown again and again. The military offered the most obvious course, one that might please his father as well as fulfill his own youthful dreams. So when Burroughs failed the examination for West Point (as did the great majority of applicants), the wound to his pride cut deep. He returned briefly to Michigan Military Academy as assistant commandant. Then with impulsive bravado he enlisted in the army, requesting a cavalry assignment in "the worst post in the United States."[11] He got his wish and quickly regretted it. Burroughs may have thought he could recapture his father's Civil War experience and also the Western cavalry's glory days (gained at horrific cost to Plains Indians) as he rose in the ranks. But despite occasional chases of renegade Apaches, garrison duty at the Seventh U.S. Cavalry at Fort Grant in the Arizona Territory resembled convict labor far more than it did Buffalo Bill's Wild West. After a bout of dysentery, Burroughs called on his father to pull the necessary strings to gain an early discharge. His military career had lasted ten months.

From 1897 until the appearance of *Tarzan of the Apes* in *The All-Story* magazine fifteen years later, Burroughs seemed inexorably pulled back to Chicago and to the world of business, try as he might to escape it. He took up his harness at American Battery under his father. A year later, when the Spanish-American War broke out in Cuba, he sought a commission. At one point he wrote directly to Theodore Roosevelt to join his Rough Riders, but he was turned down. (His dreams of military glory died hard: as late as 1906 he was inquiring about a position in the Chinese army.) Seeking then the escape route of his elder brothers and to recover the intoxicating summer of his adolescence, he returned on several occasions to Idaho—only to discover that his brothers' cattle and gold-dredging operations represented not frontier adventure but a financial noose tightening around their necks. He briefly ran a stationery shop in Pocatello, Idaho, then gladly sold it back to its previous owner, concluding, "God never intended me for a retail merchant."[12] His marriage in 1900 to Emma

Hulbert, daughter of a prominent Chicago hotel manager, only increased the pressures of career. He made a final attempt to fit into his father's designs at American Battery, where he served as treasurer, then fled west once again, with his wife, in an abortive effort to start a new life with his brothers or on his own. Even two decades later, he wrote, "It gives me a distinct sensation of nausea, accompanied by acute depression every time I think of my experience at the plant." He added sarcastically, "I have about the same pleasant recollections of each and every business connection I had in the past."[13]

Back in Chicago after 1904, Burroughs struggled like a character in an O. Henry short story or, more desperately, a Dreiser novel to stay afloat amid the hordes of scrambling white-collar workers who by the end of the decade represented one-fifth of the entire male labor force.[14] He started as timekeeper on a construction site, then took "a series of horrible jobs" as salesman. "I sold electric light bulbs to janitors, candy to drug stores and [multivolume sets of the author John L.] Stoddard's Lectures from door to door. . . . My main object in life was to get my foot in somebody's door and then recite my sales talk like a sick parrot."[15] He put in longer stints as an office manager for one firm and then "as a very minor cog in the machinery" of Sears, Roebuck's enormous mail-order business, supervising a large group of (mostly female) stenographers as they cranked out thousands of letters a day.[16] None of these positions suited his restless, independent nature. Attempts to start a small business and thrive as his father had done—in advertising, patent medicine, a correspondence course in "scientific salesmanship"—all failed miserably. The birth of his first two children in 1908 and 1909 quickened his downward plunge. He felt near bottom, financially and emotionally. "I had worked steadily for six years without a vacation," he later wrote, "and for fully half of my working hours . . . I had suffered tortures from headaches. Economize as we would, the expenses of our little family were far beyond our income. Three cents worth of ginger snaps constituted my daily lunches for months." He pawned his wife's jewelry and his watch to buy food. He "loathed poverty" and loathed himself for being in it. With the damning judgment of a conservative businessman, he wrote: "It is an indication of inefficiency, and nothing more."[17]

Burroughs's frustrations were shared by countless millions; indeed, they would become a prominent theme in twentieth-century American literature: from Theodore Dreiser's *Sister Carrie* to Saul Bellow's *Seize the Day*. Willy Loman's son Biff voiced them at mid-century in Arthur Miller's play *Death of a Salesman* when he exclaims: "It's a measly manner of existence. To get on that subway on the hot mornings in summer. To devote your whole life to keeping stock, or making phone calls, or selling or buying. To suffer fifty weeks of the year for the sake of a two-week vacation, when all you really desire is to be outdoors, with your shirt off. And always to have to get ahead of the next fella."[18]

Burroughs tried other, almost parodically marginal businesses with no better success: a sales agency for lead-pencil sharpeners; then, under his brother Coleman, a manufacturer of scratch pads. In the office doldrums, he tried another moneymaking scheme that might have seemed still more chimerical: writing commercial fiction for the "pulps."

Pulp magazines were so called because of the inexpensive, porous paper on which they were printed. They specialized in stories that were formulaic concoctions, long on twisting plot, offered in double-columned monthly installments to a mass readership. Tales of adventure, mystery, war, the Wild West, and science fiction were their stock-in-trade. These attracted a predominantly male following of adolescent boys and both blue- and white-collar men, as well as a significant number of women, as readers' letters attest. They were read at home, especially on Sundays, while traveling to and from work, and in idle moments on the job. In some respects, writers for the pulps might be compared to performers in the small-time vaudeville in which Harry Houdini began his career. Both worked hard for low wages and tried to entertain a diverse, unpretentious public. If vaudeville was industrialized in its specialized acts, systematized format, and centralized management, pulp magazines were fiction factories dominated by big publishers that demanded from authors a combination of literary facility, stamina, and speed. Pulp writers received as little as a tenth of a cent per word. And just as small-time vaudevillians dreamed of hitting the big-time houses, many pulp writers aspired to break into the "slicks," the more prestigious mass-circulation magazines printed on smooth stock, such as *Collier's* and *The Saturday Evening Post*, that paid thousands of dollars for a single story. Vaudeville achieved its height between the 1890s and the Great War. But as successors to the cheap story papers of the nineteenth century, pulp magazines early in the second decade of the twentieth century were just entering their golden age, which continued through the 1930s.[19]

Burroughs himself derided pulp fiction and claimed to have stooped to it only because he needed the money. Keenly aware of the divide between "good" literature addressing a "gentle reader" and sensational fiction with no cultural pretensions, he knew that the pulps were not aesthetically respectable. In fact, he said he became acquainted with their contents by happenstance, though his quick mastery of their formulas suggests a longer and deeper acquaintance. Because one of his shaky business ventures took advertising in their pages, the office received copies of magazines to check the ads. Burroughs brought some of them home to read. "It was at that time," he later recalled, "that I made up my mind that if people were paid for writing rot such as I read in some of those magazines that I could write stories just as rotten."[20]

His first novel, *A Princess of Mars*, begun in July 1911 on leftover stationery from his failed enterprises, portrays the adventures of John Carter, a Virginia gentleman, Civil War veteran, and Indian fighter who falls into a trance in Arizona and wakes up on Mars. Carter was a kind of dream self into whom Burroughs poured many of the masculine endowments and accomplishments he most admired:

> a splendid specimen of manhood, standing a good two inches over six feet, broad of shoulder and narrow of hip, with the carriage of the trained fighting man. His features were regular and clear cut, his hair black and closely cropped, while his eyes were a steel gray, reflecting a strong and loyal character, filled with fire and initiative. His manners were perfect, and his courtliness was that of a typical southern gentleman of the highest type.

His Mars is inhabited by two races: a reddish one, who resemble earthly humans; and a hideous green one, whose warriors are fifteen feet tall, with an extra set of limbs and curved tusks. Except for ornaments, all go naked, as does Carter himself. He soon falls in love with a beautiful copper-skinned princess, and the first-person account describes his swashbuckling adventures on behalf of her and her people as he seeks to save her from the cruel, lustful monster who commands the green race. Finally, after slaying multitudes and proving himself the finest warrior on the planet, he has the satisfactions of restoring order, being proclaimed a hero, and marrying the princess. "Was there ever such a man!" she marvels. "Alone, a stranger, hunted, threatened, persecuted, you have done in a few short months what in all the past ages [on Mars] . . . no man has ever done." Though the tale ends on a note of longing, its great theme is manly triumph both in combat and in romance.[21]

So self-conscious was Burroughs about setting down such an extravagant fantasy and about being a writer at all that he wrote surreptitiously and under the pen name Normal Bean (that is, normal brain). He sent the first forty-three thousand words of the story to the editors of *The Argosy*, one of several magazines in the publishing stable of Frank Munsey, the man who started the modern pulp-magazine revolution. Ten days later, he received a highly encouraging letter from Thomas Metcalf, an editor of *The All-Story*, a sister publication. Spurred by Metcalf, Burroughs finished the story the following month and sold it for four hundred dollars. This amounted to barely more than half a cent a word, but in his autobiographical sketch Burroughs still savored the thrill of this, "the first big event in my life."[22]

Clearly, such writing tapped both a talent and a need in Burroughs. Aside from a crude "historical fairy-tale" called "Minidoka" that he had concocted for his nephew and niece in Idaho a decade earlier, he appears not to have written fiction before and certainly none of any length. Now it seemed he could not stop. Already, while Metcalf deliberated over the Martian romance, Burroughs wrote a second novel-length story, a medieval swashbuckler called "The Outlaw of Torn." Then, with an office manager's precision, he noted that on December 1, 1911, at eight in the evening he began to write the novel that would become *Tarzan of the Apes*.

MANLINESS IN THE PAGES OF *SYSTEM*

To appreciate fully the meaning of Burroughs's dreams of manly triumph in Africa, we should first look more closely at the magazine he so eagerly left to plunge into pulp fiction. After the scratch-pad business, like the lead-pencil sharpener agency, collapsed, Burroughs took what turned out to be his last job other than that as a self-employed writer. From shortly after he began writing stories in the summer of 1911 until early in 1913, when he felt his sales could support his growing family, he worked as manager of the business service department of *System*, a business magazine run by A. W. Shaw. Though Burroughs had almost nothing good to say about any business in which he worked, the experience at *System* aroused by far his sharpest invective. "I never so thoroughly disliked any employer as I did Shaw," he remembered, as if rubbing a wound that refused to heal. Perhaps at the root of Burroughs's disgust lay his sense of fraudulence and incompetence in dispensing business advice in response to individual requests, a service the magazine provided for an annual fee of fifty dollars. "I recall one milling company in Minneapolis or St. Paul who submitted a bunch of intricate business problems for me to solve. Had God asked me to tell Him how to run heaven, I would have known just as much about it." His boss's indifference to Burroughs's lack of qualifications only confirmed the fraud. Burroughs scornfully remembered, "Shaw also had a young man about nineteen giving advice to bankers. This lad's banking experience consisted in his having beaten his way around the world."[23]

In three crucial respects, *System* was the mirror image of the masculine world of pulp magazines in which Burroughs sought refuge and profit. First, to a startling degree, issues of manliness suffused its depiction of modern business. To read its pages is to discover an ethic of intense work and competition that both shaped and repelled Burroughs—to discover, that is, the "iron cage," in the sociologist Max Weber's phrase, from which he strove to escape.[24] If magazines such as *The All-Story* divulged a world of primarily (though not exclusively) masculine fantasy, offering satisfactions denied on the job, *System* presented an alternative world in which masculine adventure lay at the core of business competition. Second, *System* proposed a hierarchy of masculine worth and ability that emerged from competition. Whether this hierarchy was due to differences in training and environment or innate differences (an issue that Burroughs explored in *Tarzan of the Apes*) was a question to which it offered an equivocal response. Third, *System* was also a magazine of stories. Though all the incidents described in its articles were allegedly true, much of the writing was either about decisive actions that businessmen had taken or about tales of adventure in the context of modern business.

Many of the narrative devices in the *System* articles borrowed from fiction. A problem would be introduced by a remark or exchange in direct, "manly" speech, and the story then proceeded with rapid-paced action to a clear outcome with a business moral. This was not a magazine concerned primarily with impersonal business processes and economic forces, though it did promise to extract underlying principles that readers could apply to their own situations. Rather, it concerned men who had the power to assess problems, chart their courses, and control events, coming out on top as one of the "big men." One might well suspect that writers contrived details, concocted dialogue, occasionally invented an informant, or even made up much of the supposedly true accounts of business advice. But even if authentic to the last detail, its stories shared a clear house style designed to appeal to readers seeking entertainment as well as information.

The November 1911 issue of *System* is one which Burroughs would have seen and, quite possibly, read just as he prepared to put his first Tarzan story on paper. Consider the title. "System" was a word that glittered with magic in the early twentieth century. It carried the promise of a scientific modern order. New system builders were eager to apply methods of rationalization, coordination, centralization, and supervision to ever-larger organizations of people and machines, including vast new office bureaucracies, immense factories, and far-flung financial empires. By this time, the great investment banker J. Pierpont Morgan, Jr., had consolidated and expanded corporations such as United States Steel (1901), International Harvester (1902), and American Telephone and Telegraph (1906). In 1911 Frederick Winslow Taylor, articulating his vision of maximum industrial efficiency, declared, "In the past, the man has been first; in the future the system must be first." In Highland Park, Michigan, Henry Ford was developing his revolutionary system of production for the Model T car. The skyscraper was the cathedral of this emerging corporate order, the modern electrified factory its palace. And regimented, synchronized movement increasingly constituted its dance. At the very same time that Ford was developing his assembly-line system, Broadway choreographers were creating its inverted image in the modern chorus line. "It is system, system, system, with me," declared a leading choreographer, Ned Wayburn, in 1913. "I believe in numbers and straight lines."[25]

How was one to operate within this modern, urban world of business and stand out? The answer of *System*'s November 1911 issue began on its cover, which shows a crowd, principally of men, walking in a business district. The man in the forefront, more fully drawn than the others, models the characteristics of the exemplary businessman thriving in the urban corporate world. Well dressed but not ostentatious, bowler snug as a helmet, newspaper furled, and walking stick at the ready, he does not need to look at the clock behind him to know that time is money. Unlike the messenger just to the right, or the stoop-shouldered man at the very center retreating down the street, or the boy with hand in pocket walking into the left margin of the picture, he strides full of purpose on his mission.

The opening article offered inspiring accounts of individual business success as part of a series, "Ideas That Have Been Put to Work." Breathlessly, the piece begins: "In a flying spark that bridged a broken wire, Edison saw not merely a manifestation of electricity, but the possibility of electric light. In the steam escaping from a kettle of water, Watt saw a power that he harnessed for the development of our industries. So many of the world's greatest ideas have been suggested by trivial observations that have been adapted to the needs of the hour."[26] The article proposed to apply this heroic view of flashing genius to the world of modern business, with vignettes demonstrating breakthroughs using analogical thinking, even as it stressed the importance of interdependence, systematization, standardization, supervision, and expansion. For example, a manufacturer discovers how to make his sales force a more cooperative team by watching a football game. A store manager at the theater notes the use of a revolving stage and realizes he can apply it to his shopwindows, vastly expanding his possibilities of exhibiting goods with a four-part revolving display. A baker learns from the success of packaged laundry starch to emphasize the hygienic values of packaged bread. These are anecdotes about active, decisive, inventive men, often (though not exclusively) attuned to machinery and certainly to organization. They are adult Tom Swifts, eager to scale the business ladder.

"What Are Profits?" asks the next article, at first glance a dusty

The cover of *System*, November 1911. The University of North Carolina at Chapel Hill

disquisition by F. W. Taussig of Harvard's economics department. Its real subject, however, is the meaning of manliness in a modern capitalist society. A leading economist, Taussig was the son of a successful physician and businessman who had immigrated to the United States from Prague. He quickly described the hierarchy of manly achievement in the business world and directly addressed the issue of why some men succeed and others fail:

> Some men seem to have a golden touch. Everything to which they turn their hand yields miraculously. They are the captains of industry, the "big men," admired, feared and followed by the business community. Others, of slightly lower degree, prosper generously, though not so miraculously—the select class of "solid business men." Thence, by imperceptible gradations, there is a descent in the industrial and social hierarchy until we

reach the small tradesman who is, indeed, a business man, but whose income is modest and whose position is not very different from that of the mechanic or the clerk.

Taussig went on to consider whether such varieties in position stem from "differences in inborn abilities" or from "training and environment." (If Burroughs were reading, his eyes must have widened with interest.) With some qualifications, Taussig answered that at the highest level they are indeed innate: "Captains of industry are doubtless born. So are great poets, musicians, men of science, lawyers. Though there may be occasional suppressed geniuses among the poorer classes, ability of the highest order usually works its way to the fore." Not surprisingly, he believed that merit thrives in a laissez-faire economy. Still, for those not touched with genius, he acknowledged, other qualities were critical, including "the advantages of capital and connection," "imagination and judgment," administrative ability, "courage," and a body "vigorous in its capacity to endure prolonged application and severe nervous strain." Surveying the various types of men who succeeded in the business world, he concluded, "Among all these different sorts of persons, a process very like natural selection is at work."[27] Implicitly, this process affirmed the essential rightness of business and other social hierarchies, which he believed reflected fundamental and progressive hierarchies of nature.

After an item on making money from waste, "What's Your Scrapheap Worth?" there was a piece by Henry Beach Needham, "How to Select the Right College Man." One might fairly say that *System* was fascinated with processes of selection—whether of kinds of scrap or kinds of men—with distinguishing the exceptional individual from the mass. The college article noted that a higher proportion of college men were going into business and quoted business leaders who wanted college graduates for executive positions. (One imagines Burroughs squirming, since he was among the more than 95 percent of American men at this time who never attended college.[28]) The article at one point casually observed that the college man "has survived [in various capacities in Western Electric] because he is 'the fittest.' " The Darwinian analogy was clearly becoming a commonplace. Enos Barton, chairman of the board of Western Electric and recently retired as its president, declared, "The college . . . is a sort of sieve—a coarse sieve wherein the best men are sifted out. . . . By our method of selection the loafers and the sports are eliminated."[29]

In the following piece, "Players in the Great Game," the subject remains the "big men," the "men who are factors in the march of progress." The first figure discussed is Irving T. Bush, who by sticking to one thing (Burroughs squirms again) is worth twenty-six million dollars at the age of forty-three. "Physically, too, Mr. Bush is big—in all some six feet and two inches, with a heart of proportionate size." He has just given a check for ten thousand dollars to his sales manager. Another "player" in the "Great Game" is Edward R. Stettinius, president of Diamond Match (and later a partner in J. P. Morgan and a key industrialist in the Allied effort during the Great War). He "sits behind his big desk in his big office. . . . As the conversation progresses, Mr. Stettinius directs it, using a half-burned cigar as a baton. . . . [H]is movements are quick and vigorous."[30] (Burroughs crunches a gingersnap.)

As a whole, the articles in *System* depicted a world of big, energetic, masterly leaders—and, implicitly, of smaller, unexceptional followers. It was a view cogently if smugly expressed by one of the largest manufacturers of the day, Cyrus McCormick, Jr., a man born with a silver reaper in his mouth. In answer to a query, "Upon what ideals, policies, programs, or specific purposes should Americans place most stress in the immediate future?" this commander of fifteen thousand workers replied: "Civilization needs leaders, but it is equally essential there should be followers. Nature has so provided that for one man capable of the larger task of brain or brawn, tens of thousands are unequal to it. In the frank recognition of this natural law, and the acceptance of it, and obedience to it, much depends."[31]

A different but equally telling perspective emerges from the advertising section of *System*. The advertisements may also be read as narratives of manliness, which directly speak to readers concerned about their inadequacy. No talent is simply innate, they seemed to say; any man can benefit from training, advice, or nostrums. The *System* articles focused on the "big men," but the advertisements promised to aid those who had fallen behind. Many offered correspondence courses and other instruction by mail. (Burroughs would hardly have glanced at these, given that one of his many failed ventures had been a correspondence course in "scientific salesmanship.")

How big a man are you?

Your weekly pay envelope will answer this question.

The dollars per week you earn prove your bigness or littleness—your importance or unimportance—whether trained or untrained.

The American School offers you a chance to become a trained man, to get a better salary and live in a better home—in fact, to change your entire life, if you only have ambition and grit and will follow our advice and instruction.

The American School makes it as easy as possible for every man to get an education who really wants one. This School was founded for just such men as you—men who have the ambition, but lack time and money.

If you want to be a **big man,** write today for our **New Deferred Tuition Plan.** Let us tell you how you can obtain the training you need—how you can pay for the tuition after your salary has been raised.

Fill in and mail the coupon. Let this coupon be your **start**—your foundation for a **big man**—a better job and a bigger salary. An agent won't bother you at your home or work. We'll send you all information by mail. We obtain our students in the same manner that we teach—by correspondence.

AMERICAN SCHOOL OF CORRESPONDENCE
CHICAGO, U. S. A.

FOUNDATION COUPON

American School of Correspondence, Chicago, U. S. A.
Please send me your Bulletin and advise me how I can qualify for the position marked "X". *System 11-11.*

....Aviator
....Draftsman
....Architect
....Building Contractor
....Structural Engineer
....Civil Engineer
....Electrical Engineer
....Elec. Light and Power Supt.
....Master Mechanic
....Steam Engineer
....Reclamation Engineer

....Lawyer
....Fire Ins. Engineer
....Telephone Expert
....Moving Picture Op'r
....Book-keeper
....Stenographer
....Accountant
....Cost Accountant
....Cert'f'd Public Acc'nt
....Auditor
....Business Manager
....College Preparatory

NAME...

ADDRESS...

OCCUPATION...

Please mention SYSTEM when writing to advertisers

"How big a man are you?" an advertisement for a correspondence school in *System*, November 1911. The University of North Carolina at Chapel Hill

—walled in, Old Man? Let Shryer help you out

Grasp the helping hand that has lifted thousands from the High Stool of Salaried Uncertainty to the Arm Chair of Successful Business Ownership.

Own a Business

Thousands of well-meaning, hard-working men are daily proving the futility of the average employee's struggle. Every today is a repetition of hundreds of yesterdays—and tomorrow nothing but a promise of another today—another lap in the wearying, grinding race that leads to nowhere.

Perhaps you too have been vainly attempting to scale the stone wall which bars the average employee from the competence which his ability, earnestness and sincerity of effort entitle him to. If so, you will be glad to know that hundreds of others—in no way different from yourself—not so capable or ambitious perhaps—have solved this problem of the employee—in the ownership of a commercial agency.

Shryer Gave Them Their Start

He knew how to do it. He had been where they were—where you are now perhaps—and knew the difficulties which prevent lots of men from "jumping the traces" and striking out for themselves.

He had taken the step from Employed Uncertainty to Business Ownership himself—and knew the worst difficulty in the way of business independence is lack of capital.

No Capital Needed

Just as he solved the problem of "no capital" for himself successfully, he is daily solving it for others—will solve it for you.

Pointers on the Collection Business

—Mr. Shryer's own book will tell you how he overcame his early handicaps—rising from a meagre $15.00 a week job to a $15,000 a year business all his own. He not only tells you how *he did it* but how he has helped hundreds of others *to succeed in the collection business* —and what he can do for you.

Earn while you learn

You don't have to make the jump suddenly. The practical knowledge his course imparts enables you to cash in on your early instruction, which you master in spare time. Shryer himself started that way. He kept it up until his spare time work was so much more profitable than his regular occupation that he was glad to give the latter up. "Pointers on the Collection Business" is a valuable book. Its worth to you depends on your willingness to strike out for business independence—at the sacrifice of only a little spare time for study. Fill out the coupon—send it to Mr. Shryer personally—TODAY.

W. A. SHRYER, Pres., American Collection Service, 495 State St., Detroit, Mich.

DEAR MR. SHRYER: Please send me "Pointers on the Collection Business" and any other facts about your course of instruction, which you think may interest me.

Name..................................... Address.....................................

City........... .... State.......................

"Walled in, Old Man?" an advertisement in *System*, November 1911. The University of North Carolina at Chapel Hill

"How big a man are you?" one ad demanded. A large, prosperous, and distinguished-looking man, with his suit coat open to reveal a vest and massive watch chain and with his hand cradling a watch, stands staring down on a smaller, thinner, balding, rumpled, and rather cringing figure. The copy declared: "Your weekly pay envelope will answer this question. The dollars per week you earn prove your bigness or littleness—your importance or unimportance—whether trained or untrained." The American School of Correspondence promised to make the difference.

Helping hands stretch forth in other advertisements for similar services. "Walled In, Old Man?" inquires one in which a clerk sits on his stool, shut in a corner of high brick walls, while from the top of the picture a strong hand reaches down. "Grasp the helping hand that has lifted thousands from the High Stool of Salaried Uncertainty to the Arm Chair of Successful Business Ownership." "Go," exhorts another as a man in suit and tie helps a more modestly dressed man up a rocky, thorny slope, and, by implication, to an office desk and a solidly middle-class life.

"Go," an advertisement for another correspondence school in *System*, November 1911. The University of North Carolina at Chapel Hill

Burroughs wanted to escape his job at *System* and the entire world it represented—in many respects, the world of his father's values, honed to a sharp competitive edge—but he was profoundly shaped by it. And though he claimed to hate business, he approached his new career in commercial fiction like a character out of the pages of *System*. The magazine celebrated charts and graphs as indexes of scientific efficiency, and from the time he began writing, Burroughs kept a graph of his word output over his desk. (It quickly rose to a peak in 1913, the first year he wrote full-time, with 413,000 words.[32]) He proved a canny bargainer with magazine editors, publishers, and film companies; a shrewd marketer of syndication and subsidiary rights; and, beginning in 1923, the successful owner of his own corporation, Edgar Rice Burroughs, Inc.

The story that made this new career possible was *Tarzan of the Apes*. Writing it, Burroughs discovered his potential as a commercial author and the possibility of a new life (his unpublished autobiography essentially ends with this new birth). More important, he discovered a rich cluster of themes with immense cultural as well as personal resonance. Their continuing fascination contributes much to Tarzan's enduring fame.

MASCULINE REVITALIZATION AND
THE REASSERTION OF HIERARCHY

On every side in the early twentieth century, age-old questions about the basis of individual merit and social hierarchy demanded new answers. Reformers and radicals of various stripes questioned the legitimacy of special privilege and entrenched power. Swept by a flood tide of immigrants, the nation swirled with an unprecedented diversity of ethnicities, religions, and cultures. Extremes of wealth and poverty, power and impotence challenged egalitarian beliefs. The sense that American society was a sharp pyramid, with figures scrambling to reach its summit or at least advance up its steep slopes—the idea projected in the pages of *System*—pervaded all classes. Those who felt themselves rightfully on top strenuously justified their positions by appeals to hierarchies, particularly those of race (whiteness), gender (masculinity), religion (Protestant Christianity), and putative superiority of body, mind, character, and merit, and they did their best to repel all radical and leveling forces. From their high fortresses, they rolled boulders down on new immigrants, African Americans, agrarian and industrial radicals, feminists, socialists, and anarchists.

Yet their assaults were not merely defensive. The contest between conservatives and reformers over the shape of the American social and economic order took place against a larger international backdrop in which new hierarchies were being violently asserted. Burroughs's generation had grown up during the great wave of European imperial expansion, when a fifth of the world's landmass (excluding Antarctica) and a tenth of its population had been seized by European powers, great and small. Britain, whose national symbol, appropriately, was the lion, claimed the largest share: one-quarter of the land and one-third of the people on the globe.[33] With the United States' own frontier exhausted, the excitement of a new global land rush with immense prizes to the victors was hard for many Americans to resist.

Particularly in the flush of the nation's triumph in the Spanish-American War, expansionists jubilantly proposed to revitalize their numbers by carrying the battle to new realms of empire. The Indiana Republican Albert Beveridge perfectly captured this spirit in his jingoistic paean on the floor of the U.S. Senate in 1899: "God has not been preparing the English-speaking and Teutonic peoples for a thousand years for nothing but vain and idle self-contemplation and self-admiration. No! He has made us *the* master organizers of the world to establish system where chaos reigns. . . . He has made us adept in government that we may administer government among savage and senile peoples." "We will renew our youth at the fountain of new and glorious deeds," Beveridge declared. Here was "system" with a vengeance.[34]

This dream of white Anglo-American revitalization and conquest not only transformed American foreign relations; it also profoundly affected American thinking, as is evident in popular fiction. Conspicuous in many popular novels of the early twentieth century are concerns with what might be called geographies of rugged masculinity: regions within which white men of northern European stock reassert their dominance over physical and moral "inferiors," including incompetents, malefactors, weaklings, and cowards.

One such realm was the West, in which Owen Wister placed his immensely popular and influential novel *The Virginian* (1902). A historical romance, the story celebrates the adventures of a homegrown noble savage, "a slim young giant, more beautiful than pictures," who is twice compared to a Bengal tiger. Like so many Westerns (and, as we shall see, other works), it both glories in wildness as the basis of masculine freedom and insists on the necessity of imposing social order. In the heyday of the cowboy in the Wyoming territory, that order was established by the individual man. The code of this society is simple: whether in bets, card games, or horse trades, "a man must take care of himself." If this code is violated, the gun and the rope are the modes of redress, lynch law and the duel the courts of justice. As the title character declares, "[E]quality is a great big bluff. . . . [A] man has got to prove himself my equal before I'll believe him." Being equal to the occasion is the only kind of equality that counts. Burroughs, who did not remark on many literary works, called *The Virginian* "one of the greatest American novels ever written."[35]

If the Western was one popular genre of masculine adventure, what might be called the Southern became another. Here the most influential work was Thomas Dixon's *The Clansman* (1905), a book immediately controversial and now infamous for its vehement espousal of white supremacy and glorification of the Ku Klux Klan. Adapted as a play, it helped to spark wholesale assaults on African Americans in the terrible race riot in Atlanta in 1906. D. W. Griffith created his brilliant, disturbing film version, *The Birth of a Nation*, in 1915.

The novel has a number of points in common with Wister's *The Virginian*: it is also a historical romance with a slender, handsome, raven-haired white Southern hero who reaffirms his manliness in mortal combat in a plot in which lynch law figures conspicuously. Here, too, the story ends with marriages symbolizing the reunion of regions—New England and the West in *The Virginian*, the North and the South in *The Clansman*. Unlike *The Virginian*, however, *The Clansman* associates wildness and animality not with natural nobility but with African American savagery and immorality. The most flagrant instance occurs in Dixon's description of the rape of a white Southern virgin by the evil mulatto Gus. The author could not decide which wild beast to invoke:

> Gus stepped closer, with an ugly leer, his flat nose dilated, his sinister bead-eyes wide apart gleaming ape-like as he laughed. . . . The girl uttered a cry, long, tremulous, heart-rending, piteous.
> A single tiger-spring, and the black claws of the beast sank into the soft white throat and she was still.[36]

At the novel's conclusion, of course, the men whom Dixon regarded as the South's and the nation's proper white leaders reassert their authority against such usurpers. Anything else, Dixon made clear, would pervert morality, politics, religion, history, and biology. In a fair fight, he believed, their triumph was inevitable: "The breed to which the Southern white man belongs has conquered every foot of soil on this earth their feet have pressed for a thousand years. A handful of them hold in subjection three hundred million in India. Place a dozen of them in the heart of Africa, and they will rule the continent unless you kill them."[37] In Dixon's fervid imagination, the rise of the "invisible empire" of the KKK was part of the march of visible white empires across the globe.

The far North was a third testing ground of masculinity in the novels and stories of Jack London. A year younger than Burroughs, London had virtually completed his extraordinary career as a writer of popular fiction before Burroughs even got started. He began publishing stories about Alaska in pulp magazines in his early twenties and wrote fifty-one books before his death at the age of forty in 1916. Burroughs both admired London's fiction and was fascinated by his turbulent life.[38] He would certainly have known *The Call of the Wild* (1903), London's first great popular success.

Buck, the hero of *The Call of the Wild*, is a dog rather than a man, a shift in species that allowed London to explore themes of savagery, violence, and primitivism with special power and directness. Half Saint Bernard and half Scotch shepherd, Buck has previously lived as a "sated aristocrat" on a California ranch, "with nothing to do but loaf and be bored." In the novel's opening pages, however, he is stolen and sent north to satisfy the demand for sled dogs created by the Klondike gold rush of 1897: "He had been suddenly jerked from the heart of civilization and flung into the heart of things primordial." The fierce demands of the life of a pack dog in the harsh Northland transform him physically, morally, and spiritually:

> His muscles became hard as iron, and he grew callous to all ordinary pain. . . . He could eat anything, no matter how loathsome or indigestible; and . . . [build] it into the toughest and stoutest of tissues. Sight and scent became remarkably keen, while his hearing developed such acuteness that in his sleep he heard the faintest sound and knew whether it heralded peace or peril.

At the same time, Buck increasingly recovers the instincts of his wild ancestors and, in reveries, the memory of his primeval companion, early man: "The hairy man could spring up into the trees and travel ahead as fast as on the ground, swinging by the arms from limb to limb, sometimes a dozen feet apart, letting go and catching, never falling, never missing his grip. In fact, he seemed as much at home among the trees as on the ground." Buck learns to compete in the "ruthless struggle for existence," "the law of club and fang." "He must master or be mastered; while to show mercy was a weakness."[39] Just as the Virginian must ultimately duel the evil cowpuncher Trampas, Buck must engage in a fight to the death with the treacherous husky Spitz. Unlike the Virginian, however, he has no Vermont schoolmarm pleading with him not to fight, and he easily learns to glory in the joy of the kill.

In the course of the story, the Northland pitilessly exposes both animal and human incompetence and weakness. Buck achieves his position as lead dog through his willingness to fight rivals to the death and maintains it through his incomparable strength and sagacity. Dogs are no more created equal in London's tale than men are in Wister's.

Like Wister and Dixon, London gave readers a romance, in his case between Buck and his "ideal master," John Thornton. Thornton, too, has joined the quest for gold, though apparently animated more by delight in the wilderness and joy in the quest than by the riches to be gained. As Buck increasingly responds to the ancestral "call of the wild," only his love of Thornton holds him back. He hungers for tougher challenges, bigger game. He kills a bear, then a moose, and when he discovers Thornton slain by members of the Yeehat tribe, he kills man, "the noblest game of all." At the novel's conclusion, he has been transmuted to legend, the great Ghost Dog fabled by the Yeehats who runs at the head of a wolf pack, "leaping gigantic above his fellows, his great throat a-bellow as he sings a song of the younger world."[40]

BURROUGHS'S LITERARY EXPERIMENT

When Burroughs dropped his infant "scion of a noble English house" into tropical Africa, another harsh and savage realm that would test the character of modern masculinity, he was adapting a well-known theme. As he later recalled, "I was mainly interested in playing with the idea of a contest between heredity and environment. For this purpose I selected an infant child of a race strongly marked by hereditary characteristics of the finer and nobler sort and at an age at which he could not have been influenced by associations with creatures of his own kind. I threw him into an environment as diametrically opposite that to which he had been born as I might well conceive."[41]

To a conservative white American of Burroughs's background and training, the jungle of Equatorial Africa brought together the starkest possible conjunction of "primitive" indigenous peoples, exotic wilderness, savage animals, and both noble and venal colonial explorers. Burroughs knew little about Africa at this point and later declared that he wrote *Tarzan* with the aid of only Henry Stanley's *In Darkest Africa* (1890) and a fifty-cent Sears dictionary.[42] Probably, his deepest direct contact with African culture had occurred on the Midway at the 1893 Chicago world's fair as he drove by the Dahomey Village in a "horseless surrey" sponsored by his father's American Battery Company. He would have grown up reading accounts of romantic European explorers, even though he was aware that in the years since his birth, Africa had quickly passed from being the object of the most lofty professions of philanthropy to being the target of the most rapacious imperial greed. More particularly, he would have read extensive newspaper accounts of one of the first modern mass atrocities, the enslavement and death of millions in the Congo Free State under the aegis of King Leopold II of Belgium. Still, Burroughs's *Tarzan* remains much more in the tradition of R. M. Ballantyne's 1862 novel for young readers, *The Gorilla Hunters* ("I say, boys, isn't it jolly to be out here living like savages?"), than in that of Joseph Conrad's *Heart of Darkness* (1902).[43] Despite Conrad's searing depiction of evil at the core of the "civilizing" enterprise, tropical Africa remained in Burroughs's and the public's imagination a great arena for white male adventure, one of the last wild places on earth.

To carry the "hereditary characteristics of the finer and nobler sort" into this demanding environment, Burroughs, who took great pride in his Anglo-Saxon ancestry, selected members of the British nobility, John and Alice Clayton, Lord and Lady Greystoke. The story opens in 1888 with John Clayton and his young, pregnant wife bound for West Africa, where he plans to investigate reports that Britain's native subjects are being exploited and enslaved by another European power (sounding much like Belgium) in pursuit of ivory and rubber. Burroughs cast Clayton from the same mold as his previous hero, John Carter, in *A Princess of Mars*. Above average height, with a military bearing and regular features, he is "a strong, virile

man—mentally, morally, and physically." By contrast, the crew of the
small vessel on which John and Alice sail from Freetown on the West
African coast toward their final destination typify the lowest elements
of society, socially, morally, biologically. The officers are "coarse, illiterate," "swarthy bullies" led by a "brute" of a captain, and the crew
that mutiny against their thuggish command are even more villainous
and animalistic.[44] In their atavistic appearance and savage proclivities,
they virtually step from the pages of Cesare Lombroso's highly influential *Criminal Man*.[45] In Burroughs's description, their leader, Black
Michael, "a huge beast of a man, with fierce black mustachios, and a
great bull neck set between massive shoulders," anticipates the apes
that will play such a prominent part in the story. Burroughs poured ice
water into Clayton's veins, allowing him to stroll across the deck of
the ship in the midst of the mutiny as casually as he might stroll
across the polished floor of a drawing room. After the crew murder the
officers, Black Michael sets Lord and Lady Greystoke, together with
abundant supplies and provisions, "alone upon . . . [the] wild and
lonely shore," castaways in a savage land.[46]

In this setting, English nobility and apes alike respond according
to their innate abilities and what Burroughs understood as the nature
of their sex. "I am but a woman," Lady Alice admits, "seeing with my
heart rather than my head, and all that I can see is too horrible, too
unthinkable to put into words." Lord Greystoke tries to stiffen her
upper lip with the reminder that they carry within themselves both
the blood of triumphant forebears and the brains of enlightened Vic-
torians: "Hundreds of thousands of years ago our ancestors of the dim
and distant past faced the same problems which we must face, possibly in these same primeval forests. That we are here today evidences
their victory. . . . What they accomplished . . . with instruments and
weapons of stone and bone, surely that may we accomplish also." He
erects a strong haven for their little family. Nonetheless, in the
trauma of an attack by a bull ape, Lady Alice's mind gives way.
Throughout the first year of their baby son's life (and the last of their
own), she imagines them back in England and their time in Africa as
merely a hideous dream. She dies as peacefully as a fading flower.
Lord Greystoke, by contrast, is violently murdered by the huge king
ape, Kerchak, who has led a cluster of apes to the Greystoke cabin.
These apes belong to a species supposedly superior to the gorilla; yet

within it, as within the human species, Burroughs emphasized innate differences. Lacking nobility of character, intelligence, or appearance, Kerchak rules over his tribe by virtue of his immense strength and fierce temper: "His forehead was extremely low and receding, his eyes bloodshot, small and close set to his coarse, flat nose; his ears large and thin, but smaller than most of his kind." By contrast, another member of the raiding party, the she-ape Kala, is "a splendid, clean-limbed animal, with a round, high forehead, which depicted more intelligence than most of her kind possessed."[47] Having just lost her offspring, she snatches the Clayton heir from the cradle and claims him for her own. In this way, Burroughs set up a plot with both mythic resonance and modern pertinence. When Kala becomes a mother to the noble waif, a host of issues rushes to the fore of Burroughs's story: nature and nurture, primate affinities and human capacities, savagery and civilization.

WILD BOYS AND MEN

Tarzan was the exemplary fictitious feral child of Burroughs's and his readers' time—as he has remained for the ninety years since. Although the fascination with them is age-old, "wild" children have exerted a special interest for Western societies since the eighteenth century, precisely because they seemed to offer special insight into the relationship between human nature and nurture. When, for example, "a naked, brownish, black-haired creature . . . about the size of a boy of twelve" emerged from the woods in northern Germany in 1724, the discovery was heralded as "more remarkable than the discovery of Uranus." He appeared alert and seemed to have especially keen hearing and sense of smell. He did not care for clothes but gradually learned to wear them. Dubbed Wild Peter, he became the pet of the royal house of Hanover, then of the duke of Hanover, King George I of England, and subsequently of his daughter, Princess Caroline. The Scottish physician and writer John Arbuthnot eagerly examined him, hoping that Peter might learn to talk, relate his feral experiences, and thus communicate the nature of the human mind in a pure state, uncontaminated by society. Arbuthnot quickly concluded, however, that Peter was an "imbecile," incapable of speech due to severe mental retardation.[48]

In 1799, seventy-five years after the discovery of Wild Peter, another feral boy of similar age was flushed by hunters in the forest near Aveyron in southern France. Like Peter, he was unaccustomed to clothes and did not speak; unlike Peter, he appeared dull rather than acute in all his senses, especially hearing and sight. The next year he was presented in Paris to the young physician Jean-Marc-Gaspard Itard, who became a pioneer in the education of the deaf and the mentally retarded. Although the Parisian public had flocked to the "savage of Aveyron" expecting to find in him the embodiment of Rousseau's noble savage, Itard encountered someone quite different: "a disgustingly dirty child affected with spasmodic movements, and often convulsions, who swayed back and forth ceaselessly like certain animals in a zoo, who bit and scratched those who opposed him, who showed no affection for those who took care of him, and who was, in short, indifferent to everything and attentive to nothing." Itard gave him the name Victor and sought to develop his senses, intellect, and emotions as well as to determine from his deficiencies what humankind owed to education and civilization. He spent five years in this effort, far longer than did Dr. Arbuthnot or any of Peter's other examiners, and though Itard claimed some successes, Victor remained profoundly a captive of his stunted early life.[49]

More immediate to Burroughs's time than this pair of "wild" boys were a pair of "wild" men. At the end of August 1911, a few months before Burroughs began writing *Tarzan*, butchers at a slaughterhouse near Oroville in north-central California discovered a "wild" man cornered by their dogs. Superficially, at least, his situation resembled Wild Peter's and Victor's when they were found. Except for a ragged scrap of canvas, which he wore like a poncho, and a frayed undershirt, he was naked. He was also fatigued, frightened, and starving. And he spoke no language that his captors could recognize. He was not a boy of twelve, however, but a man who appeared perhaps sixty years old. (He was, in fact, about fifty.) But the greatest difference that immediately set his case apart from the feral children's, long before his intelligence could be assessed or his emotional development determined, was race. When the local sheriff arrived, he perceived the "wild" man

as an Indian. To hold him and at the same time to shield him from the
curious stares of people streaming to the jail at Oroville, the sheriff
locked him up in a cell for the insane. Despite this setting, his appeared to be a striking case not of individual isolation and retardation,
as with Wild Peter and Victor, but of cultural primitivism and isolation
from the modern world. Newspapers trumpeted news of this last wild
Indian, a figure who seemed to have stepped directly from the Stone
Age into the age of airplanes.[50]

When Alfred Kroeber and Thomas Waterman, two anthropologists
at the University of California at Berkeley, read these stories, they
thought this "wild" man might be a survivor of the Yahi tribe whose
last recorded members had been massacred almost a half century earlier. Two days after the "discovery" of the strange man, Waterman
traveled to the Oroville jail. He sat in the inmate's cell and read down
a list of phonetically transcribed Yana words, until at last, with *siunini*,
yellow pine, the man's face lit up. He was, it gradually emerged, the
last surviving member of the Yahi, a southern tribe of the Yana.[51] Almost his entire life, he had lived in concealment as part of a tiny and
ever dwindling remnant in the foothills of Mount Lassen. For three
years, since the death of his mother, sister, and an old man, he had existed entirely on his own. Now he was officially a ward of the federal
government. Wearing a shirt, coat, and trousers provided for him but
spurning shoes, he traveled with Waterman by train and ferry from
Oroville to San Francisco. Until his death from tuberculosis four and a
half years later, he lived in the University of California's new Anthropological Museum near Golden Gate Park, where he demonstrated
Yahi crafts such as arrowhead making on Sunday afternoons and
worked as a janitor's assistant during the week. He never revealed his
name, but Kroeber called him Ishi, which means man in Yana.

With his gentle, friendly disposition, Ishi played the role of
Rousseauian noble savage far better than had Wild Peter or Victor.
His reactions to modern civilization aroused keen interest. Traveling
around San Francisco shortly after his arrival, he was unnerved by the
crowds. The exclamation *"Hansi saltu!"* burst from his lips: "Many
white people, many white people!"[52] A few days later, a reporter invited Ishi to attend a vaudeville performance. From his box seat, during the first two acts, Ishi watched the audience exclusively, which to
his mind was far more interesting than anything onstage. In time, he

learned white San Franciscans' names for the people around him: "English, Chinaman, Japanese, Wild Indian, Nigger, Irishman, Dutchman, policeman." He appeared impressed less with airplanes than with technologies nearer at hand and of direct use to him—matches, running water, roller window shades. According to those close to him, he blamed contemporary illnesses on "the excessive amount of time men spent cooped up in automobiles, in offices, and in their own houses. It is not a man's nature to be too much indoors and especially in his own house with women constantly about," he believed.[53]

Ishi appealed to the modern longing for a more rugged, "primitive" existence that would revitalize masculinity. This longing emerged most vividly when he returned to his home ground in May 1914, almost three years after his emergence near Oroville. The im-

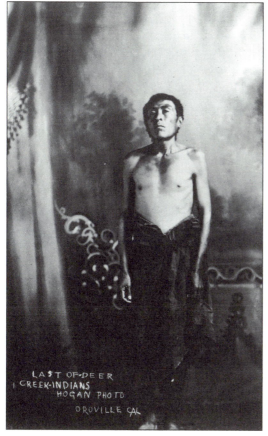

Ishi in Oroville, California, August 1911. Photograph by Hogan. Phoebe A. Hearst Museum of Anthropology, University of California at Berkeley

Ishi with bow and arrow,
Deer Creek, 1914.
Phoebe A. Hearst Museum of
Anthropology, University of
California at Berkeley

petus for the trip came not from Ishi, who was at first reluctant to re-
visit the place of his ancestors, but from Kroeber and Waterman and
their physician-friend Saxton Pope. Ultimately, Ishi agreed, and the
outing took on the aspect of a male-bonding retreat as much as an
ethnographic study. Once back in his homeland, Ishi, who had refused to be photographed without Western dress in San Francisco, re-
verted to his native breechcloth. Still he refused to shed clothing
entirely, even while swimming, unlike his "civilized" companions, all
of whom reveled in their nakedness and the opportunity to "play Indian."[54] As he demonstrated his great skills as hunter and fisherman
and his deep reverence for the natural world, he seemed a time trav-
eler from an ancient and alien realm.

The desire to strip off civilization with one's clothes and to experience primitive life firsthand in contact with nature was, of course, a
masculine Romantic impulse that recurred with astonishing force and
variety in the late nineteenth and early twentieth centuries—from

the French artist Paul Gauguin's removal to Tahiti to the German nudist movement. In addition, at the time Ishi was discovered, millions of buttoned-up American boys and men were taking to the woods in organizations such as the Sierra Club and the Boy Scouts of America. Ernest Thompson Seton declared, in the first Boy Scout handbook, "Those live longest who live nearest to the ground, . . . who live the simple life of primitive times, divested, however, of the evils that ignorance in those times begot." Seton proposed that everyone spend at least one month a year outdoors.[55]

Perhaps the American figure who most grandiosely struck the primitivist pose in this period was a minor Boston illustrator, Joseph Knowles. Beginning in early August 1913, Knowles conducted an "experiment" that both reversed Ishi's passage from wilderness to modern technological civilization and, more than any contemporary effort, paralleled Edgar Rice Burroughs's literary experiment in *Tarzan of the Apes*. What Knowles proposed was to test whether a modern man, stripped naked and without any implements, could enter the woods and live the primitive life successfully, depending solely upon his own individual resources.[56] The wilderness he chose was not in Equatorial Africa but in darkest Maine, and he was not a noble foundling but an experienced woodsman and guide on the eve of his forty-fourth birthday. Even so, the rather pudgy, cigarette-smoking Knowles made an unlikely exemplar of savage virility. The surprising celebrity he achieved testifies to how much a public adapting to modern technological civilization craved the reassurance that the urban white man could face the elements on his own and triumph.

Knowles's experiment recalls Sandow's and Houdini's feats, even as it resonates with *Tarzan*. Knowles sought the limelight as assiduously as any vaudevillian, though even he was dazzled by his success. As if conducting a Houdini escape, on August 4, 1913, he stripped off his clothes before reporters and photographers near the Spencer Mountains in northeastern Maine, vowing to stay in the wilderness for two months. He had arranged with the *Boston Sunday Post* to file weekly reports, written with charcoal on birch bark, chronicling his adventures. The week before, Harvard's Dudley A. Sargent, the physical-culture expert who twenty years earlier accorded Sandow the title "perfect man," had examined him. The best Sargent could say

Joseph Knowles stripping for
his wilderness experiment,
1913. From *Alone in the
Wilderness*. The University of North
Carolina at Chapel Hill

Knowles bidding his friends goodbye. From *Alone in the Wilderness*. The University of
North Carolina at Chapel Hill

was that Knowles "showed considerable fat, which will aid him in resisting cold." Still, the doctor struck exactly the note of cultural urgency that Knowles desired: "There is no question that in our advancement from primeval life we have dropped through disuse a great deal of natural knowledge; our artificial life has robbed us of some of our greatest powers and has stunted others." Under the circumstances, he applauded Knowles's "attempt to live like a primeval man" as being of both scientific interest and practical value.[57]

Over the next two months, the activities of the "forest man" became headline news in the *Boston Post*. Readers learned of his struggle to build a fire, catch trout, and contrive leggings out of moss. On August 24, the *Post* excitedly titled his dispatch "Knowles Catches Bear in Pit." The painter turned primitivist furnished readers with a blow-by-blow description of how he caught and killed a young black bear so that he might have its skin as a covering at night and as clothing when he finally reemerged to civilization. Later, he reported how he killed a small deer, grabbing it by its horns and breaking its neck. These exploits were double-edged. On the one hand, they testified to Knowles's prowess as primordial man, recapitulating the Darwinian struggle by which his ancestors had ascended the ladder of civilization. ("In the wilderness," he declared, "the one great law is the survival of the fittest."[58]) On the other hand, these kills violated the Maine game laws, from which Knowles had unsuccessfully sought an exemption. During his last weeks, he grew worried that game wardens might seek him out and arrest him; he spent his last days in the wild fleeing across the Canadian border so that he would not be taken prematurely.

When, scratched, bruised, thirty pounds lighter, and garbed in animal skins, Knowles emerged on October 4 near Megantic, in Quebec, he looked like primordial man come to life. He seemed to have transformed his very race in the process: a reporter described him as "tanned like an Indian, almost black." The size and enthusiasm of the waiting crowd stunned him. When he came down the steps from his train, he thought the horde "would tear the skins from [his] body." It was a foretaste of the tremendous receptions to come. All the way through Maine and down to Boston, crowds cheered his passage. Schools released their charges so that they might glimpse the great man. When he arrived in Boston, once again clad in animal skins,

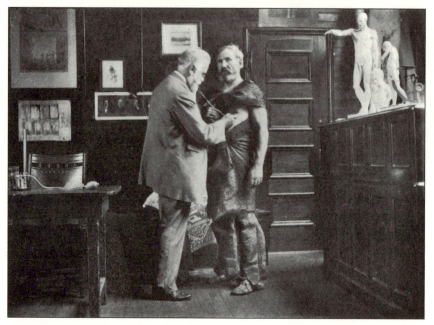

Knowles in wilderness garb as examined by Dudley A. Sargent. From *Alone in the Wilderness*. The University of North Carolina at Chapel Hill

crowds mobbed him. For a celebration on Boston Common, they swelled to an estimated fifteen to twenty thousand people. At Harvard, Dr. Sargent examined Knowles again and pronounced him stronger in every respect than before he entered the woods. Afterward, the staff of Filene's Men's Store promised to turn him into a modern man once more through "barbering, manicuring, chiropody and complete outfitting in new and fashionable clothes."

Knowles's metamorphoses from civilized to primitive man and back again seemed to fascinate the public as much as had Houdini's great magical metamorphoses. At a lavish banquet honoring Knowles, Sargent declared, "A dress shirt is not becoming to him with such a splendid body hidden away underneath." Yet it was Knowles's ability to inhabit both worlds that captured the public's imagination. He served as a primitive proxy for modern men, who liked to imagine that they, too, had splendid bodies hidden underneath their dress shirts. Two months after his return, he completed a book based on his dispatches to the *Post* called *Alone in the Wilderness*. A rival newspaper, William Randolph Hearst's *Boston American*, charged that Knowles was a fraud who actually bought his celebrated bearskin and slept in a snug, secret cabin while in the woods, but it failed to prick the bubble of his celebrity. Knowles briefly toured on the vaudeville circuit retelling his feat, and his book sold 300,000 copies.[59]

PRIMATE RELATIONS

Burroughs's "wild child" was of course a fictional hero in an adventure story rather than a historical object of scientific examination. It is doubtful that Burroughs knew of Wild Peter, Victor, or other feral children when he wrote *Tarzan*. Nor does he appear to have been aware of Ishi or, in the interval between *Tarzan*'s publication in *The All-Story* and in book form, to have remarked on the feat of Joseph Knowles. As he later said, the legend of Romulus and Remus suckled by a wolf and of Kipling's animal stories came more to his mind.[60] In time, Burroughs did learn more about the fate of feral children and acknowledged that Tarzan's adventures were fictional entertainments, not literal possibilities. He wrote in 1927:

I do not believe that any human infant or child, unprotected by adults of its own species, could survive a fortnight in such an African environment as I describe in the Tarzan stories, and if he did, he would develop into a cunning, cowardly beast, as he would have to spend most of his waking hours fleeing for his life. He would be under-developed from lack of proper and sufficient nourishment, from exposure to the inclemencies of the weather, and from lack of sufficient restful sleep.

Burroughs intended Tarzan as "merely an interesting experiment in the mental laboratory which we call imagination."[61]

Even with this retrospective caveat, Burroughs's story could be read in two alternative yet overlapping ways. It might be understood, first, as a novel diversion, an experiment in storytelling that aimed only to entertain. At the same time, *Tarzan* could be read as an allegory that in miniature recounted and explained why its hero (and those like him) triumphed where others failed. In this sense, the workings of the narrative revealed truths about the reader's world, not just the fictional characters'. Although he denied that the events in his imaginative laboratory could literally happen (which many a reader of *Tarzan* has contested), Burroughs still permitted a considerable area within which the story might be understood to be true.[62]

In this imaginative laboratory, Burroughs created a figure whose hereditary advantages, as he conceived them, are severely tested in the harsh environment of the African jungle. At the outset his situation in some ways reverses that of Wild Peter and of Victor. Apes rather than cultured savants regard him as developmentally backward, and both his foster father, Tublat, and the tribal leader, Kerchak, argue that he should be abandoned as hopeless. By the age of ten, he can claim some accomplishments, including superior cunning and ability on the ground, but he remains ashamed of his deficiencies, such as his hairless body, "pinched nose," and "puny white teeth."[63] The name the apes give him marks his difference (and, ultimately, Burroughs believed, his superiority): Tarzan means white skin.

In this way Burroughs sought to test the nature of white Anglo-Saxon masculinity. A literary fantasy rather than a scientific inquiry, *Tarzan* nonetheless resonated with the social and natural sciences of the day, which were, of course, much more deeply implicated in Western cultural fantasies than their practitioners realized. What was the nature of the human species, and how was it related to other higher primates? And within the human species, was modern Anglo-Saxon man's putative superiority intrinsic (biological) or extrinsic (the product of collective social and cultural achievements)? Taken out of their environments, how would modern man fare in the wild and "primitive" man fare in modern civilization? Was primitive man, as exemplified by Ishi, passing with the rise of modern civilization? Or was the racial stock that had created modern man in the first place passing? This last view was exemplified by Theodore Roosevelt's dire warnings of "race suicide" and Madison Grant's still more extremist *The Passing of the Great Race* (1916).[64] Each view—and at times a combination of both—was widely embraced by European and American scientists at the time. Relations between humans and their fellow primates and between modern and "primitive" man were especially topical when Burroughs was writing.

In many respects, interest in higher primates picked up where interest in feral children left off. (Indeed, both etymologically and biologically, the line between the two frequently blurred.[65]) Especially after the publication of Charles Darwin's *On the Origin of Species* (1859) and *The Descent of Man* (1871), determining human nature became intimately connected with humanity's relation to fellow primates and their ongoing struggle for existence. What was distinctively human, it appeared, could be illuminated by determining what was common to members of the primate order. How human beings learned could be clarified by discovering how other primates learned in the wild—and, perhaps, in the laboratory. Comparisons were hampered, however, by the difficulty Western scientists experienced in studying chimpanzees and especially gorillas, which were hard to locate, capture, tame, and maintain in captivity.

A pioneering effort in this regard was made by Richard L. Garner, an early researcher of animal speech who claimed to have observed more chimpanzees and gorillas in their natural state than any other white man. In his desire to forge intellectual and emotional links with these primates—and in his persistent adherence to racial categories—he provides to some degree a flesh-and-blood anticipation of Tarzan. Garner, who was born in Virginia in 1848, declared, "From childhood, I have believed that all kinds of animals have some mode of speech by which they can talk among their own kind, and I have often wondered why man has never tried to learn it."[66] Largely on his own, in 1884 he started to study the speech of monkeys and the comparatively few apes (including orangutans, gibbons, gorillas, and chimpanzees) available in American zoological gardens and circuses. He conceived of this task "as very much the same as learning [the speech] of some strange race of mankind—more difficult in the degree of its inferiority, but less in volume."[67] In this effort he made the first phonograph recordings of monkeys and played them to other monkeys to observe their reactions. Reasoning that the primates with the greatest physical development would display the greatest linguistic development as well, he set sail in 1892 for what was then French Gabon and French Congo in Equatorial Africa to study chimpanzees and gorillas "in a state of freedom."[68]

To discover firsthand how chimpanzees and gorillas behaved in the wild, outside human cages, Garner placed himself in a cage. He built a small cubicle, six feet six inches on each side, out of steel mesh, painted it a dingy green, covered it with bamboo leaves, and dubbed it "Fort Gorilla."[69] For 112 days in 1893, he made observations from this outpost. He did not prove so inconspicuous as he had hoped, however, and ultimately he had to rely on secondhand reports to augment his researches.

In his account of this expedition, *Gorillas and Chimpanzees* (1896), Garner stressed the kinship between apes and humans as well as their essential differences. He granted that if one measured an ape's intelligence along a human scale, its "mental horizon" would resemble a one-year-old child's. "But," he continued, with a twist that Burroughs would have appreciated, "if the operation were reversed, and man were placed under the natural conditions of the ape, the comparison would be much less in his favour. There is no common mental unit between them." Garner cast a skeptical eye on a number of previous reports about the gorilla, especially his belligerent assaults on human beings: "He is shy and timid, and shrinks alike from man and other large animals. I have no doubt that when he is in a rage he is both fierce and powerful, but his ferocity and strength are rated above their true value."[70] Nonetheless, with his interest in speech, Garner concentrated on chimpanzees, finding them more sociable, easier to teach, and more manageable. They also had a considerably larger vocabulary than gorillas, he believed, though still "not more than twenty words." (He could discern only two among gorillas.) He claimed to learn about ten of these words well enough to speak to chimpanzees in their native tongue. He went one step further. Although he emphasized that the true test of an animal's intelligence is its ability not to learn a human trick but to solve a new problem using its powers of reasoning, he could not resist teaching a chimpanzee to talk.

His pupil in this experiment had been found orphaned in a swamp, and so Garner named him Moses. In a way that recalls Itard's relation to Victor and Kala's to Tarzan, Garner became Moses's tutor and foster father. "I designed to bring Moses up in the way that good chimpanzees ought to be brought up," he wrote, "so I began to teach him good manners in the hope that some day he would be a shining light to his race, and aid me in my work among them." One senses Garner's dry humor here, as well as a hint of the "white man's burden." But if a paternalistic twinkle shines through his description of Moses's tutelage, so does a serious desire to determine to what degree the chimpanzee might be instructed in the refinements of civilization, down to the niceties of table manners. Garner gave Moses "a tin plate and a wooden spoon, but he did not like to use the latter, and seemed to think that it was pure affectation for any one to eat with such an awkward thing," though Garner kept trying to break Moses of the habit of "putting his fingers in the dish to help himself." Ultimately, Garner claimed that Moses "was the first of his race that ever spoke a word of human speech," though in fact the most the animal ever accomplished was to repeat uncomprehendingly two or three chimpanzee sounds that vaguely approximated words known to Garner (none of them English). Garner quickly developed a great affection for Moses and treasured signs of the animal's devotion to him. If he did not fully succeed in creating an intellectual bond, he certainly established an emotional one.[71]

After Moses's death Garner acquired two other chimpanzees, Aaron, whom he prized and loved, and Elisheba, whom he disliked but tolerated. In his homeward voyage he took both to Liverpool, England, where their response to civilized Western dress surprised him. As he opened their cage in the waiting room at the pier and "they beheld the throng of huge figures with white faces, long skirts and big coats, they were almost frantic with fear. They had never before seen anything like it, and they crouched back in the corner of the cage, clinging to each other and screaming in terror." "In their own country," Garner explained, "they had never seen any thing like this, for the natives to whom they were accustomed wear no clothing as a rule, except a small piece of cloth tied round the waist, and the few white men they had seen were mostly dressed in white; but here was a great crowd in skirts and overcoats, and I have no doubt that to them it was a startling sight for the first time."[72]

Though in moments such as this Garner was able to see the clothes and bodies of Westerners through new eyes, he was never tempted to "go native" himself. Indeed, in the photographs illustrating his account, his appearance is iconic of the commanding, masculine Western explorer. The image captioned "Starting for a Stroll," for example, shows him standing in front of his cage with a native boy whose name, unlike those of many of the chimpanzees and some of the gorillas, is never given. The boy is covered from waist to just below the knees by a piece of cloth tied in front. He wears a pendant on his neck and chest. He carries a spear, held in his lowered left hand and his raised right. Garner towers over him. The white man protects himself with a pith helmet, a jacket tightly buttoned at wrist and neck, and trousers tucked into high boots. He holds what appears to be a double-barreled rifle in a fashion roughly symmetrical to the boy's spear. Together, the two embody the types of "primitive" and "civilized" man in paternalistic colonial relationship, and except for the backdrop, they might as well be the British-American explorer Henry Stanley and his native servant in a similar illustration from the period.

Just as Garner left his native servant unnamed, though the two spent a great deal of time together in and out of the cage, he said little about the native peoples of the areas in which he worked. Nonetheless, his attitudes toward them appear highly conventional (much more so than his scientific researches). Although he sought to qualify a patronizingly hierarchical view of apes, he clearly retained one of *Homo sapiens*, with white men on top. Indeed, this conviction of white superiority over blacks served as a template as he considered differences among the apes he encountered. Speaking of two distinct types of chimpanzees (the *kulu* and the *ntyigo*) that others had considered separate species, for example, he invoked the analogies of race and caste: "I believe them to be two well-defined varieties of the same species; they are the white man and the negro of a common stock. They are the patrician and plebeian of one race, or the nobility and yeomanry of one tribe. . . . The *kulu-kamba* is simply a high order of chimpanzee."[73] Garner's research, like Burroughs's *Tarzan of the Apes*, suggests that when white Westerners around the turn of the century thought about their relation to apes, they could not avoid thinking about their relation to their fellowmen or resist reasserting supposedly natural hierarchies in which they stood at the summit. Though Garner was tempted to hang portraits of chimpanzees in his gallery of family relations, metaphorically speaking, he expressed no similar inclination with regard to black Africans.

A comparable attitude may be seen in Burroughs's *Tarzan of the Apes*. The story appeals powerfully to the fantasy of a reunion with the natural world and hence with one's authentic self. Growing up amid apes in the African jungle, Tarzan achieves a healing of the "bitter bifurcation" of modern Western culture: between civilization and

Richard Garner and an
unidentified African boy
"Starting for a Stroll."
From *Gorillas and
Chimpanzees*. The University
of North Carolina at Chapel Hill

Henry Stanley and an African
boy. From Stanley's *How I Found
Livingston* (New York: Scribner's,
1899). The University of North Carolina
at Chapel Hill

nature, man and animal, mind and body, thought and feeling, idea and act. He exults in the immediate, palpable challenges of the wild, in which "life was never monotonous or stale." Such an existence prepares him to be an exemplary savage and, ultimately, to become a superb bearer of white Anglo-Saxon civilization. As Burroughs conceived his character, both these capacities were innate, and the jungle environment made them especially robust. Discovering the cabin erected by his father and examining its books as a boy of ten, Tarzan gradually teaches himself to read and to write. In so doing, he recapitulates what Burroughs took to be the process of civilization. The narrator makes sure no reader misses the point:

> Squatting upon his haunches on the table top in the cabin his father had built—his smooth, brown, naked little body bent over the book which he rested in his strong slender hands, and his great shock of long, black hair falling about his well shaped head and bright, intelligent eyes—Tarzan of the apes, little primitive man, presented a picture filled, at once, with pathos and with promise—an allegorical figure of the primordial groping through the black night of ignorance toward the light of learning.[74]

More immediately, Tarzan's innate capacities allow him to rise above the physically more powerful apes and other animals and to become lord of the jungle. Descended from "the best of a race of mighty fighters," he delights in battle and the pleasure of the kill. Being from "a race of meat-eaters," he "craves flesh," another sign of his vigorous masculinity and racial superiority. Burroughs's stress on this appetite accords with the view of the physician Woods Hutchinson, who contended that "vegetarianism is the diet of the enslaved, stagnant, and conquered races, and a diet rich in meat is that of the progressive, the dominant, and the conquering strains." Tarzan enthusiastically devours raw gorilla and lion meat; and when he first sees a black native cook a boar, he cannot imagine "ruin[ing] good meat in any such foolish manner." Tarzan proves a mighty hunter through his innate intelligence and facility with rope and knife and, later, bow and arrow. His easy mastery of the noose to trap his enemies recalls Burroughs's own experience in the West as well as those described in novels such as *The Virginian* and *The Clansman*. With such weapons, Tarzan triumphs over rivals within the colony and the colony's most feared enemies: other apes, a lion, and his fellowmen.[75]

TARZAN AND THE REDISCOVERY OF
WHITE MALE IDENTITY

The degree to which they *are* his fellowmen and the obligations of such fellowship become the great driving questions of the novel. Like Dumas's *The Man in the Iron Mask* and similar melodramas of a captive denied the knowledge of his noble birth, this is essentially a story of Tarzan's unfolding realization of his identity as a white Anglo-Saxon and, more specifically, as the rightful Lord Greystoke. The reader is in on the secret from the beginning, of course, but as Burroughs develops his plot, Tarzan must discover the nature of his "own kind" and the truth of his noble ancestry. He answers the first of these questions largely intuitively, though his uncertainty whether he is truly a man or the son of Kala and perhaps "a strange white ape" adds a titillation not completely dispelled until the book's final pages.[76]

Growing up in a Darwinian Eden, glorying in the struggle for existence, Tarzan nibbles on the apple that will provide the knowledge of his humanity in his father's cabin. First from an illustrated primer, then from other books, he sees pictures of white boys and men and gradually realizes why he is different from the apes around him. Like Adam, with this knowledge he becomes aware of his nakedness; yet he feels no shame. He proudly displays his "sleek skin" and covets clothing only as an ungainly emblem of human superiority over other animals.[77]

From Tarzan's first sight of another live human being, however, his sense of commonality is checked by visceral racial antipathy. A remnant of a once powerful tribe moves into the area, fleeing the brutal oppression wrought by King Leopold II of Belgium. Burroughs's initial description of the black warriors anticipates Tarzan's response:

On their backs were oval shields, in their noses huge rings, while from the kinky wool of their heads protruded tufts of gay feathers.

Across their foreheads were tattooed three parallel lines of color, and on each breast three concentric circles. Their yellow teeth were filed to sharp points, and their great protruding lips added still further to the low and bestial brutishness of their appearance.

Almost immediately, Kulonga, their chief's son, slays Tarzan's foster mother, Kala. Without knowing the nature of Kala's killer, Tarzan determines to avenge her death. Kulonga is the first human he has encountered since infancy; still, when Tarzan sees him, he immediately identifies him from his father's books as "the *negro*," "so like him in form and yet so different in face and color." He tracks the black warrior to the edge of his village, then throws a "quick noose" over his head and, acting as a one-man vigilante party, lynches him:

Hand over hand Tarzan drew the struggling black until he had him hanging by his neck in midair; then Tarzan climbed to a larger branch drawing the still threshing victim well up into the sheltering verdure of the tree.

Here he fastened the rope securely to a stout branch, and then descending, plunged his hunting knife into Kulonga's heart. Kala was avenged.[78]

Whatever Burroughs's intentions were in this graphic description (reiterated when Tarzan kills other natives), it recalls in especially disturbing ways the racial lynchings that raged across the South from the 1880s through the 1920s.

Tarzan strips the dead body of possessions. Then, following apes' custom in dealing with slain enemies from outside their tribe, he prepares to eat the corpse. At this crucial moment, however, a minimal sense of shared humanity, fortified by ancestral instinct, overcomes both the chasm of race and the training of apes. For Burroughs, this instinct is by no means universal; rather, it flows from Tarzan's Anglo-Saxon blood. Kulonga's people have no such inhibitions, readers soon learn: to torture and devour their enemies are their greatest delights. Spying on their cannibal revels from a perch high in a tree, Tarzan "saw that these people were more wicked than his own apes" and "began to hold his own kind in but low esteem." Except for his admiration of their body ornaments, Tarzan's view of black Africans seems little different from the views of most whites of his day: he is repulsed by their cruelty, contemptuous of their superstitions, and happy to terrorize them for his amusement and to steal from them whatever he wants. In *The Descent of Man* (a book in Burroughs's library), Darwin consoled his readers with the thought that mankind's fellow primates were in many respects ancestors as noble as present-day savages: "For my own part, I would as soon be descended from that heroic little monkey, who braved his dreaded enemy in order to save the life of his keeper, . . . as from a savage who delights to torture his enemies, offers up bloody sacrifices, practices infanticide without remorse, treats his wives like slaves, knows no decency, and is haunted by the grossest superstitions." These natives may be of a common species, but they are not truly Tarzan's kind at all.[79]

Still, Tarzan is a climber both of trees and of the evolutionary and social ladder. Shortly after he kills Kulonga and sends a wave of fright into the native village, he stabs the great ape-king Kerchak in a fierce fight and assumes command of the colony. Although he rules wisely, ape administration proves dull work. Even the excitement of defeating a challenger such as his stepbrother Terkoz cannot curb his restlessness. He abdicates his throne to search for "other white men like himself."[80]

Coincidentally, another mutiny is brewing nearby, remarkably similar to the one that cast Tarzan's parents onshore twenty years earlier. In their swarthy, bestial appearance, the mutineers are virtual copies of the earlier crew, except that this time the giant stand-in for Black Michael is immediately shot by a rat-faced little villain named Snipes. To Tarzan these men seem "no different from the black men" in their lack of civilization, and he feels no kinship toward them.[81]

The five hapless passengers, however, form a different category. Tarzan finds ample reason to consider them stupid and ridiculous, although to a great extent these are faults of overcivilization. The most absurd of the lot is Archimedes Q. Porter, an elderly, pedantic professor who wears a frock coat and silk hat even in the African jungle and constantly loses both his train of thought and his way. His assistant, the fussy Samuel T. Philander, is scarcely more practical. The professor's daughter, however, provides the novel's love interest and Tarzan's reason for caring about them. She is Jane Porter, a beautiful,

The cover of the October 1912 issue of *The All-Story*, featuring *Tarzan of the Apes: A Romance of the Jungle*. Illustration by Clinton Pettee. Edgar Rice Burroughs Memorial Collection, University of Louisville

golden-haired, snowy-white Southern belle almost exactly Tarzan's age. Her immense black mammy, a minstrel caricature named Esmeralda who spouts malaprop nonsense and faints in every crisis, accompanies her. Fifth, and last, wearing white ducks as if plucked from a lawn-tennis match, is Jane's English suitor, the tall, handsome, and proper William Cecil Clayton, who just happens to be the son of the current Lord Greystoke and so is Tarzan's first cousin.

At last, then, Tarzan discovers his own kind, the race, class, and even kin from which he springs, though he does not learn the secret of his birth until virtually the last page. Even so, differences divide them: not only differences of language (Tarzan can read and write in English but knows only animal speech) but, more important, immense differences between Tarzan's brute training and modern Anglo-American civilization. That this contrast works overwhelmingly to Tarzan's advantage constitutes the great twist and appeal of Burroughs's story. Faced with the basic challenges of survival in the wild, the passengers' education proves worthless. The jungle that is an open book to Tarzan is to them an unknown and frightening hieroglyph. Most especially, due to the fateful combination of his innate attributes and his savage upbringing, Tarzan possesses virile virtues to a peerless degree. None can match him in physical prowess, sensory keenness, quick thinking, courage, or selflessness. The difference between Tarzan and his cousin measures the exact degree to which he has been shaped by the jungle. The two have virtually the same heredity but completely different training. Whereas Clayton has become pampered and privileged, Tarzan is the ultimate self-taught, self-made man. In ordinary company Clayton would stand out, but next to this paragon of primal masculinity he is utterly eclipsed.

Indeed, for the rest of the book, Tarzan's chief occupation is to rescue these characters from one near disaster after another. Their assignment, in turn, is to admire his beautiful and powerful body while he does so. Burroughs has already held that body up for his readers' admiration many times, insisting that here at last is truly the perfect man, a Sandovian combination of Hercules and Adonis: "His straight and perfect figure, muscled as the best of the ancient Roman gladiators must have been muscled, and yet with the soft and sinuous curves of a Greek god, told at a glance the wondrous combination of enormous strength with suppleness and speed." In lieu of wearing a fig leaf, Tarzan has donned a doeskin breechcloth (stripped from another black native he has killed) and meets members of the Porter party with minimally decent attire. He drops in on Cecil Clayton first, to save him from an attacking lion. A "naked giant," "the embodiment of physical perfection," he leaps from a tree directly onto the lion's back. Through Clayton's eyes, Burroughs's description continues: "With lightning speed an arm that was banded layers of iron muscle encircled the huge neck, and the great beast was raised from behind, roaring and pawing the air—raised as easily as Clayton would have lifted a pet dog." Not surprisingly, the *All-Story* illustrator Clinton Pettee chose this scene for the cover of the *Tarzan* issue.[82]

At this point Burroughs starts releasing lions as rapidly as a dispatcher does taxis in a thunderstorm. Back at Tarzan's cabin, another lion (originally a tiger in the *All-Story* version) is crawling through the window to devour Jane Porter and the hysterical Esmeralda. With Clayton in tow, Tarzan races back, pulls the beast out the window by the tail, and gets it in a full nelson. Clayton stands ineffectually to the side, as if taking notes: "At last Clayton saw the immense muscles of Tarzan's shoulders and biceps leap into corded knots beneath the silver moonlight. There was a long sustained and supreme effort on the ape-man's part—and the vertebrae of Sabor's neck parted with a sharp snap." Such a feat calls for a little celebration, and, as is his custom, Tarzan sounds "the bull ape's savage roar of victory," the African analogue to Buck's call of the wild. Then, leaving everyone within earshot quivering with fright from his yell, he is off to rescue Professor Porter and his assistant from yet another lion.[83]

The first time Jane sees Tarzan for herself, however, he is saving her from a more titillating and fearful menace. Tarzan's old rival Terkoz has been driven out of the ape colony, only to discover Jane and Esmeralda in the jungle. The "horrible man-like beast" carries Jane off, intending her for the first of his new harem, "a fate a thousand times worse than death." Here, within the conventions of melodrama, Burroughs transformed fears of the predatory black rapist and the specter of miscegenation into fears of hybridity between human beings and apes. Although nineteenth-century European naturalists stressed the "law" of nature by which animals refused to mate with those not of their kind, a fascination with exceptions persisted. In 1865 the British Anthropological Society republished a summary of travelers' reports that described "lascivious male apes attack[ing] women," who "perish miserably in the brutal embraces of their ravishers."[84] Other popular accounts, such as Paul Du Chaillu's *Explorations and Adventures in Equatorial Africa* (1861), reported similar legends, if only to debunk them.[85] (As with miscegenation, there was a double standard at work in these fears; the thought that Tarzan's mother might be an ape was apparently far less dreadful than the idea of his having been fathered by an ape and a white woman.) In Burroughs's story, of course, Tarzan intercepts the abductor in the nick of time, and the two square off for a duel to the death. Burroughs charges the violent scene with eroticism. Jane breathlessly watches the struggle, "her lithe, young form flattened against the trunk of a great tree, her hands tight pressed against her rising and falling bosom, and her eyes wide with mingled horror, fascination, fear, and admiration." The sight of Tarzan's body, locked in mortal combat with the monstrous ape, proves irresistible:

> As the great muscles of the man's back and shoulders knotted beneath the tension of his efforts, and the huge biceps and forearm held at bay those mighty tusks, the veil of centuries of civilization and culture was swept from the blurred vision of the Baltimore girl.
>
> When the long knife drank deep a dozen times of Terkoz' heart's blood, and the great carcass rolled lifeless upon the ground, it was a primeval woman who sprang forward with outstretched arms toward the primeval man who had fought for her and won her.[86]

Where will this romance between wild man and professor's daughter end? That is the question for the rest of the novel. In reality, wild boys and men rarely if ever brimmed with sexual passion and allure. Both Wild Peter's and Victor's examiners noted their indifference to women; and Ishi, who had very little sexual experience, "blushed furiously" whenever the subject of sex cropped up. Yet Tarzan, Burroughs assured his readers, is a "red-blooded man"; so, with Jane, he experiences a conflict between his savage training and his innate nobility comparable to his deliberation over whether to dine on Kulonga: "The order of the jungle [was] for the male to take his mate by force; but could Tarzan be guided by the laws of the beasts?" Only after wringing every delicious drop of suspense from the situation does Burroughs conclude, No. With inborn courtliness, Tarzan protects Jane and returns her to her father and friends unharmed.[87]

Jane's response is more conflicted and confused. After she first throws herself into his arms, her "outraged conscience" compels her to repulse him. When, nonetheless, Tarzan carries her off into the forest, she feels blissfully secure in the arms of her "forest god." She has fallen deeply in love. Cecil Clayton feels the shift in her affections and jealously taunts her that Tarzan is "some half-demented castaway," "beast of the jungle," or savage cannibal. These are in fact her own fears as well. When she tries to imagine Tarzan with her in civilized society—eating like an animal on an ocean liner, acting like an uncouth illiterate in front of her friends—she shudders with disgust. Can a girl from a genteel Baltimore family truly find happiness with "this jungle waif"? Still, he appeals to "the primeval woman in her nature," and she longs to be possessed by him; if need be, she will plunge into the jungle with him forever.[88]

It is not necessary to follow all the twists and turns of Burroughs's plot to the story's end. Suffice it to say that Tarzan determines to win Jane any way he can, even if it means becoming civilized. Thus he accomplishes one more astonishing metamorphosis: from savage noble to suave socialite. As yet he cannot speak English, though he can read and write it fluently. In a matter of weeks, a French navy lieutenant, Paul D'Arnot (whose life he also saves), coaches him (as Itard did Victor and Garner did Moses) with dazzling success. Tarzan quickly acquires the French language and manners (though, like Garner's Moses, he longs at times to throw his cutlery aside and to attack his food with hands and teeth). D'Arnot also teaches him not to kill every black man he meets as the two make their way to an African port. Now "Monsieur Tarzan," he dons shirt and trousers, although he is happy to shed them on a bet and, naked, to slay a lion. Swinging through the trees once more, he strongly feels the call of the wild and, even more intensely, the constrictions of civilization: "This was life! Ah! how he loved it! . . . At last he was free. He had not realized what a prisoner he had been."[89] What holds him for the moment to civilization is the hope of marrying Jane. Finally, in a dizzying rush of events, he digs up the buried treasure that Professor Porter has sought, follows Jane to America, and rescues her from a Wisconsin forest fire, swinging through the trees as of old.

But problems remain. To satisfy her father's financial obligation, Jane has reluctantly agreed to marry a scheming businessman twice her age. Still, Tarzan, who has fought Terkoz for Jane, is not about to lose her to this polished villain. "I am still a wild beast at heart," he reminds her. Gripping his rival by the throat, he persuades him to release Jane from her promise. Yet no sooner is his back turned than Jane pledges herself to his cousin Cecil Clayton, the safe, "civilized" choice. What's a jungle lord to do? The noble thing, of course. He forbears showing Clayton the proof he has just obtained that he is indeed the rightful Lord Greystoke. When Clayton naively asks him how he came to be in the African jungle in the first place, Tarzan replies, "I was born there. . . . My mother was an Ape, and of course she couldn't tell me much about it. I never knew who my father was." And it's back to the jungle once more.[90]

The selfless renunciation at the story's end provided the final hook for many readers. Knowing that they would "read for the ending," Burroughs deliberately withheld the anticipated romantic union of Tarzan and Jane. Letters poured into *The All-Story* demanding a sequel. Yet, as an American soldier in Panama wrote to the editor on behalf of "hundreds" in his unit, some regretted that Tarzan "lost the girl—while others wonder if he can get used to living in 'civilization.' "[91]

They were right to wonder. Burroughs intended *Tarzan of the Apes* as a romantic adventure story, not as a formal meditation on civilization and its discontents. Nevertheless, his tale gave powerful narrative force to a widespread sense that modern technological civilization created restrictions, frustrations, ordinariness that entailed special losses for men. Like Wister and London, Theodore Roosevelt and Frederick Jackson Turner in his own time, and like earlier American writers such as James Fenimore Cooper, Ralph Waldo Emerson, Henry David Thoreau, and Herman Melville, Burroughs celebrated untamed masculine individualism. More particularly, he created in Tarzan a figure who embodied the enduring impulse, in Emerson's words, to "enjoy an original relation to the universe," to raw nature, with all its primal, anarchic force. The desire for unmediated contact with nature and occasions to test oneself against it constitutes an overriding element of American masculine identity. It is hardly surprising that in the early twentieth century, when an increasingly impersonal, bureaucratic, and corporate society dominated the everyday life of individual citizens, that desire flared with new brightness and heat.[92]

What is more problematic in Burroughs's story and in the works of many of his contemporaries is that this assertion of masculine wildness is often explicitly tied to whiteness. Earlier writers were hardly free from bigotry, but to a notable extent writers such as Emerson and Thoreau at least tried to put their affirmations of individual wildness in the service of democratic inclusiveness and against systems of oppression, of which slavery was the most glaring and hateful.[93] In Burroughs's *Tarzan* as in Wister's *The Virginian*, however, all men are not created equal. True, Tarzan does not depend on outward hereditary privilege; indeed, the book ends with his refusing to claim his title and estate. As a self-made man, he could appeal to many readers. Yet Burroughs, in line with the predominant thought of influential whites of his time, believed that Tarzan carries his most valuable hereditary privilege, his innate superiority, in his very blood. He could be strengthened rather than degraded by the wild precisely because he holds the best of Western civilization within him. Others less favored by heredity, such as the African natives and atavistic crew members, in Burroughs's eyes do not.

If for Burroughs and his readers wildness enhanced white Anglo-Saxons but debased black Africans, it also enhanced masculinity—but not, in the same way, femininity. Tarzan's murmured statement to Jane in the story's concluding pages, "I am still a wild beast at heart," is as much a reassurance as a warning. His wildness is the basis of his virility, power, and authority, and for him to become truly civilized, to lock himself within the "iron cage" of modern capitalist society, would be tantamount to emasculation. With Jane it is another story. Burroughs allows her to submit to her awakened primal passions only in fleeting and fantastic moments. Perhaps he sensed that to make her as wild as Tarzan would be to replace her teasing oscillation between submission and resistance with an independent sexuality less acceptable to his readers and, perhaps, to himself. The metamorphosis that accompanied moving between civilization and the wild remained, above all, a masculine performance. Just as Houdini's substitute trunk trick ended with him free and Bess locked inside, the drama of Tarzan's escape art shines most brilliantly if Jane remains locked within the conventions of civilization and is released only on his initiative. It is lucky for him, then, that she plays it safe and chooses Clayton. To continue as Burroughs's "perfect man" at the top of the natural hierarchy, Tarzan must be free and unencumbered, alone and in the wild.

The gender issues of wildness may be further illuminated by considering *Tarzan* in relation to a novel published three years later, Charlotte Perkins Gilman's *Herland*. Even though we have no evidence that Gilman, the most prominent feminist theorist of this period, ever read *Tarzan*, we may regard her novel as a kind of rejoinder to it. Though a socialist as well as a feminist, Gilman had much in common with Burroughs in her views on race. Indeed, she pursued far more seriously than he did the subjects of primitivism, evolution, eugenics, and the superiority of white Anglo-Saxon civilization. She differed markedly, however, in one respect: she was convinced that the sharp division between the sexes and women's dependence on men—far from being hallmarks of advanced civilization—were perversions that led to social and racial decadence.[94] Undoubtedly, she would have distrusted Burroughs's hypermasculine ideal of Tarzan, believing as she did that primitive man behaved more like the rapist Terkoz than like the chivalrous "forest god." Certainly, too, she would have seized on the character of Jane Porter as a damning example of an overly delicate woman, economically, socially, and psychologically dependent on men. Gilman presented her startling ideas in *Women and Economics* (1898), *The Man-Made World* (1911), and many other writings. Then in *Herland*, a story serialized in Gilman's self-authored monthly *The Forerunner* in 1915, she set forth her own fictional geography of feminism, a utopian view that stands as a retort to the works of Wister, London, and Burroughs.

Gilman's story begins as another tale about white males exploring an exotic and uncharted territory. Three young American bachelors on a scientific expedition learn from neighboring "savages" of an isolated mountain country where "no men lived—only women and girl children."[95] Equipped with a private yacht, motorboat, and biplane, they set out to discover Herland for themselves. Although close friends and former classmates, the three differ in both their training and their attitudes toward women. Jeff Margrave, a physician, is a dewy-eyed idealist who longs to place women on a pedestal and worship at their feet. Terry Nicholson, a rich explorer who finances the excursion, prefers to seduce and dominate women. In a country of women, he jokes, he will be crowned king in no time. The narrator of the story, Vandyck Jennings, tries to steer a middle course. A sociologist, he sees himself as an open-minded investigator, although he enters Herland doubting the very possibility of women's independence.

What the three discover confounds their expectations—and challenges the very notion of savage virility on which *Tarzan* was based. Far from a primitive wilderness, the entire land appears to them "an enormous garden," perfectly cultivated, immaculately ordered, utterly devoid of wild beasts—or wildness of any kind. The population is equally well tended. Two thousand years earlier, after the country was sealed off by a volcanic eruption, its men died out, but through a miraculous mutation, women developed the capacity for virgin birth, producing only girls. Gradually they created a eugenic utopia, limiting the population and choosing mothers of the finest Aryan stock so as to avoid the "degenerate" and "unfit" and to breed out "the lowest types." The result is a "clean-bred, vigorous lot," a race as remarkable for its intelligence as for its health, strength, and beauty. There has not been a criminal for six hundred years. With only one sex, there is no sense of what is "manly" and what "womanly," a situation that unnerves the male visitors. With no predatory beasts to slay, no savages to kill, no villains to foil, no helpless women to rescue or even assist, no struggle of any kind, there is no opportunity to display white masculine prowess. As Terry complains: "I like Something Doing. Here it's all done."[96]

The contrast between *Tarzan* and *Herland* emerges most vividly in the stories' attempted rapes. The dark, hairy ape Terkoz provides an occasion for Tarzan to display the courage, strength, chivalry, and sexual self-restraint that supposedly distinguished the finest Anglo-Saxons from the darker races and beasts. In Gilman's story, the situation is quite different. The arrival of the three men gives Herland the opportunity to reestablish its ancient bisexual order and to rejoin with other lands. By permitting the three men to marry local women and to conceive children, the nation also hopes to enlarge its ethic of Motherhood to include a new Fatherhood and Brotherhood as well. The men eagerly assent, but, once wed, they discover that Herland's idea of marriage is very different from theirs. Their wives still live apart, and they limit sexual relations to the minimum for procreation. Van and Jeff gradually adjust to the new order, but Terry cannot. He believes that a woman wishes to be mastered, and, like a hunter, he approaches her as "some quarry he was pursuing, something to catch and conquer." However, his wife, Alima, even if she has an "atavistic" element of femininity, is no swooning, delicate "girl" but "a big, handsome creature, rather exceptionally strong even in that race of strong women." In a desperate effort to reassert his mastery and what he regards as his conjugal rights, Terry tries to rape her. Alima fights back, kicking him in the groin. Two or three women aid her in repulsing his attack. They easily force him to the floor, tie him "hand and foot, and then, in sheer pity for his futile rage, . . . anesthetize him."[97] Here is a metamorphosis indeed, in which man is tied up and rendered unconscious like a captured animal (or as in a Houdini nightmare) and women are free and in power. Alima initially wants Terry killed—Terkoz's fate—but the court banishes him instead. Though Herland apparently continues with its "Great Change" to heterosexuality, some readers may have wondered why.

THE *TARZAN* MACHINE

Herland reached only loyal readers of Gilman's slender magazine in 1915. By that time, through Burroughs's unflagging efforts, Tarzan had already found millions of fans. His success developed from the bottom up, beginning with magazine and newspaper readers and rising like an irresistible tide to the book-buying public. After the tale appeared in its entirety in the October 1912 issue of *The All-Story*, which had a circulation of perhaps 200,000, Burroughs approached several publishers, including A. C. McClurg, Bobbs-Merrill, Reilly & Britton, and Dodd, Mead, seeking a book contract. All turned him down flat. However, the Munsey Company, publishers of *The All-Story*, arranged with the New York *Evening World* for *Tarzan* to be serialized in that and other newspapers across the country. *Tarzan* thus reached an enormous readership, including members of the working

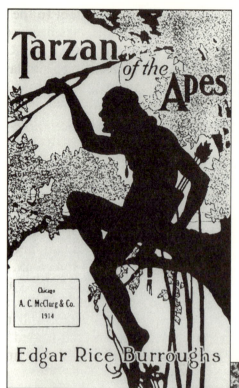

The title page of the first edition of *Tarzan of the Apes* (1914), adapted from a drawing by Fred J. Arting. Edgar Rice Burroughs Memorial Collection, University of Louisville

Elmo Lincoln, the first film Tarzan. Edgar Rice Burroughs Memorial Collection, University of Louisville

class, immigrants, and ethnic minorities. Its hero became a cultural icon before the story ever appeared in book form and for readers who would never enter a bookshop.

Though Burroughs was of mixed minds about attempting a sequel, at the urging of *The All-Story*'s editor Thomas Metcalf, he completed *The Return of Tarzan* in January 1913. Here the formerly laconic jungle lord, having tasted civilization, moralizes freely about its effeminacy and corruption as he foils dastardly villains on several continents, escapes from a tomb in a manner reminiscent of Houdini, and, once again, rescues a marooned Jane Porter on the African coast. Giving readers the satisfaction he had withheld in the first Tarzan novel, Burroughs contrived to marry Tarzan and Jane in the tale's closing lines. But inevitable as were Tarzan's triumphs within his fictional realm, he still encountered formidable challenges within the harsh world of publishing. The enthusiastic Metcalf, who had trumpeted the original Tarzan story to readers ("Zowie! but things happen!") and elaborately whetted their appetites for a sequel, rejected Burroughs's tale outright. It suffered from "lack of balance," he explained cryptically, a charge particularly unsettling for Burroughs, who worried how far to let his imagination carry him. "A well balanced mind would not turn out my kind of stuff," he replied defensively. But a rival pulp magazine, *New Story*, snapped up Burroughs's sequel with the rapacity of a crocodile and paid him one thousand dollars, far more than he had expected from *The All-Story*.[98]

With this crowning success, Burroughs finally quit his job at *System* to work in the "fiction factory" full-time and to become a veritable Tarzan machine. Early the next year he dashed off *The Beasts of Tarzan* in just over a month and sold it to *The All-Story* for twenty-five hundred dollars, the most the magazine had ever paid for a story. Then at last he found a book publisher for the original *Tarzan of the Apes*, McClurg and Company, which repented its earlier decision. The novel appeared in June 1914, illustrated by Fred J. Arting, who depicted Tarzan in silhouette with a Plains Indian profile and a posture both languid and alert. Tarzan still had to struggle for readers. The print run of the first edition was ten thousand copies. Although the novel never topped the sales charts in any one year, it achieved remarkable success over time both in the United States and abroad with sales that swelled into the millions before Burroughs's death.[99]

A succession of film versions powered the Tarzan machine, beginning with the release of the first *Tarzan of the Apes* in January 1918. With a coordinated publicity campaign of film distribution, newspaper serialization, and book sales, the movie proved one of the most profitable in the history of the nascent industry, and sales of Burroughs's Tarzan books soared. The film's star, barrel-chested Elmo Lincoln, attempted to embody the Arting illustration with the help of a wig. Reviewers generally applauded his efforts, though Burroughs thought he looked more like a "prize bear."[100]

For a quarter century, from 1914 to 1939, Burroughs turned out a new Tarzan book virtually every year. In failing health, he produced his last in 1947, three years before his death. During his lifetime, he also published eleven Martian adventures, four stories set on Venus, six "Pellucidar" tales taking place within Earth, several Westerns, and numerous other works. "I want to be known as Edgar Rice Burroughs the author, not Edgar Rice Burroughs the author of *Tarzan*," he declared, but he never truly got his wish. Instead, for all his success, he found himself a captive of his fictional creation. Ironically, in committing himself to manufacture a never-ending series of adventures celebrating masculine wildness and freedom, he discovered that he had exchanged one punishing regimen for another, albeit much more profitable, one. As early as December 1919, he was complaining, "I feel now that I can never write another Tarzan story and I . . . do not see how the reading public can stand for any more of them. . . . I have said and re-said a dozen times everything that there is to say about Tarzan—this is why the work is so hard." Similar moans accompanied the writing of later Tarzan adventures. Twenty years after the initial appearance of *Tarzan of the Apes*, at the height of his success, he wrote, "The only thing about the marketing of my stories that ever surprises me is when they sell. I have never written a story yet but that deep down in my heart I was positive that it would be refused."[101] Though he commanded his literary empire with stern authority and claimed a "big" man's income, he never escaped the self-doubt and tedium of the walled-in clerk.

CONCLUSION

It is easiest to say what happened to their bodies.

Sandow died first, in October 1925. After funeral services at a Baptist church in Holland Park, his body was buried in a cemetery at Putney Vale, near London. Yet surprisingly, given his immense fame and prosperity, no stone ever marked his grave. Wrapping herself in a tight silence, his widow appears to have forbidden any memorial.[1]

Houdini made sure he would not suffer a similar fate. That any great magician, let alone himself, might not have a suitable grave site deeply disturbed him, and over the course of his career he spent considerable effort and expense refurbishing the graves of other conjurers, including John Henry Anderson, Bartolomeo Bosco, William Davenport, Robert Heller, and "the Great Lafayette" (Sigmund Neuberger). He lavished still greater care over the arrangements for his own family. As early as 1904 he had exhumed the bodies of his father and half brother to rebury them in a family plot he had purchased at Machpelah Cemetery in Queens, New York. Always fascinated with the macabre, he wrote in his diary, "Saw what was left of poor father and Hermann. Nothing but skull and bones. Hermann's teeth were in splendid condition."[2] After the death in 1913 of his mother, with whom his identity was so intensely bound, he began to plan his own

Houdini's widow, Bess, and his brother Theo at his grave, c. 1928. Library of Congress

grave site in earnest. With an ostentatious display of graven images that is startling in a Jewish cemetery, he erected a massive granite monument, ornamented with figures carved from Italian marble. To cap the structure, he arranged for a commanding bronze bust of himself. Ever the headliner, he had written in large letters above the Weiss name HOUDINI. Among his meticulous instructions for his own burial, he specified that all his mother's letters be interred with him as a pillow for his head.

Tarzan, of course, never died. As for Burroughs, he was the only one of the three to live to "damn[ed] old age."[3] His heart ailed for years and finally gave out on March 19, 1950, when he was seventy-four. After his death, in obedience to his instructions, his body was cremated and his ashes buried next to his mother's remains under a black walnut tree outside the offices of Edgar Rice Burroughs, Inc., in the Los Angeles suburb that bears the name of his most famous creation, Tarzana, California.

The larger cultural legacies of Sandow, Houdini, and Burroughs are much more difficult to specify. Even in their lifetimes, their presentations of the triumphant white male body evolved significantly, and each figure showed notable agility in adapting his message to changing circumstances.

Undoubtedly, the greatest change, to which all three responded, was the coming of the Great War. Sandow, now retired from performing and living in England, faced it first. Even when the war lay several years in the future, he contributed time, prizes, and his immense prestige to training eleven thousand recruits to guard the English home front. Once again, reporters marveled at the bodily metamorphosis he achieved by his training and competitions. *The Times* of London reported, "Each of the 104 prize-winners added no less than 12 inches to their combined neck, chest, and leg measurements, while the winner of the first prize of £500 obtained in all an improvement of 27½ inches, 5¾ inches being added to his chest girth." Throughout the war, Sandow urged the importance of physical training and gloried in his status as "the greatest 'recruiting sergeant' the Army has ever had."[4]

When the United States entered the war in April 1917, Houdini immediately registered for military service, exulting, "HURRAH, now I am one of the boys." Despite his many performances in Germany, he declared, "WE MUST WIN, and that is all there is to it." Although he was too old to serve directly, he contributed both his talents as entertainer and some of his stratagems as escape artist to support the cause.

A year younger than Houdini, Burroughs also found himself too old for active duty. Instead, he joined the Illinois reserve militia and rose to the rank of captain. With his pen, he was still more bellicose. Targeting German Americans in the drive to sell Liberty bonds, for example, he declared, "Each and every one of us pines to go over the top and spear a Hun. . . . Next to sticking a bayonet through a Hun's gizzard, you can inflict the greatest pain upon him by jabbing him in the pocket-book." Workers who thought this a "rich man's war" equally aroused his ire. He contemptuously described one who declined to join the militia because of its history of brutally repressing workers as a "narrow chested, pimple-faced, chinless, anthropoid creature." Indeed, even at the conclusion of the war, he itched to purge subversive elements at home: "We have thrashed the trouble makers of Europe and it is within the range of possibilities that we may have to deal with similar cattle here."[5]

Tarzan fully shared Burroughs's rabid anti-German sentiments. At the outset of *Tarzan the Untamed*, the major Tarzan novel written during the war, a sadistic German officer apparently kills Tarzan's Jane (in response to pleas from his editor and his wife, Burroughs ultimately revived her). This brutal assault sets the spring for a plot in which Tarzan pursues an insatiable appetite for revenge, sadistically reveling in each German death and hungering for the next: "[N]ever could she be entirely avenged. Life was too short and there were too many Germans." A few years later, as Burroughs contemplated losing German royalties with the translation of his wartime Tarzan tales, he wrote to his editor, "How would it be to make the Germans Austrians, or will these volumes circulate also in Austria . . . ?"[6]

The war offered scant opportunity for the kinds of individual heroism, freedom, and prowess that Sandow, Houdini, and Burroughs had celebrated. On the contrary, it represented the powers of modern depersonalization and mechanization at their most ghastly. Overall, approximately 10 million died in the conflict, including more than 112,000 Americans. In the war's aftermath a new generation of writers, preeminently Ernest Hemingway, attempted to put manly courage back together again. To do so, they endeavored to purge its emphasis on romantic patriotism and heroic transcendence in favor of private tests and qualified triumphs.

Nonetheless, key elements in the work of Sandow, Houdini, and Burroughs endure. Sandow offered a compelling if controversial new standard of masculine strength, muscular development, and beauty to face the challenges of modern life, and Houdini had an aura of courage, miraculous powers, and invincibility. To these Burroughs added a narrative of the unclad white male body filled with wildness, engaged in violent combat, and inviting romance. Together, these three figures helped to shape conceptions of manliness and the white male body that proved immensely popular in their own day and have shown remarkable resilience.

History never repeats itself, but it is an avid recycler. With the end of the Vietnam War and the advent of an information-based, global economy in the 1970s, as well as new waves of immigration, the emergence of modern feminism, and other developments, came a new "crisis" of masculinity. Responses to that crisis have taken many forms, but no cultural observer could miss the reemergence of body-building, stage magic, and adventure stories and films. Often with a high degree of self-consciousness, new popular heroes assumed the places of the old: Arnold Schwarzenegger as the great heir to Sandow; David Copperfield and Doug Henning among the many rivals for Houdini's legacy; Miles O'Keeffe and Christopher Lambert as new Tarzan hopefuls. The cultural needs at the turn of the twentieth century remain very much with us as we enter a new millennium.

The value of this legacy remains highly controversial, though. The bodily spectacles offered by Sandow, Houdini, and Burroughs always existed in dialogue with audiences who brought their own imaginative concerns and experiences to the entertainments, so that the meanings of their work are necessarily fluid. They appealed to immense and diverse publics, across class, across nation, across gender. Clearly, they spoke powerfully to individual aspirations for palpable challenge and heroic achievement. They offered compelling dramas of bodily risk as a means of self-realization. Yet their work easily fortified images of white male superiority that were used to dominate women, people of color, and less technologically advanced societies. To some degree, all spoke to the longing for a restitution of manly authority and power that appeared threatened by the coming of a more impersonal modern order. By stressing the centrality of the unclad white male body, each in effect reasserted that gender and racial divisions were fundamentally based on innate and natural differences. At the same time, each appealed to the dream of masculine metamorphosis, the possibilities for bodily transformation and, by implication, for a transformation of self and of social standing. The challenge that remains is to conceive of transformations in which freedom, wholeness, and heroism are available to all.

NOTES

INTRODUCTION

1. Theodore Roosevelt, *An Autobiography* (New York: Charles Scribner's Sons, 1920).
2. Carleton Putnam, *Theodore Roosevelt*, vol. 1, *The Formative Years* (New York: Charles Scribner's Sons, 1958), 198; Edmund Morris, *The Rise of Theodore Roosevelt* (New York: Coward, McCann, and Geoghegan, 1979), 129; David McCullough, *Mornings on Horseback* (New York: Simon and Schuster, 1981), 229.
3. See "Snap-Shots of the Presidential Candidates," *Harper's Weekly*, July 30, 1904, 1174–75.
4. Max Weber, *The Protestant Ethic and the Spirit of Capitalism*, trans. Talcott Parsons (New York: Charles Scribner's Sons, 1958); originally published in essay form in German, 1904–1905.
5. Theodore Roosevelt to Edgar Rice Burroughs, San Antonio, Tex., May 19, 1898, Irwin Porges Papers, Edgar Rice Burroughs Memorial Collection, University of Louisville, Louisville, Ky. (This letter is reproduced in Irwin Porges, *Edgar Rice Burroughs: The Man Who Created Tarzan* [Provo, Utah: Brigham Young University Press, 1975], 70.) David L. Chapman, *Sandow the Magnificent: Eugen Sandow and the Beginnings of Bodybuilding* (Urbana: University of Illinois Press, 1994), 151; Kenneth Silverman, *Houdini!!! The Career of Ehrich Weiss* (New York: HarperCollins, 1996), 189–90.
6. Kristin L. Hoganson, *Fighting for American Manhood: How Gender Politics Provoked the Spanish-American and Philippine-American Wars* (New Haven, Conn.: Yale University Press, 1998).

7. Francis A. Walker, *Discussions in Economics and Statistics*, ed. Davis R. Dewey (1899; reprint, New York: Augustus M. Kelley, 1971), 2:446–47.

8. Harvey Green, *Fit for America: Health, Fitness, Sport, and American Society* (New York: Pantheon, 1986), 224–25.

9. George M. Beard, *American Nervousness, Its Causes and Consequence* (1881; reprint, New York: Arno Press, 1972), esp. 96–138.

10. See esp. Alfred D. Chandler, Jr., *The Visible Hand: The Managerial Revolution in American Business* (Cambridge, Mass.: Belknap Press of Harvard University Press, 1977).

11. Olivier Zunz, *Making America Corporate, 1870–1920* (Chicago: University of Chicago Press, 1990), 126–27; "The Fate of the Salaried Man," *Independent*, Aug. 20, 1903, 2002–3.

12. William D. Haywood and Frank Bohn, *Industrial Socialism* (Chicago, n.d.), 25, quoted in David Montgomery, *Workers' Control in America: Studies in the History of Work, Technology, and Labor Struggle* (Cambridge, U.K.: Cambridge University Press, 1979), 9.

13. Alfred D. Chandler, Jr., "*Fin de Siècle*: Industrial Transformation," in Mikuláš Teich and Roy Porter, eds., *Fin de Siècle and Its Legacy* (Cambridge, U.K.: Cambridge University Press, 1990), 28, 31.

14. Reed Ueda, *Postwar Immigrant America: A Social History* (Boston: Bedford Books of St. Martin's Press, 1994), 2.

15. D. W. Meinig, *The Shaping of America*, vol. 3, *Transcontinental America, 1850–1915* (New Haven, Conn.: Yale University Press, 1998), 278.

16. Howard P. Chudacoff, *The Age of the Bachelor: Creating an American Subculture* (Princeton, N.J.: Princeton University Press, 1999), esp. 48, 217–50; George Chauncey, *Gay New York: Gender, Urban Culture, and the Making of the Gay Male World, 1890–1940* (New York: Basic Books, 1994); Elliott J. Gorn, *The Manly Art: Bare-Knuckle Prize Fighting in America* (Ithaca, N.Y.: Cornell University Press, 1986), esp. 179–247.

17. Caroline Ticknor, "The Steel-Engraving Lady and the Gibson Girl," *Atlantic Monthly*, July 1901, 106; Peter G. Filene, *Him/Her/Self: Gender Identities in Modern America*, 3rd ed. (Baltimore, Md.: Johns Hopkins University Press, 1998), 19–22; Nancy F. Cott, *The Grounding of Modern Feminism* (New Haven, Conn.: Yale University Press, 1987), esp. 9.

18. Edwin Milton Royle, "The Vaudeville Theatre," *Scribner's*, Oct. 1899, 489.

19. Duffield Osborne, "A Defense of Pugilism," *North American Review*, Apr. 1888, 433–35.

20. For a cogent overview of sports in this period, see Elliott J. Gorn and Warren Goldstein, *A Brief History of American Sports* (New York: Hill and Wang, 1993), 98–182.

21. Frank Luther Mott, *American Journalism: A History, 1690–1960*, 3rd ed. (New York: Macmillan, 1962), esp. 436, 547, 549.

22. Frank Luther Mott, *A History of American Magazines, 1885–1905* (Cambridge, Mass.: Belknap Press of Harvard University Press, 1957), 5–6; John Tebbell, *The*

American Magazine: A Compact History (New York: Hawthorn Books, 1969), 106–81. See Frank A. Munsey, "Impressions by the Way," *Munsey's Magazine*, Oct. 1903, 51–52; "Cheap Magazines," *Independent*, June 27, 1895, 867.

23. Mott, *American Journalism*, 593; James Collins, testimony before congressional committee, quoted in Jackson Lears, *Fables of Abundance: A Cultural History of American Advertising* (New York: Basic Books, 1994), 201.

24. Neil Harris, "Iconography and Intellectual History: The Halftone Effect," in *Cultural Excursions: Marketing Appetites and Cultural Tastes in Modern America* (Chicago: University of Chicago Press, 1990), 304–17.

25. Robert C. Allen, *Horrible Prettiness: Burlesque and American Culture* (Chapel Hill: University of North Carolina Press, 1991); Susan A. Glenn, *Female Spectacle: The Theatrical Roots of Modern Feminism* (Cambridge, Mass.: Harvard University Press, 2000).

1. WHO IS THE PERFECT MAN?

1. For this famous distinction, see Kenneth Clark, *The Nude: A Study in Ideal Form* (Princeton, N.J.: Bollingen Series XXXV [2], Princeton University Press, 1956), esp. 3. See also Kenneth R. Dutton, *The Perfectible Body: The Western Ideal of Male Physical Development* (New York: Continuum, 1995), esp. 101; Emmanuel Cooper, *Fully Exposed: The Male Nude in Photography*, 2nd ed. (New York: Routledge, 1995), 8–71.

2. On gender as performance, see especially Judith Butler, *Gender Trouble: Feminism and the Subversion of Identity* (New York: Routledge, 1990).

3. Rudolph Aronson, *Theatrical and Musical Memoirs* (New York: McBridge, Nast and Company, 1913), 82–83; Harold U. Faulkner, *Politics, Reform, and Expansion, 1890–1900* (New York: Harper & Brothers, 1959), 141–81.

4. Lewis C. Strang, *Celebrated Comedians of Light Opera and Musical Comedy in America* (Boston: L. C. Page, 1901), 191. For a discussion of *Adonis* and the text of the play, see Gerald Bordman, *American Musical Comedy: From "Adonis" to "Dreamgirls"* (New York: Oxford University Press, 1982), chap. 2 and app. 2, from which my quotations from the play are taken.

5. On this point, see David Scobey, "Nymphs and Satyrs: Sex and the Bourgeois Public Sphere in Victorian New York," unpublished essay.

6. "The Strongest Man in the World," *New York World*, June 18, 1893, 16; George C. D. Odell, *Annals of the New York Stage*, vol. 15, *1891–1894* (New York: Columbia University Press, 1949), 333; *New York Herald*, June 18, 1893; "The Strongest Man in the World," *Frank Leslie's Illustrated Weekly*, July 6, 1893, 7.

7. "Strongest Man in the World," *Leslie's Weekly*, 7; *New York Herald*, June 18, 1893, 23. The latter gives the figure of twenty-six hundred pounds; the writer for *Leslie's* estimates the weight as "nearly a ton."

8. See George Chauncey, *Gay New York: Gender, Urban Culture, and the Making of the Gay Male World, 1890–1940* (New York: Basic Books, 1994), esp. 1–127.

9. G. Mercer Adam, *Sandow on Physical Training; A Study in the Perfect Type of the Human Form* (New York: J. Selwin Tait & Sons, 1894).

10. *Chicago Tribune*, Aug. 20, 1893, 16; compare with *San Francisco Examiner*, Apr. 17, 1894, 9. But note that in one of the first newspaper pieces on Sandow after his New York debut, he described himself as so "delicate" that "his parents feared that he would not grow into manhood" (*New York Herald*, June 18, 1893, 23).

11. Theodore Roosevelt, *An Autobiography* (New York: Charles Scribner's Sons, 1920), 13, 27–28, 122.

12. George Butler and Charles Gaines, *Yours in Perfect Manhood: Charles Atlas* (New York: Simon and Schuster, 1982), 17, 19–20.

13. Eugen Sandow, "My Reminiscences," *Strand Magazine*, Feb. 1910, 144. See also "Strongest Man in the World," *New York World*, 16; and Adam, *Sandow on Physical Training*, 24–25.

14. Sandow, "My Reminiscences," 145. See Horst Ueberhorst, *Friedrich Ludwig Jahn, 1778/1978* (Munich: Moos, 1978).

15. On *tableaux vivants*, also known as "model artists," see Timothy J. Gilfoyle, *City of Eros: New York City, Prostitution, and the Commercialization of Sex, 1790–1920* (New York: W. W. Norton, 1992), 124.

16. This is the reverse side of the analysis of class and the female body offered by T. J. Clark, *The Painting of Modern Life: Paris in the Art of Manet and His Followers* (New York: Knopf, 1984), esp. 118.

17. David L. Chapman, *Sandow the Magnificent: Eugen Sandow and the Beginnings of Bodybuilding* (Urbana: University of Illinois Press, 1994), 9.

18. On challenges and boxing, see Elliott J. Gorn, *The Manly Art: Bare-Knuckle Prize Fighting in America* (Ithaca, N.Y.: Cornell University Press, 1986), 99–100.

19. Chapman, *Sandow the Magnificent*, 23–30.

20. "Strongest Man in the World," *New York World*, 16; "Great Gnarls of Muscle," *San Francisco Examiner*, Apr. 17, 1894, 9. The reporter for the *New York World*, however, noted that Sandow's clothes failed to conceal his physical development altogether: "His coat bulges out about the chest and back, in curious contrast to the waist, which is as small as a woman's."

21. For Sandow's dimensions, see "Sandow a Mighty Man of Muscle," *New York Herald*, June 18, 1893, 23; for the comparisons with Langtry and Cleveland and the reporter's description of the size of Sandow's muscles, see "Strongest Man in the World," *New York World*, 16.

22. "Sandow a Mighty Man of Muscle," *New York Herald*, 23.

23. John L. Sullivan, *Life and Reminiscences of a 19th Century Gladiator* (Boston: Jas. A. Hearn, 1892), 29.

24. *New York Herald*, Dec. 22, 1885; on Sullivan's career, see especially Michael T. Isenberg, *John L. Sullivan and His America* (Urbana: University of Illinois Press, 1988); Gorn, *Manly Art*, 210–47.

25. Roberta J. Park, "Healthy, Moral, and Strong: Educational Views of Exercise and Athletics in Nineteenth-Century America," in Kathryn Grover, ed., *Fitness*

in American Culture: Images of Health, Sport, and the Body, 1830–1940 (Amherst: University of Massachusetts Press and Margaret Woodbury Strong Museum, 1989), 151–52.

26. D. A. Sargent, "The Physical Proportions of the Typical Man," in D. A. Sargent, et al., *Athletic Sports* (New York: Charles Scribner's Sons, 1897), 16–17; *Statistics, Medical and Anthropological of the Provost-Marshal-General Bureau, Washington, D.C.,* quoted in D. A. Sargent, "The Physical Characteristics of the Athlete," *Scribner's Magazine,* Nov. 1887, 558; David J. Mrozek, *Sport and American Mentality, 1880–1919* (Knoxville: University of Tennessee Press, 1983), 194.

27. Sargent, "Physical Characteristics of Athlete," 542.

28. Mrozek, *Sport and American Mentality,* 219.

29. Gorn, *Manly Art,* 225–29.

30. "Report of Dr. D. A. Sargent's Examination," in Sullivan, *Life and Reminiscences,* 286, 294.

31. Ibid., 290.

32. In 1897 Sandow claimed a height of five feet nine and a quarter inches. See Eugen Sandow, *Strength and How to Obtain It* (London: Gale & Polden, 1897), 157.

33. *New York World,* June 25, 1893, 21.

34. Sargent's opinion was later supported by a similar examination of Sandow in San Francisco by Dr. Leverett Sweany. See "Sandow Examined," *San Francisco Examiner,* May 6, 1894, 4.

35. "Strongest Man in the World," *New York World,* 16.

36. "Lurline Lashes Sandow," *New York World,* July 2, 1893; "Lurline Whipped Eugene Sandow," *New York Herald,* July 2, 1893, 22; "Attila against Sandow," *New York Times,* July 25, 1893, 9.

37. *National Police Gazette,* Feb. 18, 1893, 14, 15.

38. Stephen D. Boyd, Jr., diary, Jan. 23, 1898, quoted in Edward L. Ayers, *The Promise of the New South* (New York: Oxford University Press, 1992), 182–83.

39. "Mirth and Muscle," *Boston Daily Globe,* July 18, 1893, 3; "Muscle and Music," *Boston Home Journal,* July 4, 1893, newspaper clipping in Dudley Sargent Papers, Harvard University Archives.

40. *Chicago Tribune,* Aug. 27, 1893, 29.

41. [Amy Leslie], "The Muscles of Sandow," *Chicago Daily News,* Aug. 2, 1893, 4; the Chicago spectator, Hunter McLean, is quoted in Chapman, *Sandow the Magnificent,* 64.

42. "Sandow in Plaster of Paris," *Strand Magazine,* Oct. 1901, 461; "Sandow Cast in Plaster," unidentified newspaper clipping in Sargent Papers.

43. Sandow, *Strength and How to Obtain It,* 124–25.

44. *New York Herald,* June 18, 1893. Another reported Sandow in the bath immediately after a performance taking his visitor's hand and placing it on Sandow's heart, "which had lately helped to support three horses." Sandow "called attention to the fact that there was no violent beating. In fact, the action of the heart could not be felt at all through the thick coating of muscle" ("Strongest Man in the World," *New York World,* 16).

45. [Leslie], "Muscles of Sandow," 4; Bertha Palmer's experience is recounted in Randolph Carter, *The World of Flo Ziegfeld* (New York: Praeger, 1974), 11.

46. David Chapman insists that Sandow had homosexual liaisons as well but offers ambiguous evidence. For example, if a *New York World* reporter's description of Sandow's relationship to his "bosom friend" the piano accompanist Martinus Sieveking truly pointed to their sexual intimacy, it seems highly unlikely that Sandow would have permitted the article's inclusion in Adam, *Sandow on Physical Training* (p. 110), the next year. See Chapman, *Sandow the Magnificent*, 19, 51–52, 189. In any case, George Chauncey's work in *Gay New York* would suggest caution in projecting modern conceptions of homosexuality back on Sandow and his time.

47. *National Police Gazette*, Jan. 27, 1894. This double legitimation is discussed in Dutton, *Perfectible Body*, 253.

48. The magistrate lectured the seven offenders, "You ought to have more respect for the women and children" ("Heat of 89.3 Here Sets Year's Mark as Summer Begins," *New York Times*, June 22, 1934, 1, 3). Similar laws prevailed in England until the late 1930s. By contrast, in 1918 the Young Men's Christian Association (YMCA) decreed that suits need not be worn in swimming pools (Cooper, *Fully Exposed*, 77–78).

49. On these tensions in the nineteenth-century female nude in art, see Clark, *Painting of Modern Life*, esp. 129–30.

50. H. P. M., "The Latest Society Fad," *Frank Leslie's Illustrated Weekly*, Mar. 29, 1894, 206.

51. For a similar instance of Sandow's posing before a group of socially prominent women, in an account charged with sexual innuendo, see "Posed for the Ladies," *San Francisco Chronicle*, May 17, 1894, 12.

52. See Samuel Wilson Fussell's discussion of the acceptability of the first pose among bodybuilders in the 1980s and their suspicion of the second as homoerotic in *Muscle: Confessions of an Unlikely Bodybuilder* (New York: Avon, 1991), 191.

53. Geraldine A. Johnson, "Introduction," 10; Michael Hatt, "Eakins's Arcadia: Sculpture, Photography, and the Redefinition of the Classical Body," 62–65; and Tamar Garb, "Modeling the Body: Photography, Physical Culture, and the Classical Ideal in Fin-de-Siècle France," 86–99, all in Geraldine A. Johnson, ed., *Sculpture and Photography: Envisioning the Third Dimension* (Cambridge, U.K.: Cambridge University Press, 1998).

54. These were the prices charged by Sarony in 1893; see Ben L. Bassham, *The Theatrical Photographs of Napoleon Sarony* (Kent, Ohio: Kent State University Press, 1978), 14.

55. Paul Bourget, *Outre-Mer: Impressions of America* (New York: Charles Scribner's Sons, 1895), 61. John Addington Symonds to Edmund Gosse, Dec. 25, 1899, in *The Letters of John Addington Symonds*, ed. Herbert M. Schueller and Robert L. Peters (Detroit: Wayne State University Press, 1969), 3:1779; Anthony Comstock, *Traps for the Young* (1883; reprint, Cambridge, Mass.: Belknap Press

of Harvard University Press, 1967), 171; Greg Mullins, "Nudes, Prudes, and Pigmies: The Desirability of Disavowal in *Physical Culture,*" *Discourse* 15 (Fall 1992): 30.

56. Dutton, *Perfectible Body,* 142, 161–62.

57. John Mack Faragher, ed., *Rereading Frederick Jackson Turner* (New York: Henry Holt, 1994), 33–34.

58. For example, *The Christian Martyrs' Last Prayer* was commissioned by William Walters in 1863 and finished in 1883; *Pollice Verso,* one of the most celebrated of all the artist's works, was purchased by A. T. Stewart in 1875. See Gerald M. Ackerman, *La vie et l'oeuvre de Jean-Léon Gérôme* (Paris: ACR Édition, 1986), 252, 232.

59. Carlin A. Barton, "The Scandal of the Arena," *Representations* 27 (Summer 1989): 1–36, esp. 14. Barton notes a contemporary analogue in Martin Scorsese's *Raging Bull* (1980).

60. For "Spartacus Sullivan," see Sullivan, *Life and Reminiscences,* 29.

61. "Where Is the Perfect Man?" *San Francisco Examiner,* May 27, 1894, 24.

62. On the first impostor, see "Eugene Sandow's Great Strength," *Chicago Times,* July 30, 1893, 9. Of Miller, a reporter for the *Chicago Tribune,* Aug. 11, 1893, wrote, he "gives a good exhibition, but he is not in Sandow's class." For the Sampson quotation, see *Chicago Tribune,* Aug. 27, 1893, 29.

63. "A Lion Is a Rank Coward," *San Francisco Examiner,* May 13, 1894.

64. Long after the event, keeping the pretense of heroic contest to the last, Sandow, in "My Reminiscences," called this "perhaps the greatest, certainly the most thrilling, of all my experiences" (p. 150). In the same article, he said there were forty thousand in the audience; the *San Francisco Chronicle* gave the figure of three thousand, and *The San Francisco Examiner* estimated twenty-five hundred. For these attendance figures and descriptions of the event, see *San Francisco Chronicle,* May 23, 1894, 14, and *San Francisco Examiner,* May 23, 1894, 12.

65. Advertisement for "Sandow's Mail System of Teaching Physical Culture," *Collier's,* Feb. 28, 1903; Dudley A. Sargent, letter to editor, *New York Herald,* c. 1902, quoted in Chapman, *Sandow the Magnificent,* 139.

66. Eugen Sandow, *Life Is Movement* (London: National Health Press, n.d. [c. 1918]), esp. x, 5, 12; Chapman, *Sandow the Magnificent,* 176–77.

67. "Sandow, Famous Strong Man, Dead," *New York Times,* Oct. 15, 1925, 23. David Chapman questions this explanation of Sandow's death, noting that his cause of death was officially recorded as "aortic aneurysia." He speculates that Sandow really died of syphilis. See Chapman, *Sandow the Magnificent,* 185–88.

2. THE MANLY ART OF ESCAPE

1. Bronislaw Malinowski, "Culture," in Edwin R. A. Seligman, ed., *Encyclopedia of the Social Sciences* (New York: Macmillan, 1931), 638; Malinowski quoted in Keith Thomas, *Religion and the Decline of Magic* (New York: Charles Scribner's Sons, 1971), 647.

2. The most complete and authoritative biography is Kenneth Silverman, *Houdini!!! The Career of Ehrich Weiss* (New York: HarperCollins, 1996), which is supplemented by Kenneth Silverman, *Notes to Houdini!!!* (Washington, D.C.: Kaufman & Greenberg, 1996). Among earlier biographies, the most useful are Harold Kellock, *Houdini: His Life-Story* (New York: Harcourt, Brace, 1928); and Milbourne Christopher, *Houdini: The Untold Story* (New York: Thomas Y. Crowell, 1969).

3. The best accounts of this sort are Walter B. Gibson, *Houdini's Escapes* (New York: Harcourt, Brace, 1930); and J. C. Cannell, *The Secrets of Houdini* (1931; reprint, New York: Dover, 1973).

4. The most determinedly psychological (though not always the most illuminating) of these have been: Bernard C. Meyer, *Houdini: A Mind in Chains: A Psychoanalytic Portrait* (New York: E. P. Dutton, 1976); Raymond Fitzsimons, *Death and the Magician: The Mystery of Houdini* (New York: Atheneum, 1981); and Ruth Brandon, *The Life and Many Deaths of Harry Houdini* (London: Secker & Warburg, 1993).

5. James Randi and Bert Randolph Sugar, *Houdini: His Life and Art* (New York: Grosset & Dunlap, 1976), 19.

6. Harry Houdini, "Harry Houdini," *Magician Annual* 3 (1909–1910): 16.

7. Quoted in Silverman, *Houdini!!!* 8. The faulty German spelling is presumably Houdini's.

8. Houdini to Quincy Kilby, Brooklyn, May 26, 1916, Quincy Kilby Scrapbook, Harvard Theatre Collection, Harvard University (hereafter cited as QKSB, HTC).

9. Christopher, *Houdini: The Untold Story*; Harry Houdini, *A Magician among the Spirits* (New York: Harper, 1924), 151.

10. Houdini's account of these efforts, *A Magician among the Spirits*, bears the dedication: "In worshipful homage I dedicate this book to the memory of my sainted mother. If God in His infinite wisdom ever sent an angel upon earth in human form, it was my mother."

11. See Houdini's account in unidentified magazine article, probably from Houdini souvenir program, c. Sept. 1926, p. 5, in Houdini Collection, Harry Ransom Humanities Center, University of Texas at Austin (hereafter cited as HRHC).

12. Undated postcard from Ehrich Weiss to Cecilia Weiss, McManus-Young Scrapbook, Library of Congress, Washington, D.C. (hereafter cited as LC); unidentified magazine article, c. Sept. 1926, in HRHC; Harry Houdini, *The Right Way to Do Wrong: An Exposé of Successful Criminals* (1906; reprint, Mattituck, N.Y.: Amereon House, n.d.), 94; Silverman, *Notes to Houdini!!!* 14.

13. This account, like all of Houdini's about his childhood, cannot be regarded uncritically. As Manny Weltman speculates, Houdini may in fact have seen an imitation of Lynn's act by a traveling medicine show and, quite possibly, without his father. Nonetheless, Houdini's account of the act—and of his father's presence—has a significance independent of scrupulous accuracy. See Manny Welt-

man, *Houdini: Escape into Legend, the Early Years, 1862–1900* (Van Nuys, Calif.: Finders/Seekers, 1993), 10–11.

14. In 1914 Houdini bought the apparatus for the trick from Lynn's son, together, he claimed, with the world rights to perform it (Silverman, *Notes to Houdini!!!* 169–70).

15. Christopher, *Houdini: The Untold Story,* 12; Meyer, *Houdini,* 11–12; for comment on Dr. Lynn's act, see also Albert A. Hopkins, *Magic: Stage Illusions and Scientific Diversions, Including Trick Photographs* (1897; reprint, New York: Arno Press, 1977), 63–64; and Edwin A. Dawes, *The Great Illusionists* (Secaucus, N.J.: Chartwell Books, 1979), 163.

16. See Meyer, *Houdini,* 130, 140–41; Louise J. Kaplan, *The Family Romance of the Impostor-Poet Thomas Chatterton* (New York: Atheneum, 1988), 157.

17. The edition he read was titled *Robert-Houdin, the Great Wizard: Celebrated French Conjurer, Author, and Ambassador,* trans. Lascelles Wraxall, introduction and index by R. Shelton Mackenzie (Philadelphia: Charles Desilver, 1859); for a modern English edition, see *Memoirs of Robert-Houdin,* trans. Lascelles Wraxall, ed. Milbourne Christopher (New York: Dover, 1964).

18. Harry Houdini, *The Unmasking of Robert-Houdin* (London: George Routledge, 1909), 7.

19. Interestingly, Houdini dedicated the book in which he attacked Robert-Houdin to his own father, bestowing on him a Ph.D. and LL.D. that he never possessed and lauding him as one "who instilled in me love of study and patience in research" (ibid., xi).

20. "Un prestidigitateur n'est point un jongleur; c'est un acteur jouant un rôle de magicien . . ." (italics added); Jean-Eugène Robert-Houdin, *Comment on devient sorcier: Les secrets de la prestidigitation et de la magie* (1878; reprint, Paris: Slatkine Reprints, 1980), 29.

21. *The Boy's Own Conjuring Book* (New York: Dick and Fitzgerald, [1860?]).

22. Kaplan, *Chatterton,* 216–17. Houdini's career as an escape artist has many aspects in common with the psychology of the impostor.

23. Houdini to John E. Waitte, Munich, Sept. 8, 1902, HTC.

24. Quotation from L. R. C. Crandon to Arthur Conan Doyle, in Silverman, *Houdini!!!* 325.

25. Quoted in Robert W. Snyder, *The Voice of the City: Vaudeville and Popular Culture in New York* (New York: Oxford University Press, 1989), 46.

26. Silverman, *Houdini!!!* 132; Silverman, *Notes to Houdini!!!* 68.

27. Kellock, *Houdini,* 59.

28. Hopkins, *Magic,* 44.

29. Fitzsimons, *Death and the Magician,* 30, 54.

30. Silverman, *Notes to Houdini!!!* 18.

31. Other substitution tricks in the 1890s also developed narratives in which a man was released and a woman confined. In one of the most famous, "Strobeika," a young Russian woman takes the place of her imprisoned fiancé and is discov-

ered shackled and tied to a horizontal plank. A New York performance by the celebrated magician Alexander Herrmann (1843–1896) is described in "Strobeika's Secret All Laid Bare," *New York Herald*, Dec. 21, 1890, 13. At this same time, the husband-and-wife team Mildred and Rouclere (Mildred May Searing and Harry Rouclere), in a spiritualist program as "Ellington and Cook," performed a variation of the substitution trick as a spirit phenomenon rather than an escape. A few years later, Horace Goldin presented an illusion, "Dreyfus Escape from Devil's Island," in which he was released from a cage, leaving a young woman in his place. See David Price, *Magic: A Pictorial History of Conjurers in the Theater* (New York: Cornwall Books, 1985), 165–66, 175, 223.

32. *New York Dramatic Mirror*, quoted in Laurence Senelick, "Lady and the Tramp: Drag Differentials in the Progressive Era," in Laurence Senelick, ed., *Gender in Performance: The Representation of Difference in the Performing Arts* (Hanover, N.H.: University Press of New England, 1992), 27.

33. Percy Hammond, quoted in Senelick, "Lady and the Tramp," 29. See also unidentified clipping, Robinson Locke Scrapbooks, New York Public Library for the Performing Arts (hereafter cited as RLSB, NYPL).

34. "Girls and More Girls Cut Work to Form Waiting Line," *Cincinnati Times Star*, Mar. 7, 1912, RLSB, NYPL.

35. *Variety*, Apr. 24, 1909, 12.

36. Rennold Wolf, "The Sort of Fellow Julian Eltinge Really Is," *Green Book Magazine*, Nov. 1913, 802. The lyrics were by Eltinge.

37. Harry B. Smith and Gus Edwards, "The Modern Sandow Girl" (New York: Gus Edwards Music Pub. Co., 1907), quoted in Senelick, "Lady and the Tramp," 29. I have slightly altered the punctuation.

38. Sharon R. Ullman, *Sex Seen: The Emergence of Modern Sexuality in America* (Berkeley: University of California Press, 1997), 53; Ullman is here apparently quoting from *The New York Dramatic Mirror*, Apr. 11, 1912.

39. "Eltinge Says He Didn't," *Variety*, Jan. 6, 1906, 12.

40. Unidentified clipping, HRHC.

41. Wolf, "Eltinge," 794; Joan N. Vale, "Tintype Ambitions: Three Vaudevillians in Search of Hollywood Fame" (master's thesis, University of San Diego, 1985), 25.

42. On this subject, see Fred Siegel, "The Vaudeville Conjuring Act" (Ph.D. diss., New York University, 1993).

43. *St. Joseph Herald*, Mar. 1, 1898, clipping in HRHC.

44. Houdini to Kilby, June 27, 1916, QKSB, HTC.

45. Kellock, *Houdini*, 135.

46. Houdini, "Harry Houdini," 17. See his pamphlet *Magic Made Easy*, c. 1898; reprinted in Walter B. Gibson, *The Original Houdini Scrapbook* (New York: Corwin Sterling, 1976), 79–95. "Metamorphosis" is item 61.

47. On the variety of conjuring acts in vaudeville, see Siegel, "Vaudeville Conjuring Act."

48. Houdini, "Harry Houdini," 16.
49. Ibid., 17.
50. *Minneapolis Times*, Feb. 21, 1899, clipping in HRHC.
51. Houdini diary, Apr. 24, 1899, quoted in Silverman, *Houdini!!!* 25.
52. *Kansas City Times*, Apr. 15, 1899, clipping in QKSB, HTC.
53. Eric H. Monkkonen, *Police in Urban America, 1860–1920* (Cambridge, U.K.: Cambridge University Press, 1981), esp. 158–60.
54. "Irons Could Not Hold Him," *San Francisco Chronicle*, June 3, 1899, 12.
55. "Exposé of Houdini's Trunk and Handcuff Trick," *San Francisco Examiner Magazine*, July 9, 1899, 25.
56. *San Francisco Report*, July 14, 1899, clipping in QKSB, HTC.
57. Harry Houdini, *Handcuff Secrets* [bound with *Unmasking of Robert-Houdin*], 81.
58. *San Francisco Report*, July 14, 1899, clipping in QKSB, HTC.
59. Harry Houdini, "Secrets of My Handcuff Tricks," *San Francisco Examiner Magazine*, July 23, 1899, 29.
60. Harry Houdini, *The Adventurous Life of a Versatile Artist*, rev. ed. (New York?: n.p., 1922), 11.
61. "A Talk with Houdini," *New York Dramatic Mirror*, June 25, 1904.
62. Houdini to Waitte, Mischi-Mowgorod, Russia, Aug. 11, 1903, HTC.
63. Houdini, *Adventurous Life of a Versatile Artist*, 14.
64. "Expert Jail Breaker Walks through Locks and Manacles," *Washington Post*, Jan. 2, 1906.
65. *Washington Post*, Jan. 7, 1906, reprinted in Houdini, *Adventurous Life of a Versatile Artist*, 25–30.
66. "Houdini Escapes from City Prison," *Boston Daily Globe*, Mar. 19, 1906, clipping in HTC; "Houdini Breaks from City Prison," *Boston Post*, Mar. 20, 1906, clipping in HTC; Milbourne Christopher, *Houdini: A Pictorial Life* (New York: Thomas Y. Crowell, 1976), 1–4.
67. "He Could Be Biggest Burglar in World," *Boston Post*, Mar. 21, 1906, clipping in HTC.
68. "Is Master of Locks and Bolts," *Appleton (Wis.) Crescent*, July 23, 1904.
69. Peter Brooks, *Body Work: Objects of Desire in Modern Narrative* (Cambridge, Mass.: Harvard University Press, 1993), 64.
70. Kellock, *Houdini*, 272.
71. Houdini, *Adventurous Life of a Versatile Artist*, 1.
72. *Complete Tales and Poems of Edgar Allan Poe* (New York: Modern Library, Random House, 1938), 246; Silverman, *Houdini!!!* 263.
73. Franz Kafka, *The Complete Stories*, ed. Nathum N. Glatzer (New York: Schocken Books, 1971), 144.
74. Houdini to Waitte, Paris, Nov. 31 [*sic*], 1901, HTC.
75. "Houdini at Harvard," *Boston Herald*, May 7, 1908, clipping in Microfilmed Scrapbook, Houdini Historical Center, Appleton, Wis. (hereafter cited as MSB, HHC). A few days earlier, at the request of audience members, he had stripped in full view of male spectators at the Boston Athletic Club before performing an

escape. "Houdini Escapes from Glass Case," *Boston Herald*, May 4, 1908, clipping in MSB, HHC.

76. "A member of the Eclectic Medical Society" [as the writer asked to be identified] to Houdini, Jan. 27, 1906, HTC. For an instance in which a prison attendant detected a concealed device under Houdini's right foot, see "Houdini Meets His Waterloo," *Boston Herald*, Sept. 10, 1906, clipping in HTC.

77. Houdini, *Adventurous Life of a Versatile Artist*, 1.

78. See Louise J. Kaplan, *Female Perversions: The Temptations of Emma Bovary* (New York: Doubleday, 1991), 11–12.

79. "A Talk with Houdini," *New York Dramatic Mirror*; Houdini to Waitte, Hanover, Germany, Feb. 22, 1903, HTC.

80. Description and quotations are drawn from three unidentified newspaper clippings, HTC.

81. "Houdini Victor in Supreme Test," unidentified newspaper clipping in HTC.

82. "Slippery Man Scorns 400 Pounds of Chains," *New York Press*, Apr. 11, 1908, clipping in MSB, HHC.

83. Handbill with challenge from Weed Chain Tire Grip Company, New York City, and Houdini's acceptance, 1908, McManus-Young Collection, LC.

84. "Houdini vs. the Pittsburg Vise," broadside in MSB, HHC.

85. Neil Harris, *Humbug: The Art of P. T. Barnum* (Boston: Little, Brown, 1973), 59–89; James W. Cook, Jr., *The Arts of Deception: Playing with Fraud in the Age of Barnum* (Cambridge, Mass.: Harvard University Press, 2001), esp. chap. 2, "The 'Feejee Mermaid' and the American Market Revolution."

86. Kellock, *Houdini*, 196.

87. I here paraphrase Peter Brooks's observation, "Since as the primacy of the body may be most dramatically felt in its failure: the deathbed is a privileged literary place" (*Body Work*, 5).

88. Houdini, *Adventurous Life of a Versatile Artist*, 5.

89. Silverman, *Houdini!!!* 162.

90. Kaplan, *Chatterton*, esp. 216–17.

91. Sydney *Daily Telegraph*, Apr. 16, 1910, quoted in Brandon, *Life and Many Deaths of Houdini*, 24.

92. "Houdini Shackled, Leaps into River, Almost Drowned," Philadelphia *North American*, May 15, 1908, 1–2. The *Philadelphia Record* for the same date reported he stayed underwater only fifty-seven seconds.

93. Harry Houdini, "Nearly Dying for a Living," *Hearst's Magazine*, Dec. 1919, 40 [?], clipping in HRHC.

94. "Shackled, Dives from the Bridge," *Detroit Journal*, Nov. 27, 1906, clipping in HTC.

95. Houdini to Waitte, New Orleans, Nov. 17, 1907, HTC.

96. Houdini diary, May 4, 1907, quoted in Silverman, *Houdini!!!* 182.

97. "Handcuffed, Houdini Goes into Canal," *Rochester Union and Advertiser*, May 7, 1907, 9. A film of this jump confirms the reporter's account; see Silverman, *Houdini!!!* 114–15.

98. Houdini to Waitte, Chicago, Feb. 12, 1908, HTC.

99. Cannell, *Secrets of Houdini*, 61–62.

100. Quoted in Mark Seltzer, *Bodies and Machines* (New York: Routledge, 1992), 160.

101. The lyrics would have been known to all Houdini's audience: "Loudly the bell in the old tower rings,/Bidding us list to the warning it brings,/Sailor, take care! . . . /Danger is near thee, Beware! . . . /Many brave hearts are asleep in the deep, so beware!"

102. Christopher, *Houdini: The Untold Story*, 105–6.

103. Houdini recording on Edison wax cylinder, Oct. 29, 1914, Flatbush, N.Y., copy at HHC, and transcription by George N. Gordon of second wax cylinder made on the same occasion in Kenneth Silverman Papers, HHC; Silverman, *Notes to Houdini!!!* 81.

104. Houdini recording on wax cylinder; J. Hewat McKenzie, *Spirit Intercourse* (London: Smith, Marshall, Hamilton Kent, 1916), 86–87; Brandon, *Life and Many Deaths of Houdini*, 157.

105. Challenge, Glasgow, Oct. 19, 1909, MSB, HHC.

106. Challenge from Grant Staff Barracks, June 3, 1904, HRHC.

107. Challenge from Liverpool Seamen, Oct. 20, 1914, MSB, HHC.

108. In fact, *Success* was never used to transport convicts to Australia and was not built until 1840. See Charles Bateson, *The Convict Ships, 1787–1868* (Glasgow: Brown, Son & Ferguson, 1959), 257–58 and illustration facing 240.

109. Elaine Scarry, *The Body in Pain: The Making and Unmaking of the World* (New York: Oxford University Press, 1985), 31.

110. *Kansas City Post*, Sept. 8, 1915, 2. Brandon describes Houdini's Kansas City aerial straitjacket escape but misdates the year as 1914. Silverman dates Houdini's first such escape as September 29, 1915, in Minneapolis (*Houdini!!!* 194). The *Kansas City Post* had been bought by the yellow-journalist publishers Fred C. Bonfils and Harry H. Tammen in 1908. See Frank Luther Mott, *American Journalism: A History, 1690–1960*, 3rd ed. (New York: Macmillan, 1962), 568.

111. *San Antonio Express*, Feb. 1, 1916, 5.

112. Transcript of Houdini lecture, Symphony Hall, Boston, Jan. 3, 1925, bound volume titled "Lectures, Articles on Spiritualism," McManus-Young Collection, LC, quoted in Silverman, *Houdini!!!* 197.

113. A Houdini imitator, Henry Huber, made the analogy to hanging explicit in his aerial straitjacket escapes with such announcements as "Man Hanged at 2:30 Today" (Price, *Magic*, 240).

114. *San Antonio Express*, Feb. 1, 1916, 5.

115. James Randi, "A Peek behind the Curtain," in Randi and Sugar, *Houdini*, 173–74; Silverman, *Houdini!!!* 196–97; see also John A. Novak, *The Art of Escape*, vol. 4, *Escapes from a Strait Jacket* (Calgary, Alberta: Micky Hades, 1979).

116. Beatrice Houdini to Theo "Dash" Weiss, Apr. 21, 1911, Sidney H. Radner Collection, HHC; on Houdini's kidney ailment, see Houdini to Waitte, Pittsburgh, Nov. 16, 1911, and Houdini to Waitte, New York, Nov. 23, 1911, both in HTC.

117. Houdini to Theo "Dash" Weiss, Nürnberg, Sept. 23, 1913, Sidney H. Radner Collection, HHC.

118. *Washington Times*, Apr. 19, 1916, 2.

119. Houdini to Karl Germain, Pittsburgh, Mar. 7, 1922, quoted in Christopher, *Houdini: The Untold Story*, 311.

120. "Houdini Secrets for U.S. Soldiers," New York *Evening Sun*, Feb. 26, 1918, clipping in MSB, HHC.

121. R. Laurence Moore, *In Search of White Crows: Spiritualism, Parapsychology, and American Culture* (New York: Oxford University Press, 1977), 102–27.

122. See Ann Braude, *Radical Spirits: Spiritualism and Women's Rights in Nineteenth-Century America* (Boston: Beacon Press, 1989).

123. Thomas Frost, *The Lives of the Conjurors* (London: Chatto & Windus, 1881), 250; Charles J. Pecor, "John Henry Anderson, the Great Wizard of the North; Nineteenth-Century Magician, Actor, Publicist," *Theatre Studies* 24/25 (1977/78–1978/79): 51–52.

124. John Nevil Maskelyne, *Modern Spiritualism* (1876), reprinted in James Webb, ed., *The Mediums and the Conjurors* (New York: Arno Press, 1976); Frost, *Lives of Conjurors*, 332–33.

125. Harry Kellar, *A Magician's Tour* (Chicago: Donohue, Henneberry, 1897), *passim*.

126. In his early pamphlet *Magic Made Easy*, Houdini offered lessons in spiritualist effects. See reprint in Gibson, *Original Houdini Scrapbook*, 85 and *passim*.

127. Thomas R. Tietze, *Margery* (New York: Harper & Row, 1973), 1. This remains the best single account of Mina Crandon's extraordinary career.

128. Mark W. Richardson, L. R. G. Crandon, et al., *Margery Harvard Veritas: A Study in Psychics* (Boston: Blanchard, 1925), 46.

129. J. Malcolm Bird, *"Margery" the Medium* (Boston: Small, Maynard, 1925), 378, 231. The reference to Keith's appears in Richardson, Crandon, et al., *Margery Harvard Veritas*, 43. This was one of the Emerson Hall sittings at Harvard in 1925.

130. J. Malcolm Bird, "Our Next Psychic," *Scientific American*, July 1924, 28ff.; *Boston Herald*, Dec. 19, 1924, quoted in Brandon, *Life and Many Deaths of Houdini*, 258.

131. Arthur Conan Doyle, quoted in "Margery Genuine, Says Conan Doyle," *Boston Herald*, Jan. 26, 1925, in Edward Saint, comp., Scrapbooks of Mounted Clippings, vol 1., Rare Book Division, LC. See also Hamlin Garland's description of Walter's personality in a 1927 séance in *Forty Years of Psychic Research* (New York: Macmillan, 1936), 309–11. On female mediums and masculine spirit-controls in the nineteenth century, see Moore, *In Search of White Crows*, 111.

132. Silverman, *Houdini!!!* 325.

133. See Le Roi Crandon's reference to "this low-minded Jew," cited in ibid., 325.

134. Harry Houdini, *Houdini Exposes the Tricks Used by the Boston Medium "Margery"* . . . (New York: Adams Press, 1924), 6–7.

135. Bird, *"Margery" the Medium*, 413.

136. Houdini, *Houdini Exposes*, 6–8.

137. Ibid., 10.

138. Bird, *"Margery" the Medium*, 430.

139. Houdini, *Houdini Exposes*, 17.

140. Bird, *"Margery" the Medium*, 433. Bird indicates the term of abuse indirectly by referring to a famous exchange in Owen Wister, *The Virginian* (1902; reprint, New York: Penguin Books, 1988), 22. Tietze gives the quotation as "bastard," perhaps misunderstanding Bird.

141. Houdini, *Houdini Exposes*, 17.

142. Ibid., 23.

143. Tietze, *Margery*, 184.

144. "Houdini Answers Prof. McDougall . . . ," *Boston Herald*, Sept. 22, 1924, clipping in Saint, comp., Scrapbooks of Mounted Clippings, vol. 1, LC.

145. Samuel J. Smilovitz [S. J. Smiley, pseud.], "Was Houdini Killed?" undated typescript, Fulton Oursler, Sr., Collection, Georgetown University.

146. Kellock, *Houdini*, 382.

3. "STILL A WILD BEAST AT HEART"

1. Burroughs to Thomas Newell Metcalf, Mar. 6, 1912, quoted in Irwin Porges, *Edgar Rice Burroughs: The Man Who Created Tarzan* (Provo, Utah: Brigham Young University Press, 1975), 123–24; John Taliaferro, *Tarzan Forever: The Life of Edgar Rice Burroughs* (New York: Scribner, 1999), 72. These two works are the best biographies of Burroughs, and I have relied on them throughout this chapter. Although I have examined photocopies of Edgar Rice Burroughs's papers in the Irwin Porges Papers, Edgar Rice Burroughs Memorial Collection, University of Louisville, Louisville, Ky., I have cited Porges, *Burroughs*, for the convenience of the reader whenever they are quoted within.

2. Metcalf to Burroughs, Mar. 11, 1912, quoted in Porges, *Burroughs*, 125–27.

3. At age nineteen as captain of the football team at Michigan Military Academy, Burroughs's height was given as five feet ten and a half inches. The next season it was reported as five feet ten inches. When he enlisted in the army a few months later, his height was listed as five feet nine inches. His son Hulbert Burroughs later said he was close to five feet nine inches. His weight was also variously reported. At his enlistment he was recorded as weighing 153 pounds stripped. Less than five months earlier, Burroughs wrote his weight in a notebook as 175 pounds, dressed. See Porges, *Burroughs*, 2–3, 38, 54.

4. Edgar Rice Burroughs, "Autobiography," typescript, Edgar Rice Burroughs Memorial Collection, 56–57.

5. Edgar Rice Burroughs, "The Tarzan Theme," *Writer's Digest*, June 1932, 31.

6. Burroughs, "Autobiography," 19.

7. Ibid., 1.

8. Burroughs appears to have misremembered the year, however, estimating that he was "in my second or third year," instead of six (Porges, *Burroughs*, 774).

9. Ibid., 13–14, 774–77.

10. Burroughs, "Autobiography," 6. On Burroughs's experiences in the West, see Phil Burger, "Glimpses of a World Past: Edgar Rice Burroughs, the West, and the Birth of an American Writer" (master's thesis, Utah State University, 1987).

11. Burroughs, "Autobiography," 23.

12. Ibid., 43.

13. Burroughs to brother Harry Burroughs, Mar. 19, 1921, quoted in notes, Porges Papers.

14. Peter G. Filene, *Him/Her/Self: Gender Identities in Modern America*, 3rd ed. (Baltimore, Md.: Johns Hopkins University Press, 1998), 78.

15. Burroughs, "Autobiography," 51.

16. Burroughs to Mr. M. R. Werner, Mar. 3, 1937, quoted in Porges Papers.

17. Burroughs, "Autobiography," 53–54.

18. Arthur Miller, *Death of a Salesman* (1949; reprint, New York: Viking Press, 1958), 22.

19. Quentin Reynolds, *Fiction Factory* (New York: Random House, 1955); Ron Goulart, *Cheap Thrills: An Informal History of the Pulp Magazines* (New Rochelle, N.Y.: Arlington House, 1972); Lee Server, *Danger Is my Business: An Illustrated History of the Fabulous Pulp Magazines* (San Francisco: Chronicle Books, 1993).

20. Burroughs, "Autobiography," 55.

21. Edgar Rice Burroughs, *A Princess of Mars* (1912; reprint, New York: Ballantine, 1963), 147.

22. Burroughs, "Autobiography," 56. The story first appeared in the magazine as "Under the Moons of Mars."

23. Ibid., 57.

24. Max Weber, *The Protestant Ethic and the Spirit of Capitalism*, trans. Talcott Parsons (New York: Charles Scribner's Sons, 1958); originally published in essay form in German, 1904–1905.

25. Frederick Winslow Taylor, *The Principles of Scientific Management* (1911; reprint, New York: W. W. Norton, 1967), 7; Wayburn quoted in Mary Morgan, "Handling Humanity in the Mass," *Theatre Magazine*, May 1913, 146. This last point is further developed in John F. Kasson, "Dances of the Machine in Early Twentieth-Century America," in Townsend Ludington, ed., *A Modern Mosaic: Art and Modernism in the United States* (Chapel Hill: University of North Carolina Press, 2000), 153–74.

26. *System*, Nov. 1911, 451.

27. Ibid., 460–63.

28. As late as 1900 only one in twenty-five men between the ages of eighteen and twenty-one was enrolled in college; in 1870, it had been one in sixty. See Burton J. Bledstein, *The Culture of Professionalism: The Middle Class and the Development of Higher Education in America* (New York: W. W. Norton, 1976), 278.

29. *System*, 470, 480.

30. Ibid., 489, 491.

31. Cyrus McCormick, Jr., to Albion Small, Feb. 3, 1915, quoted in Olivier Zunz,

Making America Corporate, 1870–1920 (Chicago: University of Chicago Press, 1990), 199.

32. Burroughs, "Autobiography," 58.

33. Scott B. Cook, *Colonial Encounters in the Age of Imperialism* (New York: Harper-Collins, 1998), 1.

34. *Congressional Record*, Jan. 9, 1900, 711, 712.

35. Owen Wister, *The Virginian: A Horseman of the Plains* (1902; reprint, New York: Penguin Books, 1988), 3, 179, 230, 111, 112. Burroughs's tribute appeared in an article he wrote for Thomas Ford, literary editor, *Los Angeles Times*, in 1922; see Porges, *Burroughs*, 368.

36. Thomas Dixon, *The Clansman: An Historical Romance of the Ku Klux Klan* (New York: Doubleday, Page, 1905), 304.

37. Ibid., 186.

38. When Burroughs heard of London's death, he briefly considered writing a biography of him. See Porges, *Burroughs*, 278.

39. Jack London, *The Call of the Wild* (1903; reprint, New York: Macmillan, 1915), 18, 43, 61, 199, 59, 60, 167.

40. Ibid., 223, 231.

41. Burroughs, "Tarzan Theme," 99–100.

42. Dolph Sharp, "Edgar Rice Burroughs, Inc.," *Writer's Digest*, Aug. 1949, 14.

43. R. M. Ballantyne, *The Gorilla Hunters* (London: Collins' Clear-Type Press, n.d.), 22.

44. Edgar Rice Burroughs, *Tarzan of the Apes* (1914; reprint, New York: Dover Books, 1997), 2, 4, 3.

45. See Gina Lombroso-Ferrero, *Criminal Man according to the Classification of Cesare Lombroso* (1911; reprint, Montclair, N.J.: Patterson Smith, 1972), esp. 3–51.

46. Burroughs, *Tarzan of the Apes*, 4, 13.

47. Ibid., 15, 25.

48. Robert M. Zingg, "Feral Man and Cases of Extreme Isolation of Individuals," in J. A. L. Singh and Robert M. Zingg, *Wolf-Children and Feral Man* (1942; reprint, Hamden, Conn.: Archon Books, 1966), 183, 195; Douglas Keith Candland, *Feral Children and Clever Animals: Reflections on Human Nature* (New York: Oxford University Press, 1993), 9–12.

49. Candland, *Feral Children and Clever Animals*, 17–37; quotation from Itard in Harlan Lane, *The Wild Boy of Aveyron* (Cambridge, Mass.: Harvard University Press, 1976), 4.

50. Robert F. Heizer and Theodora Kroeber, eds., *Ishi, the Last Yahi: A Documentary History* (Berkeley: University of California Press, 1979), 92; Theodora Kroeber, *Ishi in Two Worlds* (Berkeley: University of California Press, 1961), 3–4.

51. Heizer and Kroeber, eds., *Ishi, the Last Yahi*, 130.

52. Ibid., 121.

53. Saxton T. Pope, "Characteristics of Ishi," in ibid., 231; Kroeber, *Ishi in Two Worlds*, 138, 176.

54. Kroeber, *Ishi in Two Worlds*, 210; Heizer and Kroeber, eds., *Ishi, the Last Yahi*, 99, 122, 227. I am indebted to Eric Combest for this point.

55. Ernest Thompson Seton, *Boy Scouts of America: Official Handbook of Woodcraft, Scouting, and Life-Craft* (New York: Doubleday, Page, 1910), 1.

56. Joseph Knowles, *Alone in the Wilderness* (Boston: Small, Maynard, 1913), 226.

57. Ibid., 229–31.

58. Ibid., 127.

59. *Boston Post*, Oct. 5, 1913, Oct. 10, 1913, Oct. 12, 1913; Knowles, *Alone in the Wilderness*, 282; *Boston American*, Dec. 2, 1913; Roderick Nash, *Wilderness and the American Mind* (New Haven, Conn.: Yale University Press, 1967), 141–43.

60. Burroughs to Rudolph Altrocchi, Mar. 31, 1937, Porges Papers; see Porges, *Burroughs*, 132.

61. Burroughs to *Daily Maroon*, Mar. 30, 1927, quoted in Porges, *Burroughs*, 135.

62. On allegory as a mode of reading popular fiction, see Michael Denning, *Mechanic Accents: Dime Novels and Working-Class Culture in America* (New York: Verso, 1987), 72–73.

63. Burroughs, *Tarzan of the Apes*, 32.

64. Madison Grant, *The Passing of the Great Race* (New York: Scribner's, 1916).

65. The word "gorilla," for example, derives from an alleged African name for a wild or hairy man; "orangutan" from the Malaysian for man of the woods; q.v. *Oxford English Dictionary*. The Swedish naturalist Carolus Linnaeus in the definitive edition of his *Systema naturae* (1758) included two species within the genus *Homo*: *Homo sapiens* and *Homo troglyte*.

66. R. L. Garner, *The Speech of Monkeys* (New York: Charles L. Webster, 1892), 3. On Garner, see Candland, *Feral Children and Clever Animals*, 207–26; and Georg Schwidetzky, *Do You Speak Chimpanzee?* trans. from the German by Margaret Gardiner (London: George Routledge, 1932), 44–47.

67. Garner, *Speech of Monkeys*, 5.

68. R. L. Garner, *Gorillas and Chimpanzees* (London: Osgood, McIlvaine, 1896), 14.

69. Ibid., 15–16, 20.

70. Ibid., 61–62, 218.

71. Ibid., 77, 79–80, 101.

72. Ibid., 136–37.

73. Ibid., 42.

74. Burroughs, *Tarzan of the Apes*, 56, 43. The phrase "bitter bifurcation" is from William H. Gass, *Finding a Form* (New York: Knopf, 1996), 138.

75. Burroughs, *Tarzan of the Apes*, 38, 48, 61; Woods Hutchinson, *Instinct and Health* (New York: Dodd and Mead, 1909), 34.

76. Burroughs, *Tarzan of the Apes*, 37.

77. Ibid., 52.

78. Ibid., 57, 60, 63.

79. Ibid., 72; Charles Darwin, *The Descent of Man* (Princeton, N.J.: Princeton University Press, 1981), 2:404–5. In his copy of the second edition, Burroughs wrote

the date Jan. 1899 on the flyleaf, together with a drawing of a large monkey or ape, which he captioned "Grandpa" (Porges, *Burroughs*, 75).

80. Burroughs, *Tarzan of the Apes*, 84.

81. Ibid., 89.

82. Ibid., 86, 99. Burroughs admired Pettee's cover illustration and at one point considered purchasing the original (Porges, *Burroughs*, 159).

83. Burroughs, *Tarzan of the Apes*, 107.

84. Ibid., 135; Johann Friedrich Blumenbach, summarizing travelers' accounts in *The Anthropological Treatises* . . . , ed. and trans. Thomas Bendyshe (London: Longman, Green, Longman, Roberts, and Green for the Anthropological Society, 1865), 73, quoted in Harriet Ritvo, *The Platypus and the Mermaid and Other Figments of the Classifying Imagination* (Cambridge, Mass.: Harvard University Press, 1997), 92. Rudolph Altrocchi offers numerous other instances of human-ape unions as well as animal-raised foundlings in a variety of literary traditions, ancient and modern, in "Ancestors of Tarzan," in *Sleuthing in the Stacks* (Cambridge, Mass.: Harvard University Press, 1944), 74–124, esp. 99.

85. Paul B. Du Chaillu, *Explorations and Adventures in Equatorial Africa* (New York: Harper & Brothers, 1861), 394.

86. Burroughs, *Tarzan of the Apes*, 137.

87. On the sexuality of Wild Peter, Victor, and Ishi, see Zingg, "Feral Man," 187, 193; Candland, *Feral Children and Clever Animals*, 35; Heizer and Kroeber, eds., *Ishi, the Last Yahi*, 234; Kroeber, *Ishi in Two Worlds*, 220; Burroughs, *Tarzan of the Apes*, 137, 144.

88. Burroughs, *Tarzan of the Apes*, 138, 161, 162, 209, 181, 216.

89. Ibid., 194.

90. Ibid., 209, 218.

91. Anonymous writer on behalf of "The Soldiers of the 10th Inf[antry], U.S. Army" to Thomas Metcalf, Sept. 14, 1912, Porges Papers.

92. Ralph Waldo Emerson, *Nature*, in Robert E. Spiller and Alfred R. Ferguson, eds., *The Collected Works of Ralph Waldo Emerson* (Cambridge, Mass.: Belknap Press of Harvard University Press, 1971), 1:7; George Kateb, "Wildness and Conscience: Thoreau and Emerson" (paper presented at Sawyer Seminar, National Humanities Center, Research Triangle Park, N.C., 1999).

93. Kateb, "Wildness and Conscience."

94. Gail Bederman, *Manliness and Civilization: A Cultural History of Gender and Race in the United States, 1880–1917* (Chicago: University of Chicago Press, 1995), 138.

95. Charlotte Perkins Gilman, *Herland* (New York: Pantheon, 1979), 2.

96. Ibid., 11, 82, 71–72, 92, 99.

97. Ibid., 131, 87, 132.

98. "Table-Talk," *All-Story*, Sept. 1912, quoted in Porges, *Burroughs*, 136; Metcalf to Burroughs, Jan. 22, 1913, and Burroughs to Metcalf, Jan. 24, 1913, quoted in Porges, *Burroughs*, 150.

99. On the printing and sales of Burroughs's early Tarzan novels by A. C. McClurg,

see Alan M. Freedman, "McClurg Speaks," *Burroughs Quarterly*, n.s., no. 3 (July 1990): 2–4; and Alan M. Freedman, "McClurg Royalty Payments," *Burroughs Quarterly*, n.s., no. 4 (Oct. 1990): 13–14.

100. Burroughs to brother Harry Burroughs, quoted in Taliaferro, *Tarzan Forever*, 144.

101. For the first two quotations, see Porges, *Burroughs*, 350, 301–2. For the last quotation, see Edgar Rice Burroughs, "The Story of Tarzan" (1932), *Burroughs Bulletin*, n.s., no. 3 (July 1990): 35.

CONCLUSION

1. David L. Chapman, *Sandow the Magnificent: Eugen Sandow and the Beginnings of Bodybuilding* (Urbana: University of Illinois Press, 1994), 187.

2. Houdini diary, 1904, quoted in Kenneth Silverman, *Houdini!!! The Career of Ehrich Weiss* (New York: HarperCollins, 1996), 178.

3. Dolph Sharp, "Edgar Rice Burroughs, Inc.," *Writer's Digest*, Aug. 1949, 51.

4. Eugen Sandow, *Life Is Movement* (London: National Health Press, n.d. [c. 1918]), 10; "Territorial Physical Development Competition," London *Times*, July 24, 1909, 12. I have spelled out abbreviations.

5. Quoted in Irwin Porges, *Edgar Rice Burroughs: The Man Who Created Tarzan* (Provo, Utah: Brigham Young University Press, 1975), 288, 289.

6. The stories that formed the basis for *Tarzan the Untamed* were written in 1918 and 1919. Edgar Rice Burroughs, *Tarzan the Untamed* (1920; reprint, New York: Ballantine Books, 1963), 69; Porges, *Burroughs*, 392, 790.

INDEX

Locators in *italic* indicate illustrations and photographs.

A. C. McClurg and Company, 215, *216*, 217

Adonis (Gill), 24–25, *26*, 27, *27*, 57

advertising: in mass-circulation magazines, 16, *17*; for men against temptations of modern life, 49–50; of Sandow by Ziegfeld, 53; in *System* magazine, 175, *176*, *177*, 177–79, *178*

Agnew Clinic, The (Eakins), 69

Albee, Edward F., 101

Alexander III, tsar of Russia, 35

All-Story, The, 7–8, 16, 170, 215; demand for *Tarzan* sequel by, 211, 217; encouragement of Burroughs by editor of, 169, 217; publication of *Tarzan* by, 195, *206*, 208

Alone in the Wilderness (Knowles), *192*, 194–95

American Battery, 161, 162, 165, 166, 184

American Can, 11

American frontier, 10, 68–69, 162, *163*, 164, 165, 180–81

American Gaiety Girls, 99

American School of Correspondence, *176*, 177

American Society for Psychic Research, 146–47, 153

American Sugar Refining, 11

American Telephone and Telegraph, 11, 171

Anderson, John Henry, 145, 219

anthropometry, 41–42, 54

Arbuthnot, John, 186–87

Argosy, The, 16, 169

Arizona Territory, 165

Armour, 11

Arrow Collar Man, 19

Arting, Fred J., 217

"Asleep in the Deep" (song), 130, 134

assembly-line system, 171–72

Atlas, Charles (Angelo Siciliano), 7, *32*

"Attila, Professor Louis," *see* Durlacher, Ludwig

bachelor subculture, 12–13, 18

Ballantyne, R. M., 184

Barnum, P. T., 123
Barton, Enos, 174
baseball, 14
Beard, George M., 11
Beasts of Tarzan, The (Burroughs),
    217
Beck, Martin, 101, 103
Bellow, Saul, 167
Bellows, George, 19
Benzon, "Professor," 105
Between Rounds (Eakins), 69
Beveridge, Albert, 180
Bienkowski, Franz, 35
Birth of a Nation, The (film), 18, 181
Blackstone, Harry, 79
Bobbs-Merrill publishers, 215
bodily risk: in Houdini's act, 124–25,
    126, 127–31, *132*, 133–38, *139*, 140–
    41; Houdini's fascination with, 125;
    Houdini's triumph over, 98; as means
    of self-realization, 223
bodybuilding, 7, 32, 38, 54, 68; *see also*
    Sandow, Eugen
body image: and classical Greece, 21,
    32–33; historical perspective on, 18–
    19, 21, 33, 58, 75–76; Houdini's, 89,
    154–55; Sandow as new ideal of, 23,
    28–30, 32, 76, 154–55
body measurements: of Eltinge, 96; of
    Houdini and Bess, 89; of Sandow, 38–
    39, 42, *43*, 45, 96; of students in Sar-
    gent's study, 41–42, 51; of Sullivan,
    42, *43*, 44
Bosco, Bartolomeo, 219
Boston, 12, 39–40, 50, 54, 73, 75, 110–
    12, 117–19, 149, 194
Boston American, 194–95
Boston Daily Globe, The, 50
Boston Journal, The, *111*
Boston Sunday Post, 191, 193
Boughton, Harry, *see* Blackstone,
    Harry
Bowdoin College, 41
boxing, 14–15, 35, 39–40, 69, 70

Boyd, Stephen D., 50
Boy Scouts of America, 191
Boy's Own Conjuring Book, The, 86
Britain, industrial output of, 12
British Anthropological Society, 208–9
British Empire, 179–80
Brooks, Peter, 113
Brothers Houdini, 89, 91
"Brownsville affair," 8
"Bull Moose" campaign, 6
burlesque, 18; *see also specific theaters*
Burne-Jones, Edward, 25
Burroughs, Arthur (brother), 162
Burroughs, Charles (brother), 162
Burroughs, Coleman (brother), 164
Burroughs, Edgar Rice: in Chicago, 158,
    165, 166; death of, 220; early employ-
    ment of, 165–67, 169–70; early years
    of, 161–62, *163*, 164–65; and feelings
    of failure, 160–61; during Great War,
    221–22; in Idaho, 162, *163*, 164, 165,
    169; Joan of Arc drawing by, 164, *164*;
    marriage of, 165–66; Normal Bean
    pseudonym of, 169; poverty experi-
    enced by, 166; as pulp-fiction writer,
    167–69, 178–79, 218; as Rough Rider
    volunteer, 8 165; at Sears, Roebuck,
    166; in Seventh U.S. Cavalry, 165;
    success of *Tarzan* and, 215, 217–18; at
    System magazine, 158–59, 170–71,
    175, 178, 217; word-output graph of,
    178; and writing of *Tarzan*, *157*, 157–
    58, 169, 178, 183–84, 195; *see also*
    Tarzan *and* Tarzan of the Apes (Bur-
    roughs)
Burroughs, George (brother), 162
Burroughs, George T. (father), 161, 162,
    164–65
Burroughs, Harry (brother), 162
Bush, Irving T., 175

Call of the Wild, The (London), 182–83
Caroline, princess of England, 186

Carrington, Hereward, 147
Casino Roof Garden, New York, 23–24,
    39, 46, 47
Cazeneuve, Bernard Marius "Le Com-
    mandeur," 91
censorship, 67
Central Leather, 11
Charley's Aunt (play), 92
Chase Theatre, Washington, D.C., 109
Chicago, 12, 50–54, 89, 158, 165, 166,
    184
Chicago Daily News, 53
Christianity, 21
circuses, 33, 63, 98–99, 100
Civil War, 161, 165
Clansman, The (Dixon), 181, 203
class, *see* social class
classical ideal of male body: in photo-
    graphs of Sandow, 58, *62*, *63*, 64, *64*,
    65–66, 67; Sandow as, 21, 32–33, 42,
    46
Cleveland, Grover, 38
College of Physical Culture, Boston, 73,
    75
Collier's, 167
commercial photography, *see* photogra-
    phy
Commodore the lion: and Sandow, 72–
    73
Comstock, Anthony, 67
Comstock, Dr. Daniel F., 147
Congo Free State, 184
Conrad, Joseph, 184
Consolidated Coal, 11
contests and challenges: for "most beau-
    tiful man" and "most perfectly devel-
    oped man" sponsored by Macfadden,
    32; for "strongest man on earth," Lon-
    don, 33–36, *34*, 38, *61*, 72; Ziegfeld's,
    53
Cooper, James Fenimore, 211
Copperfield, David, 223
Corbett, James "Gentleman Jim," 15,
    39, 41, 42

corporate power and wealth, 11–12, 171
Cosmopolitan, 16
Count of Monte Cristo, The (Dumas), 113
Crandon, Dr. Le Roi, 147
Crandon, Mina ("Margery" the
    medium), 145–53, *146*, *151*
Criminal Man (Lombroso), 185
cultural and historical perspective: on
    advertising, 16, *17*; on body image, 21,
    58, 75–76; on entertainment, 13–15,
    223; on Houdini's themes of control
    and mastery, 79–80; on journalism,
    15–16; on manliness, 10–11, 222; on
    Sandow, 21, 75–76; on stage magic,
    77; on transition from Victorian to
    modern culture, 75; *see also* masculin-
    ity
Curtis, Tony, 7
Cyclops (strongman), 35

Dahomey Village at World's Columbian
    Exposition, 51, 89, 184
Dakota Territory, 31
Dalton, William, *see* Eltinge, Julian
danger, *see* bodily risk
Darwin, Charles, 197, 205
Davenport, Ira, 143, *144*, 145
Davenport, William, 143, *144*, 145,
    219
Death of a Salesman (Miller), 167
depressions, U.S., 12, 23, 24
Derby Desk Company, 119
Descent of Man, The (Darwin), 197, 205
Diamond Match, 175
Dickson, W. K. L., 73
dime museums, 80, 98, 100
Discobolus: Montgomery as, *71*
Dixey, Henry, 24–25, *26*, *27*, 27–28, 39,
    46, 57, 92
Dixon, Thomas, 181
Dodd, Mead, publishers, 215
Doyle, Sir Arthur Conan, 134, 145,
    147

Dreiser, Theodore, 167
Du Chaillu, Paul, 209
Dumas, Alexandre, 113, 203
Du Pont de Nemours, 11
Durlacher, Ludwig ("Professor Louis Attila"), 33, 35–36, 48

Eakins, Thomas, 69
Eastman, George, 18
Eastman Kodak, 11, 18
ectoplasm, 148
Edgar Rice Burroughs, Inc., 178, 220
Edison, Thomas A., 18, 73, *74*
Edward VII, king of England, 35
elite theatergoers: Sandow's appeal to, 24, 29; *see also* social class
Eltinge, Julian, 92–96, *94*, *97*, 98
Emerson, Ralph Waldo, 211
Erie Railroad, 24
eroticism, 1, 8, 29, 57, *59*, 67–68, 76
exhibitionism: by Houdini, 80; by Sandow, 58
Explorations and Adventures in Equatorial Africa (Du Chaillu), 209

Falk, Benjamin J., *34*, 63, *63*
female impersonation, 93, 96–98; *see also* Dixey, Henry; Eltinge, Julian
feminism, 94–95, 96, 222; *see also* gender issues
Ferber, Edna, 112
Filene's Men's Store, Boston, 194
Film Development Corporation, 142
Ford, Henry, 171
Forerunner, The, 213
Fortesque, George K., 25
Fort Grant, Arizona Territory, 165
Foucault, Michel, 114
Fox, Catherine, 143
Fox, Leah, 143
Fox, Margaret, 143

Fox, Richard Kyle, 19
Frank Leslie's Illustrated Weekly, 57, *59*, 68
Frank Merriwell at Yale (Standish), 19

Garfield, James, 109
Garland, Hamlin, 153
Garner, Richard L., 197–200, *201*
Gauguin, Paul, 191
gender issues: in *Adonis*, 27; and bachelor subculture, 12–13; in Burroughs's depiction of Jane in *Tarzan*, 205, 207, 208, 209–11, 212–13; and Dixey's transformations, 24–25, *26*, *27*, 27–28, 39, 46, 57, 92; during 1893 depression, 23; and Eltinge's transformation, 92–96, *94*, *97*, 98; and female response to Sandow's phallic power, 54, 56–57, *59*; in Gilman's *Herland*, 213–15; in Houdini's feminine-like vulnerability, 116–17; in the Houdinis' "Metamorphosis," 92; and men assaulted by women, *47*, 47–48; and "New Woman," 12–13; in 1970s, 222; in period images of manliness, 8, 10; in photographs of Sandow, 67–68; in professional magic, 141–53; raised by Sandow, 29–30, 76; in reactions to strains of modern life, 49–50, 60; in theatrical display of male and female bodies, 18–19, 33; as themes in performances and *Tarzan*, 8; and wildness in *Tarzan*, 8, 212–15; *see also* masculinity
General Electric, 11
George, king of Greece, 35
George I, king of England, 186
George V, king of England, 75
German Americans: during Great War, 75, 142–43, 221–22
Germany, 6, 12, 30, 33, 75, 108, 115, 118, 142–43, 221–22
Gérôme, Jean-Léon, 25, 69

Gilbert, W. S., 25
Gill, William, 24
Gilman, Charlotte Perkins, 213–15
gladiator image, 60, 68–73
Golden Gate Park, San Francisco, 73
Gorilla Hunters, The (Ballantyne), 184
Gorillas and Chimpanzees (Garner), 199, *201*
Grace Hospital, Detroit, 154
Grant, Madison, 196
Grape-Nuts advertisement, 16, *17*
"Great Lafayette," *see* Neuberger, Sigmund
Great War, 6, 75, 142–43, 221–22; and concept of freedom, *222*
Greek Slave (Powers), 58
Griffith, D. W., 18, 181
Gross Clinic, The (Eakins), 69
Grotto Theatre, Chicago, 70–71
Guiteau, Charles, 109, 113
Guiteras, Dr. Raymond, 39
gymnastic movement in Germany, 33

halftone photoengraving, 18
Hammerstein's Roof Garden, New York, 131
Harper's Weekly, 6
Harvard University, 4; 5, *5*; 41, 51, 54; 115, 146–47, 173
Haymarket bombers, 162
Haywood, William "Big Bill," 11
Hearst, William Randolph, 15, 16, 19, 105, 194
Heart of Darkness (Conrad), 184
Hebrew Relief Society, 82
Heller, Robert, 145, 219
Hemingway, Ernest, 222
Henning, Doug, 223
heredity versus environment: in determining masculine worth, 170–71, 179–83; in *System* magazine, 170, 174–75; in *Tarzan of the Apes*, 184–86
Herland (Gilman), 213–15

historical perspective, *see* cultural and historical perspective
HMS *Success*, 135
homosexuality, 12, 29, 95, 98
Honest Hearts and Willing Hands (play), 41
Houdini, Harry: adolescence of, 82, 85–87; aerial straitjacket escapes of, 124–25, 136–38, *137*, *139*, *140*, 140–41; Atlantic City pier jump of, 129; Belle Island Bridge jump of, 127, 128; in Berlin, *107*, 108, 131; birth and early childhood of, 80–84; bridge jumps of, 124, *126*, 127–31; campaign against mediums and spiritualist frauds by, 82–83, 141, 143, *144*, 145–47, 150–53, *151*; as "Cardo," 99; challenges for, 117–21, *122*, 123–24; in *Cheer Up*, 142–43; "Chinese Water Torture Cell" of, 7, 124, 131, *132–33*, 133–35, *134*; as daredevil, 124–25, *126*, 127–31, *132*, 133–38, *139*, 140–41; death of, 153–54, 219–20; early career of, 13, 87, *88*, 89, *90*, 91–92; in Europe, 108, 109, 115; factory employment of, 85; fearlessness of, 123, 128, *222*; in films, 142; freedom as concept in performances of, 114–15, 116, 123–24, 125, 136; grave refurbishing by, 219–20; during Great War, 142–43, 221; hamper escape of, 117–19, *118*; as "Handcuff King," *78*, 101, *102*, 103–6, *107*, 108, 117, 125; Harvard Bridge Jump of, *126*; as historical embodiment of manliness, 6, 7, 19; influence of freaks and oddities on, 100; innovations of, 125, 127–41; invitations to touch body of, 112, 123; Jewish issues for, 81–83, 87, 89; lobby displays designed by, *122*, 123; from magician to escape artist, 98–101; marriage of, *88*, 89, *90*, 91, 92, 98–99; milk-can escape of, *129*, 129–31; modified bridge jump in New York

Houdini, Harry (*cont.*)
harbor by, 131; needle-swallowing trick of, 101, 103; onstage straitjacket escapes, 105–6; operational aesthetic of, 123; political implications of acts of, 114–15, 116; as "Prison Defier," 108, 109–17, *110*, *111*, 125; as "Professor Murat," 99; proposed jump from East River Pier of, 131; relationship with mother, 82–83, 128, 141, 143, 219; rivals of, 104–5; Robert-Houdin's influence on, 85–87; with Roosevelt, 8, *9*; sadomasochistic themes in work of, 114; Scotland Yard handcuff escape by, 108; Somerset Street "Tombs" escape of, *110*, 110–12, *111*, 117; special handcuff escape in Blackburn, England, of, 118; speculations on hiding places in body of, 116; spiritualism and, 99–100; straitjacket escape in Hanover, Germany, of, 118; strip searches of, 105, 106, 115; suspension from U.S. Treasury Building of, *137*, 138; themes of control and mastery as crucial to success of, 79–80; and torture, *134*, 135; trunk trick of, 89, 91–92; and victimization theme, 106, 108, 113–17; Washington, D.C., federal prison escape of, 109–10; with Welsh Brothers Circus, 98–99, *99*, 100; Whitehead's assault on, 153–54
Houdini, Wilhelmina Beatrice Rahner "Bess" (wife), *83*, *88*, 89, *90*, 92, 98–100, 128, 141, *220*
Houdini (film), 7, 127
How I Found Livingston (Stanley), *201*
"How to Select the Right College Man" (Needham), 174
Hulbert, Emma (Burroughs's wife), 165–66
Hunting Trips of a Ranchman (Roosevelt), 6
Hutchinson, Woods, 202

Hyman, Jacob, 85, 89
Hyman, Joe, 89

"Ideas That Have Been Put to Work" (series in *System* magazine), 172
immigration, 10, 12, 75, 80–81, 222
In Darkest Africa (Stanley), 184
Independent, The, 11, 16
Industrial Workers of the World, 11
insane asylums: Houdini's interest in, 105–6, 114, 138
International Harvester, 11, 171
International Paper, 11
"In the Penal Colony" (Kafka), 114
Iolanthe (Gilbert & Sullivan), 25
"iron cage," 8, 170
Ishi the Yahi, 187–90, *190*, *191*, 195
Itard, Jean-Marc-Gaspard, 187

Jackson, Peter, 40
Jahn, Friedrich Ludwig, 33
Johnson, Jack, 15
journalism: transformation in, 15–16; *see also* press coverage
Julian Eltinge Magazine, 94

Kafka, Franz, 114
Kansas City Post, The, 136
Kansas City Times, The, 103
Keith, B. F., 54, 101, 109, 111, 116
Keith & Proctor's 125th Street Theatre, 120–21
Keith's Theatre, Boston, 54, 117–19, *118*, 149
Kellar, Harry, 145
Kettle Hill, Cuba, 6
kinetoscope, 18, *74*
Kipling, Rudyard, 195
Klondike gold rush, 182–83
Knowles, Joseph, 191, *192*, 193–95, *194*
Kodak camera, 18

Kroeber, Alfred, 188, 190
Ku Klux Klan (KKK), 181–82

Ladies' Home Journal, *139*, *140*
Lambert, Christopher, 223
Langtry, Lillie, 38
Laocoön, 124
Leopold II, king of Belgium, 184, 203
Le Roy, William "the Human Claw
    Hammer," 100
Leslie, Amy, 53, 56
Leyendecker, J. C., 19
*Life and Reminiscences of a 19th Century
    Gladiator* (Sullivan), 44, 69
Lincoln, Elmo, *216*, 218
living statue: in *Adonis* (Gill), 24–25, *26*,
    27, *27*; Sandow as, 27–28; Sullivan as,
    40; at World's Columbian Exposition,
    51
Lloyd George, David, 75
Lombroso, Cesare, 185
London, England, 33–36, 38, 72, 108,
    118, 219, 221
London, Jack, 19, 182–83, 211
London Stereoscopic, *61*, 63
"Lurline, the Water Queen," 71; assault
    on Sandow by, 46–49
Lynn, H. S., 84–85, 145

Macfadden, Bernarr, 31–32, 67–68; pose
    as Mercury by, *31*
Machpelah Cemetery, New York, 219,
    220
magazines: mass-circulation, 15–16; *see
    also specific magazines*
Magician among the Spirits, A (Houdini),
    145
Malinowski, Bronislaw, 77, 79
Man in the Iron Mask (Dumas), 203
Man-Made World, The (Gilman), 213
"Margery" the medium, see Crandon,
    Mina

Marquis of Queensberry Rules, 15
marriage: deferment by men of, 12–13
Marx, Minnie, 89
Marx Brothers, 89
masculinity: and American frontier, 68–
    69, 165; and danger, 128; and fantasy
    in pulp magazines, 170; Houdini's
    dramatization of, 80, 87, 96, 98, 112–
    17; in 1970s, 222–23; as performance,
    23; and professional magic, 143; Roo-
    sevelt as embodiment of, 4–6, *5*; of
    Sandow, 29–32, 36, 39, 46, 58, 64,
    75–76; and *System* magazine, 169–75,
    176, 178–79; and white male body,
    222; wildness and, 189–95, *192*,
    211–12
Maskelyne, J. N., 91, 145
Massachusetts Institute of Technology,
    147
Masses, The, 19
Master Mystery, The (film), 142
Matthews, Albert G., 3, *4*, 7
McClure, S. S., 15–16
McCormick, Cyrus, Jr., 175
McDougall, Dr. William, 146
McGill University, 153–54
McKenzie, J. Hewat, 134
measurement, *see* body measurements
Melville, Herman, 211
metamorphosis: in *Adonis* (Gill), 24–25,
    26, 27, *27*; in Crandon's séances, 149–
    50; in Eltinge's performances, 92–96,
    94, *97*, 98; and the Houdinis' "Meta-
    morphosis," *88*, 89, *90*, 91–92, 96, *99*;
    in Knowles's appearence, 194;
    Sandow as inspiration for male, 32, 36,
    38; in Tarzan's transformation from
    savage to socialite, 210–11; as theme
    in work of Burroughs, Houdini, and
    Sandow, 8
Metcalf, Thomas, 157, 169, 217
Michigan Military Academy, *163*, 164–
    65
middle class, *see* social class

Midway at World's Columbian Exposi-
tion, 51, 89, 184
Miller, Arthur, 167
Miller, Sebastian, 70–71
"Minidoka" (Burroughs), 169
Minneapolis Times, 103
miscegenation, 208, 209
Model T automobile, 171
modern life: as cause of renewed inter-
est in stage magic, 77, 79; during
Great War, 222; as reflected in *System*
magazine, 169–75, *176*, 178–79; as
threat to masculinity, 49–50, 60, 75
"Modern Sandow Girl, The" (Eltinge), 95
Modern Spiritualism (Maskelyne), 145
Montgomery, Irving, 71, *71*
Morgan, J. Pierpont, Jr., 171
Mr. Wix of Wickham (play), 92
Muldoon, William, 69–70, *70*
Müller, Friedrich Wilhelm, *see* Sandow,
Eugen
Munsey, Frank, 7, 16, 169
Munsey Company, 215, 217
Munsey's, 16

nakedness, *see* nudity
National Police Gazette, 19, 47–48, 49, 56,
56
"Nearly Dying for a Living" (Houdini),
128
Needham, Henry Beach, 174
Neuberger, Sigmund ("the Great
Lafayette"), 219
neurasthenia, 10–11
New Journalism, 15
New Story, 217
"New Woman," 12–13, 18, 19; and self-
development, 13
New York Athletic Club, 39
New York City, 12, 15, 23–25, 27–28,
39, 46, 47, 82–83, 85, 131, 219
New York Society for the Suppression of
Vice, 67

New York World, 44
North American Review, The, 14
nudity: of Houdini, 80, 108, 112–17; and
images of white manliness, 8, 10; versus nakedness in visual arts and history, 21, 58; social credentialing of, 33;
as subject of academic study, 21, 33,
58; as subject of artistic study, 21, 33,
58; as subject of ethnography, 21; as
subject of science, 21, 33, 58; as symbol of Sandow's power, 57, *59*; in visual arts and history, 21, 58; *see also*
body image

O'Keeffe, Miles, 223
On the Origin of Species (Darwin), 197
"organization" men and women, 11,
166–67, 170–71
Orpheum circuit, 101, 103
Orpheum Theatre, San Francisco, 71
Osborne, Duffield, 14
"Outlaw of Torn, The" (Burroughs), 169

"Palingenesia" (Lynn), 84–85, 125
Palmer, Bertha Honoré, 53, 56
Palmer, Potter, 53
Passing of the Great Race, The (Grant), 196
Pettee, Clinton, *206*, 208
Philippine-American War, 10
Phillips Academy, 164
photography: culturally acceptable nude
images in, 21; and Houdini's bridge
jumps, *126*, 127; and images of masculinity, 3–6, *4*, *5*; in a kinetoscope,
18, *74*; proliferation of, 16, 18;
Sandow's image in, 29–30, 60, *61–66*,
63–64, 67–68
Physical Culture, 31–32
physical fitness: and Jahn's gymnasium
movement, 33; Macfadden on, *31*,
31–32; Sandow's encouragement of, 7,
73, 75

physical strength: decline of white male, 10, 14–15; of Houdini, 112, 154–55; as manifestation of manliness, 8; of Sandow, 28, 30, 33–36, *34*, 38, 45, *61*, 72, *222*; as self-determined, 30–31, 38
"Pit and the Pendulum, The" (Poe), 114
Pittsburg Auto Vise and Tool, 121
Pittsburgh Plate Glass, 11
"Players in the Great Game" (article in *System* magazine), 175
Plessy v. Ferguson, 54
Poe, Edgar Allan, 114
Pollice Verso ("Thumbs Down") (Gérôme), 69
Pope, Saxton, 190
Powers, Hiram, 58
press coverage: of Eltinge's "ambisextrous abilities," 93, 95–96; of Houdini, 99–100, 103–6, 108, *111*, 112–17, 127–28, 131, 136, 138, *139*, *140*; of Lurline's assault on Sandow, 47–48, 49; of Sandow, 24, 27–28, 30, 36, 38–39, 50, 53–55, 58, *59*, 60, *71*, 71–72, 75; of Sullivan, 39
Prince, Walter Franklin, 147, 152
Princess of Mars, A (Burroughs), 168–69, 184
Princess Theatre, Montreal, 153–54
private showings and receptions: for nude sculptures, 58; for Sandow, 24, 53
Proctor, F. F., 16
psychic communication, 147–48
Pulitzer, Joseph, 15, 16, 19, 44
Pulitzer Building, New York, 15
Pullman, George, 53
Pullman, Harriet S., 53
pulp fiction, 13, 16, 167–69, 178–79
Pure Food and Drug Law (1906), 159
Putney Vale cemetery, London, 219
Pygmalion, Greek myth of, 24–25

"race suicide": warnings of, 10, 196
racial issues: in boxing, 40; as evident in

Roosevelt's views, 8, 10; in *Tarzan*, 203–5, 208, 212
Radcliffe students: body measurements of, 41, 51
Rahner, Wilhelmina, *see* Houdini, Wilhelmina Beatrice Rahner "Bess"
railroad bankruptcies and 1893 depression, 24
Reeves, Steve, 68
Reilly & Britton, publishers, 215
Remington, Frederic, 162
Return of Tarzan (Burroughs), 217
Richet, Charles-Robert, 147
Robert-Houdin, Jean-Eugène, 85–86, 144
Rome, classical, 21, 32, 68–73
Roosevelt, Theodore: in Africa, 6; *Autobiography* of, 4; manliness and spectacle of, 5, 6, 19, 211; and Rough Riders, 4, 6, 8, 165; sickly childhood of, 30–31; views on race of, 8, 10; warnings of "race suicide" by, 196; western ranch life of, 31, 162
Rough Riders, 4, 6, 8, 165
Royal Aquarium theatre, London, 35–36

Sacher-Masoch, Leopold von, 130
Salutat (Eakins), 69
Sampson, Charles A., *34*, 35, 36, 38, 48, 63, 71
Sandow, Eugen: American debut of, 7, 14, 23–24, 27–28, 32, 38, 44; as Apollo, 44; arrival on *Elbe* of, 23; assault by "Lurline, the Water Queen" on, 46–49, *47*; birth, parents, and background of, 30, 32–33; body measurements and display of, 38–39, 42, *43*, 45, 96; in Boston, 50; as British subject 75; and classical ideal, *22*, 32–33, 38; complexion of, 54; cultivation of gentleman image by, 29, 33, 36, *37*, 46, 68, 76; death of, 75, 219; as Dying Gaul, 64, *66*, 67; in Edison's filmstrips

Sandow, Eugen (*cont.*)
and films, 73, *74*; as example of freedom, 22–23, 58; as Farnese Hercules,
64, *65*, 67; and fig-leaf attire, *22, 62,
63, 64*; as first male pinup, *63*, 63–64,
64, 65, 66, 67–68; and gladiator ideal,
72–73; and Great War, 75, 221; as
heroic ideal of manhood, 29–30, 39,
58, 64; as historical embodiment of
manliness, 6–7, 19; as icon of hyper-
masculinity, *22*, 29; impostors of, *71*,
71–72; in India, 54; invitations to
touch body of, 54, *56*, 56–58, *59*, 60;
in leopard-skin leotard, *63*; as model
for statue of European man, 54, *55*; as
modern Hercules, 36, 38, 46, 72, 124;
as "perfect man," 7, 23, 27–28, 32,
38, 44, 46, 72; physical examination
of, 38–39, 45–46, 54, 56–58, *59*; with
Roosevelt, 8; self-differentiation from
circus performers of, 33, 63; souvenir
photographs of, 60, 63, 67; in
"strongest man on earth" contest,
London, 33–36, *34*, 38, *61*, 72; and
strongman Attila, 33, 35; in "Tomb of
Hercules" position, 28; at Trocadero
Theatre, Chicago, 50–54, *51, 52*, 89;
in wrestling match with Commodore
the lion, 72–73
"Sandowe" (Sandow impostor), *see*
Montgomery, Irving
Sandow on Physical Training (Sandow), 30
San Francisco Chronicle, 73
San Francisco Examiner, The, 105, 106,
107
San Juan Hill, Cuba, 6
Sargent, Dr. Dudley A., *40*, 41–42; body
measurements of students by, 41–42,
51; examination of Knowles by, 191,
193, 194, *194*; examination of Roosevelt by, 5; examination of Sandow
by, 45–46, 75; examination of Sullivan
by, 41–42, *43*, 44; statue of Sandow
presented to, 54, *55*

Sarony, Napoleon, *43, 59, 62*, 63, *64–66*
Saturday Evening Post, The, 167
Scarry, Elaine, 136
Schwarzenegger, Arnold, 223
Scientific American, 146, 148, 150, 151,
153
séances and spiritualism, 147–53
Seize the Day (Bellow), 167
self-liberation: Houdini's theme of, 114–
15, 116, 123–24, 125, 136; *Tarzan* as
act of, 159–60
self-made man: Houdini as, 80–87;
Sandow as, 32–33, 38
Seton, Ernest Thompson, 191
sexuality: and Eltinge's "ambisextrous
abilities," 93, 95–96; and eroticism, 1,
8, 29, 57, *59*, 67–68, 76; in *Tarzan*
and *Herland*, 214–15; of wild men,
209–10
Shaw, A. W., 170
Sherlock Holmes, 134
Siciliano, Angelo, *see* Atlas, Charles
Sierra Club, 191
"Significance of the Frontier in American History, The" (Turner), 68–69
Sister Carrie (Dreiser), 167
sleight of hand, 79, 100
social class: and importance of privileged social credentials, 33; and religion, 179; and Sandow's appeal, 24,
29, 33, 53, 76; and strongman contests
and challenges, 35; and Sullivan's appeal, 39–41; in *Tarzan of the Apes*,
183–84; and vaudeville's appeal, 18;
and white-collar workers, 11
Society of American Magicians, 147
Spanish-American War, 4, 10, 165, 180
sports: and bachelor subculture, 13, 14–
15, 35, 39–40, 69, 70
Standard Oil, 11
Standish, Burt L., 19
Stanley, Henry, 184, *201*
Steckel, George, 63
Stettinius, Edward R., 175

Stoddard, John L., 166
strength, *see* physical strength
strongmen, 29, 100; *see also* Sandow,
    Eugen
Sullivan, John L. (the Boston Strong
    Boy), 13, 15, 19, 35, 39–46, *43*; as
    Hercules, 39, 44; and nickname
    "Spartacus Sullivan," 69
Sullivan, Sir Arthur, 25
Summerville, Amelia, 25
Sweetser, Lew, 162
Swift, Sarah E., *see* "Lurline, the Water
    Queen"
System: The Magazine of Business, 158–59,
    169–75, *176*, 178–79, 217

Taft, William Howard, 6
Taking the Count (Eakins), 69
Tarzan: as historical embodiment of
    manliness, 6–8, 19; as "perfect man,"
    156–60, 213; as primate-like, 202–3;
    and urge to recover wildness, 7, 160,
    200, 222
Tarzan of the Apes (Burroughs): anti-
    German attitudes in, 222; and concept
    of freedom, 159–60; in film, 7, *216*,
    218, 223; heredity versus environ-
    ment in, 184–86, 196; idea for, 157,
    178–79; importance of privileged so-
    cial credentials in, 33; as means of
    imaginative escape, 159–60; and pri-
    mate behavior, 195–200, *201*, 202–3;
    publication in *All-Story* of, 7, 16, 169,
    170, 195, *206*, 208, 211, 215, 217;
    sequels to, 217–18, 222; story of,
    184–86, 203–5, 207–15
Taussig, F. W., 173–74
Taylor, Frederick Winslow, 171
Terror Island (film), 142
Thoreau, Henry David, 211
Thurston, Howard, 79
Times, The (London), 221
transformation, *see* metamorphosis

Tremont Theatre, Boston, 50
Trocadero Theatre, Chicago, 50–54, *51*,
    52, 70–71, 89
Turner, Frederick Jackson, 68–69, 211

United Booking Office, 14
United Fruit, 11
United States Steel, 11, 171
U.S. Rubber, 11
U.S. Supreme Court, 54

Van der Weyde, Henry, 63
vaudeville: female performers in, 18;
    golden age of, 77; as popular new en-
    tertainment, 13–14, 18; Sandow's suc-
    cess in, 36, 76; theater circuits for, 14,
    101, 103
Victor (the "savage of Aveyron"), 187,
    195, 209
Vietnam War, 222
violence: as evidence of masculinity, 31;
    by Sandow against black bellboy, 54;
    of Sullivan, 39–40; *see also* bodily risk
Virginian, The (Wister), 180, 181, 203, 212

Walter (Crandon's brother and spirit-
    control), 148–52
Washington, Booker T., 8
Washington Times, 142
Waterman, Thomas, 188, 190
Watts, G. F., 25
Wayburn, Ned, 172
weakness: as male concern, 49, 50, 154–55
Weber, Max, 170
Weed Chain Tire Grip Company, *120*,
    120–21
Weiss, Ehrich, *see* Houdini, Harry
Weiss, Theo (Houdini's brother), 85, 89,
    141, *220*
Weisz, Cecilia (Houdini's mother), 80–
    84, *83*, 128, 219; death of, 141, 143

Weisz, Erik, *see* Houdini, Harry
Weisz, Rabbi Mayer Samuel (Houdini's father), 80–84, *81*, 85, 86, 87, 219; death of, 82; as *moyel* and *shocher*, 82, 85
Welsh Brothers Circus, 98–99, *99*, 100
Western Electric, 174
West Point, 165
Weyerhaeuser Timber, 11
"What Are Profits?" (Taussig), 172–74
white-collar workers, 11, 166–67, 170–71
white male identity: historical perspective on, 18–19; images of, 8, 10; Tarzan and rediscovery of, 203–5, *206*, 207–15, 222; *see also* Houdini, Harry; Sandow, Eugen
wild boys and men, 8, 186–95, *189*, *190*, *192*, *194*, 209
Wild Peter, 187, 195, 209

Willard, Jess, 15
Wilson, Woodrow, 6
Winckelmann, Johann, 333
Wister, Owen, 162, 180, 181, 183, 211, 212
woman suffrage, 94
women, *see* gender issues
Women and Economics (Gilman), 213
World's Columbian Exposition, Chicago, 50–51, 89, 184
writers for pulp fiction, 167–68

Yahi Indians, 188
Yale University, 41
Yeats, William Butler, 7, 153

Ziegfeld, Florenz, Jr., *51*, *52*, 52–53, 72